Microeconomics of Interactive Economies

For my wife Angelika,
who gave so much for this book.

W.E.

Microeconomics of Interactive Economies

Evolutionary, Institutional, and Complexity Perspectives

A 'Non-Toxic' Intermediate Textbook

- Interdependencies & Complexity
- Uncertainty, Search & Learning
- Interaction & Cumulative Process
- Evolutionary Process & Multiple Equilibria
- Coordination & Cooperation
- Institutions, Rules & Routines
- Real-World Markets: Firm Size & Power, Oligopoly & Monopolistic Competition
- Neoclassical 'Perfect Markets' and Their Critique
- Modern Core Models of Complexity Economics
- The Universe of Economic Forms and Dynamics
- Game Theory and Simulation Methods

Wolfram Elsner

Professor of Economics, iino – Institute for Institutional and Innovation Economics, Faculty of Business Studies and Economics, University of Bremen, Germany

In collaboration with Torsten Heinrich, Henning Schwardt, and Matthias Greiff

Edward Elgar
Cheltenham, UK • Northampton, MA, USA

Published by
Edward Elgar Publishing Limited
The Lypiatts
15 Lansdown Road
Cheltenham
Glos GL50 2JA
UK

Edward Elgar Publishing, Inc.
William Pratt House
9 Dewey Court
Northampton
Massachusetts 01060
USA

Paperback edition reprinted 2013

A catalogue record for this book
is available from the British Library

Library of Congress Control Number: 2012938049

ISBN 978 1 84064 522 4 (cased)
     978 1 78100 903 1 (paperback)

Printed and bound in Great Britain by T.J. International Ltd, Padstow

Overview

Contents

Figures

Tables

Preface – Microeconomics in Times of Crisis: A 'Post-2008' Textbook, its Aims and Scope

A famous joke told by Franco Modigliani, famous economist and Nobel laureate, in his lecture 'My evolution as an economist' at Trinity University, San Antonio, TX, USA, 24 March 1987, goes as follows: 'A surgeon, an engineer and an economist are discussing which of the three disciplines would be the oldest: The surgeon spoke first and said, "Remember at the beginning when God took a rib out of Adam and made Eve? Who do you think did that? Obviously, a surgeon." The engineer was undaunted by this and said, "You remember that God made the world before that. He separated the land from the sea. Who do you think did that except an engineer?" "Just a moment," protested the economist, "Before God made the world, what was there? Chaos. Who do you think was responsible for that?"

Economics being responsible for chaos? In fact, 'mainstream' economics has not been really successful in recent times in contributing to the solution of the exploding problems of mankind.

Contributing to the solution of the increasing problems of the world would mean to provide, with the authority of a leading scientific discipline, useful advice for a sustainable, socially inclusive, spatially even, a stable, reliable and crises-free economic development that could survive beyond the 21st century, in which all people could make long-run plans and thus would become capable of learning, investing, and innovating. But many, including professional practitioners, entrepreneurs, and even some politicians, supported by an increasing number of 'dissidents' from the ranks of academic economics itself, nowadays state that so-called neoclassical mainstream economics, with its dominant 'neoliberal' policy orientation with 'markets' and de-regulation for everything, has failed to inform such action as indicated – and even more so, the more *complex* problems have become. Among these problems are the sustainable use of resources, climate protection, safe food, health, education, workplace-safety, and old-age care provisions for all, a socially acceptable income and wealth distribution, social inclusion and justice for all, power control, limiting bureaucracies (private and public), equal chances to develop one's capabilities, freedom of speech even at the workplace, democratic participation, etc.

The *neo-liberal recipe* given by a 'mainstream' of economists for nearly forty years was a 'one size fits all' simplistic postulate: 'De-régularisez! Privatisez! Le marché va de lui-même'. The oversimplification leaves no room for complexity; it does not foresee financial fragility, turbulence, and 'panickiness' and it could not anticipate the *2008 financial crisis*. Essentially being a crisis of the 'speculation industry', the financial meltdown has caused or aggravated severe food and resource, climate, health, social, political, and moral crises and indeed, wherever we look, there are those that are '*too big to fail*', and are thus saved and provided with a full comprehensive insurance by the governments, to be paid by future generations.

While the orthodox 'mainstream' theories have for many years been criticized by more heterodox economists for their oversimplifications, all criticisms were dismissed by a great majority of economists. Countless critical declarations of economists have come out since the burst of the financial bubble. For example, D. Colander, H. Foellmer, A. Kirman and other well-known complexity economists and evolutionary economists launched the so-called *Dahlem Report* in February 2009, 'The Financial Crisis and the Systemic Failure of Academic Economics' (see also, e.g., Kirman, 2010). Others have argued that thinking like a 'mainstream' economist would undermine community (Marglin, 2008).

No wonder that economics appears to be a divided science and a *contested discipline*, where the dominating 'mainstream' has been qualified by physicist and publicist M. Buchanan as the only scientific discipline that is still not modern, since it is not yet complex but *simplistic* with its 'market-optimality and -equilibrium' assumptions (Buchanan, 2008). That economics 'mainstream' has in fact been considered responsible – as far as science can be responsible – for the ongoing financial crises, has been suggested even in conservative newspapers such as *The Times* (Kaletsky, 2009), the *Financial Times* (Buiter, 2009) and the *Scientific American* (Nadeau, 2008).

The dramatic and aggravating real-world problems would require an opening up of the 'mainstream' axioms and perspectives, mostly based on the relatively simple core model of the 'optimal, equilibrating, and stable market economy'. Nonetheless, the economics 'mainstream' is still dominating *higher education*, and related textbooks. In fact, there was a growing relative dominance of more complex 'heterodoxies' in terms of research questions, approaches, and methodologies over the last 30 years – after the neoclassical research program had reached its limits through some most critical proofs (by G. Debreu, R.R. Mantel, and H. Sonnenschein) in the early 1970s. This has not forcefully spilled over into the areas of the curricula of academic mass teaching and thus textbooks, which largely leave untouched the 'mainstream's' general world view and dominant policy orientation and postulates. On the contrary, it appears that the 'Ivory tower [remains] unswayed by [the] Crashing Economy, [...] The basic curriculum will not change' (Cohen, 2009).

But also, many textbooks do hesitate to draw the general consequence of thoroughly revising basic assumptions, perspectives, theories, models, and methods of received ('mainstream') economics from scratch. While the people using them would agree that there is little evidence for self-equilibrating, stabilizing, and 'efficient' 'market' economies to be found in any concrete investigation, they would rarely state this in a more general way and with all consequences required in front of their classes, in their political comments, advice, or recommendations – or in their textbooks. Established textbooks, therefore, sometimes appear to follow a strange overall argument: The basics of the 'perfect market economy' remain untouched while increasing parts of the book present all kinds of complexity issues and approaches just 'on top', as 'exemptions', 'deviations', 'specific cases', 'peculiarities', 'add-ons' or 'other views' – thus, overall, implying that the complex world outside basically leaves the ideal of a 'market' untouched, and making students learn the somewhat peculiar 'message' that 'first there is the market' – and second ... a whole lot of 'disturbing things' without relevance for the genuinely positive workings of the 'market mechanism'.

Against this background, students will learn in the *present textbook* that the economic problem is both more basic and more manifold in structures and 'solutions' than just 'the market'. And the 'market' itself is nothing – unless specified by a concrete set of informal and/or formal, societally learned and habituated rules.

A *real-world* market economy will have to be conceptualized as a complex phenomenon, itself defined and embedded in a set of mechanisms and entities that basically are its counter principles, such as private and public bureaucracies (hierarchies), networks, and learned informal *social rules* and *social institutions*. Only all of these together give life, sense, meaning, and 'workability' to a spontaneous decentralized mechanism 'with prices' that we are used to calling a 'market', while both limiting and enabling agents. These factors are most likely precisely those crucial mechanisms that allow a 'market' to come into being at all. What remains of the 'market' can no longer be considered purely equilibrating, optimizing, stabilizing, or coordinated by prices alone. In this textbook, we will look at, and explain, a variety of decision structures and allocation mechanisms, among them models of real-world markets.

This textbook, thus, may become a most productive challenge for those economists and academic teachers who still have to use textbooks that present economics as being about a 'market' economy that in principle is 'efficiently' allocating resources, generating meaningful price signals, resulting in equilibrium and stability, and working to '*the greatest happiness of the greatest number*'. Many economists will come to agree with the overall complexity perspective, approaches, models, analytical results, and implications in this book. In fact, much research undertaken by economists that consider themselves 'mainstream' economists deviates more or less in its assumptions or results from that 'perfect', general-equilibrium 'market economy' core model, and, as indicated before, increasingly addresses complexity issues in a broad array of applications and approaches.

The present textbook, therefore, *rebuilds basic microeconomic modeling and teaching* 'from scratch', on the basis of the wealth and breadth of *complexity economics* that have evolved in the last three decades – in fact based on a more than 300-year-old tradition of complex *evolutionary* and *institutional* economic thinking. The 'market' becomes a special case in the universe of complex structures, their potential processes and system orbits. Microeconomics is no longer exclusively about 'markets' but rather contains a much broader set of coordination problems and potential coordination forms. The real world is more diverse in its agents, problem structures, mechanisms, processes, and (interim) outcomes than reflected in the conventional core of microeconomics.

To be sure, microeconomics does not lose its accessibility for *rigor* and *formal modeling* nor for *teachability* in this way, and it even gains in relevance and professional usefulness. Note that the Nobel Prize 2009 went to one of the leading representatives of complexity economics, *Elinor Ostrom* (who received it together with Oliver Williamson), who has focused on social dilemma and collective-good problems in a broad array of real-world applications, theoretically, by formal modeling, by computer simulation, laboratory experiment, and field studies – applying game theory, doing empirical research, and deriving highly relevant policy advice. We consider this and earlier Nobel Prizes for evolutionary, institutional, and complexity economists in a wide sense (including 'original' institutionalists and game theorists), such as Gunnar Myrdal, Herbert Simon, Douglass North, John Harsanyi, John Nash, Reinhard Selten, Amartya Sen, George Akerlof, Daniel Kahnemann, Robert Aumann, and Thomas Schelling – all of them working beyond the theoretical core of the 'perfect market', and its usual neoliberal policy implications – a welcome encouragement of this kind of post-crisis textbook. In that sense this also is a *non-toxic* textbook as often called for in the post-2008 period. And, finally, this textbook is considered by its authors a contribution to a more pluralistic culture in the whole discipline of economics and in economics education in particular, as has been much required and suggested in broader disciplinary discussions in recent years (see, e.g., Reardon (ed.), 2009; Fullbrook (ed.), 2009).

ABOUT THE AUTHORS

Wolfram Elsner studied economics at the University of Cologne, Germany, received his PhD at the University of Bielefeld, Germany, in 1977 and the *venia legendi* ('Habilitation' as used in German-speaking academia, also called '*venia docendi*') in 1985. He then left academia to work in the 'real world' for ten years. He has worked as the head of a city economic development agency for four years. Later he worked as the head of the planning division of a Ministry for Economic Affairs in a German state ('Land') and as director of that state government's economic research institute for six years (until 1995). He also served as that state's official for industrial defense restructuring (conversion) policy through the nineties (1992-2001), managing a state proactive industrial-conversion program and EU funds allocated to this purpose. During this time he returned to academia as a full professor of economics at the University of Bremen in 1995 and has served in many academic functions and in associations, locally, nationally, and internationally, since then. He is adjunct professor of the doctoral faculty at the economics department of the University of Missouri at Kansas City, and head of the iino – Institute for Institutional and Innovation Economics, University of Bremen. He has taught at foreign universities in the U.S., Australia, South Africa, and European countries. He has edited and co-edited many books and edits several book series, among them 'Advances of Heterodox Economics' (Routledge), he has served and still serves on many editorial boards, and he is managing editor of the *Forum for Social Economics*.

Torsten Heinrich, studied at the Dresden University of Technology, Germany, and the Universidad Autónoma de Madrid, Spain, and received his PhD at the University of Bremen in 2011 with a thesis on technological change and growth patterns under network effects, which includes complex modeling and computer simulations. He holds a post-doc (assistant professor) position at the University of Bremen.

Henning Schwardt, studied at the Universities of Kiel, Germany, Stockholm, Sweden, and Universidad Autónoma de Madrid, Spain, and received his PhD at the University of Bremen in 2012 with a thesis on the modern institutional theory of economic development with special reference to Latin America. He holds a post-doc (assistant professor) position at the University of Bremen.

Matthias Greiff, studied economics at the University of Frankfurt, Germany, and the New School for Social Research, New York. He received his PhD at the University of Bremen in 2011 with a thesis on social approval as an incentive to the voluntary production of collective goods and on open-source communities, which included complex modeling and lab experiments.

He holds a post-doc (assistant professor) position at the University of Giessen, Germany.

ACKNOWLEDGEMENTS

The authors are grateful to *Miriam de Blasi*, M.A., *Shuanping Dai*, M.A, *Yasar Damar*, M.A., *Yanlong Zhang*, M.A., and *Tim Oppermann*, M.A., who contributed to particular chapters or sections.

Many have commented on earlier versions of this text. We are grateful to Prof. *Ping Chen* (Fudan University, Shanghai and Peking University, Beijing, formerly of University of Texas, Austin), Prof. *Philip A. O'Hara* (Curtis University, Perth, AUS), Prof. *Paul D. Bush* (Emeritus at CSU, Fresno), Prof. *Duncan K. Foley* (New School for Social Research, NY), Prof. *Alexander Lascaux* (Russian Academy of the National Economy, University of Hertfordshire, UK), further to *Malgorzata Wiklinska* (a leading corporate manager and PhD candidate at University of Bremen) and Dr. *Francis Woehrling* for comments, encouragement, and support.

Finally, we would like to thank generations of students who have worked with and often commented on this text. *Till Frischmuth*, B.Sc., *Philipp Kroemer*, and *Thomas Hoffmann*, B.Sc., have compiled and formatted the sometimes 'wicked' text files to create a readable text.

You may contact the authors for any questions, critique, comments, or suggestions anytime at the textbook website

www.microeconomics.us.

Furthermore, the website provides you with

- further texts,
- further references and readings,
- teaching materials (slides) for the courses 'microeconomics' and 'evolutionary and institutional economics', and finally,
- further exercises and exams,
- the opportunity to discuss with the authors and readers.

Didactics – How to Work with this Textbook

There is about a dozen more recent micro textbooks out that are trying to break free of the 'demand – supply – equilibrium' scheme and to integrate the dominant research questions and discourses of the last 30 years more or less 'from scratch'– thus reorganizing microeconomics bottom-up. Some few of these textbooks have already made a significant career within a few years after their publication. However, in all, the requirement for new perspectives is still not fully met on a broad scale, both quantitatively and qualitatively (i.e., in terms of the breadth of textbook choices for teachers and students and in terms of the strictness of the reconstruction of the field according to complex structure and process). Textbooks that are consequently based on the most important characteristic of the modern economy, i.e., 'direct' interdependence and complexity, 'strong' uncertainty and interactivity, complex modeling and complex process, are still rare.

We list and discuss most of the micro textbooks of this new kind under 'further reading' for this section in the supplementary material to this textbook at the *textbook website* www.microeconomics.us.

This textbook, as one of the latter kind, might relatively rarely be used as the prime textbook source in undergraduate micro teaching, for the time being, insofar as many curricula just prescribe to teach the conventional wisdom, even if teachers are not convinced of that. Its specific role will then be at first to serve as a supplementary source and further reading that may help introducing evolutionary, institutional, and complexity perspectives into otherwise more conventional micro teaching.

To be sure, this book can of course be used – and, in fact, was developed – as a stand-alone textbook aiming at dealing with modern perspectives and at a high practical and professional relevance of economic education, while aspiring both to a high theoretical level and a new and more realistic view on economies.

Since the problem sets, questions, approaches, core models, material, examples, references, perspectives, etc. in this textbook often considerably deviate from conventional textbooks, from the 'mainstream' of 'conventional wisdom', from attitudes, opinions, and ways to argue as often received from mass media and everyday consciousness and communication, this textbook must also be different in *style*. It will be more demanding with its new perspectives that offer alternatives to preconceived patterns of perception and thought. More complex and uncommon issues require, and will be more properly represented by, longer explanations, by and large. Thus, we may often start from different angles than is typically the case in textbooks that convey a more settled, standardized, codified, and 'obvious' body of knowledge. The body of knowledge of this textbook is on average less standardized (as yet), and thus often more unfamiliar or even surprising for everyday perceptions, thought patterns, and language. We also may more often repeat issues, propositions, terms, or examples and look at them from different angles.

This is also why we strive to inform students about the often surprisingly extensive body of new critical literature in order to demonstrate that there indeed is a whole world to learn. We would not expect students to read and learn more than they usually are required to by more conventional courses and textbooks.

Complexity economics is about continuing and self-reproducing complexity, about unfamiliar structures with pending tensions, lasting contradictions and trade-offs, resulting in unknown processes with multiple equilibria, often with open results, and often never-ending. This often includes surprising results. Nevertheless, we will see that a lot of concrete and specific things can be learned under such circumstances for a proper, 'good' (rather than 'perfect' or 'efficient') behavior in economic reality and for the future professional reality of current students.

Therefore, as said, we make intensive use of suggestions for *further reading*, quite different from the conventional textbook format, where usually only a minimum of endorsing standard references will be given. While usual textbooks tend not to 'disturb' and 'confound' students with 'too much' literature, we think it is most important for students to learn how much, how diverse and how rich the critical complexity literature 'outside there' really is: An important didactical issue – and an important corresponding attitude to be learned for profession and life in general.

The ideal 'stand-alone' use of this textbook can be applied to *undergraduate* and *graduate micro*, depending on the specific givens of a department's, college's or school's program, according to the following Table 0.1.

Table 0.1   A possible use of this textbook for undergraduate and graduate courses

Chapters for Use in *Undergraduate Courses*	Chapters for Use in *Graduate Courses*
1. Introduction to the Microeconomics of Interactive Economies	
2. Methods for Analyzing Interactive Economies: An Introduction to Game Theory	
3. Problem Structures and Processes of Interactive Economies	3. Problem Structures and Processes of Interactive Economies
4. Real-World Markets: Hierarchy, Size, Power, and Direct Interdependence	4. Real-World Markets: Hierarchy, Size, Power, and Direct Interdependence
5. Ideal Neoclassical Market and General-Equilibrium	5. (parts of) Ideal Neoclassical Market and General-Equilibrium
	6. Critique of the Neoclassical 'Perfect Market' Economy and Alternative Price Theories
	7. Methods for Analyzing Complex Processes: An Introduction to Computer Simulation
	8. Recent Core Models of Complexity Economics
	9. A Universe of Economies: Interdependence and Complexity, System Trajectories, Chaos, and Self-Organization

We particularly assume in this matrix that graduate students have learned about the game-theoretic tools. However, should this not have included evolutionary game theory and other evolutionary formal modules (such as the replicator), the corresponding sections of Chapter 2 can be introduced in that particular graduate course. The particular curriculum is, of course, subject to specific local specifications and requirements and to the discretion of the lecturer.

Note that the courses as outlined above might also serve for two-semester courses. In that case, also some of the supplementary chapters of this textbook not printed here but available at the textbook website www.microeconomics.us may appropriately be added to the course.

1. Introduction to the Microeconomics of Interactive Economies

Many economic situations are characterized by a *direct interdependence* of the agents involved. The behavior of one, or some, of them influences the options that are open to the others and the results they can achieve. Given different options for behaviors in a certain situation, then, which one do agents choose? And will their choices result in an outcome that they can be satisfied with, for themselves or even as a group? Or are situations conceivable in which individuals who make individually optimal decisions can generate outcomes that leave them all, or at least some, worse off in an interdependent setting? As you may infer from these questions, it is important to be aware that economic situations cover a much broader range of circumstances than the mere exchange of goods and services for money. Rather, they include companies having to decide on how to handle joint research and development projects, or firms choosing price and quality of product varieties in competitive set-ups, but also such situations as taking up studies and attending lectures in an effort to acquire knowledge and skills that may amongst other things serve to increase future earnings potential, and many more. All such situations involve *several behavioral options* that are open to the agents as well as results that depend on *decisions made by other agents*. Such interdependent and interactive situations and their consequences in a socio-economy are at the center of this textbook.

1.1 DIFFERENT PROBLEM STRUCTURES IN INTERDEPENDENT SOCIAL SITUATIONS

Social situations, where interdependent agents exercise a mutual influence on their respective results, can be differentiated by the *degree of conflict* that is inherent to them. When referring to degree of conflict here, we mean the tension that can arise between an individually optimal decision and the eventual result on an aggregate level, the outcome that individually optimal decisions may produce when exercised together, that in turn feeds back to individual results.

The simplest case is one where individually optimal (rational) behavior by each agent leads to a result that is the best for each agent involved in the optimal social, collective outcome. On the other side of the spectrum lie situations in which individually rational behavior results in a socially suboptimal outcome that is reflected in comparatively worse individual results as well. This means, decision criteria beyond a sole focus on immediate individual optimization, would allow the group members to realize superior results. How to solve such situations, how to transform them so that even narrowly conceived rational individuals can attain improved results, is a question that we will return to repeatedly throughout the book.

Note that the concept of rationality as utilized in mainstream economics differs somewhat from the general use of the term, and from the use of the term in other disciplines. Beyond the coherence of behavior and assumptions, and the purposefulness of behavior with regard to a specific objective, in economics the rationality concept includes the assumption that individual behavior is optimal for reaching an objective (the maximization of an economic outcome captured in terms of costs and benefits of an action). The optimality of behavior is governed by certain mathematical conditions that we will explain in detail below (in Chapters 2 and 5). A rational decision in these circumstances is thus by definition also an optimal decision which introduces a dimension that people may not be aware of when listening to economists but that in fact results in a significant difference between different concepts of rationality. As a baseline and reference point, we follow this understanding of rationality. However, eventually it will be necessary to adapt a rationality concept that is more closely oriented on its use in other disciplines.

In economies, a commonly used criterion for evaluating and comparing situations is the *Pareto*-criterion. A situation is defined as Pareto-optimal if no agent's situation can be improved without reducing the payoff of someone else at the same time. Note that this criterion does not include a broader judgment regarding the desirability of an outcome. A situation where one agent controls all available resources, or receives the entire payoff in a given set-up, while the rest of the group have or receive nothing, is Pareto-optimal, just as is a situation where all agents control or receive equal shares. If a situation is not Pareto-optimal, if it is Pareto-inferior compared to another Pareto-superior one, at least one agent's payoff can be improved without a concurrent reduction in anyone else's payoff. If the individually optimal decisions lead to an outcome that is Pareto-optimal, we assume the degree of conflict to be low. If individually optimal decisions lead to a Pareto-inferior outcome, in turn, the degree of conflict is assumed to be high as agents' interests in others' decisions and their preferred choices do not concur.

You may imagine these situations along the following lines. As we consider agents and their behaviors, and the overall result to be expected from their decisions, every agent needs to have at least two behavioral options, A and B. If individually optimal decisions result in a Pareto-optimum, we can say that every agent rationally wants to choose option A and that this choice leads to an optimum on the group level as a side-effect. In the second case, every agent's individually optimal choice is B, but the outcome is not optimal. In fact, they would all prefer everyone would choose A. But no one has an individual incentive for this choice. Even if all other agents choose A, an individual can attain her best payoff by opting for B. However, if all agents choose B, the result will be suboptimal, on a group level as well as for every one of them. But as they all individually prefer B, rational and individualistic agents deciding freely will not be able to solve the situation and reach the Pareto-superior result. Such situations are thus called *social dilemmas*.

In between these two types of outcomes lie a variety of situations, in which individually optimal behavior cannot be defined without knowing about the choices of the other agents in a situation. That is to say, within the set-up as described above, if all other agents choose their option B, the last agent would also choose B, but if the others opt for A, so would the last one choosing. There is no clearly optimal behavior for an individual, but different options become more or less attractive, depending on what the other agents in a group opt for. Such problem-situation is therefore called a *coordination problem*. Once the agents in a group have coordinated on a type of behavior, they have no reason to change their behaviors, at least not individually. Note, however, that there is no guarantee that the coordinated situation would be the best among the possible outcomes. It is, by definition of the problem-structure, superior to uncoordinated outcomes, though.

Such different types of interdependent situations can be represented with the help of game-theoretic tools. Once these have been introduced in Chapter 2, we will return to these social decision situations for a more detailed analysis.

1.2 COMPETING PARADIGMS IN ECONOMICS: INVISIBLE HAND VS. FALLACY OF AGGREGATION

Many economists have been and continue to be very optimistic about the structures of social situations. The assumption from which a broad strand of economic theory has been developed is that individually rational behavior would automatically result in a social optimum as well. This *invisible hand* paradigm certainly served its purpose of developing a narrative based on which newly emerging merchant and trading classes could emancipate themselves against their feudal overlords. A concept of a *self-organizing* social and economic system leading to desirable social outcomes without the need for supervision served the articulation of their interests very well. *Adam Smith* who gave the idea its attractive 'invisible hand' capture, did not believe in its general validity, though. In fact, for him, pure individual self-interest as the sole motivation would lead to overall undesirable results. Rather, agents were socially embedded actors, who were generally willing to contribute to the public welfare, if only they were allowed sufficient room to choose and felt sufficiently empowered. The embeddedness in the social structures of their environment was a crucial factor for a functioning social and economic sphere. This second aspect has been pushed to the background of much of economic theory, however, and the focus has generally been directed to situations in which individual optimality and social desirability (presumably) coincide. It has become increasingly clear that the optimality of results in self-organizing economic systems is by no means certain, though, and that situations in which the results can be improved by properly structuring the decision-problem to enable agents to achieve superior results are the rule rather than an uncommon exception.

Other possible situations, related to the dilemma situations referred to above, can be described in terms of the *fallacy of aggregation* concept (sometimes also called the fallacy of composition). This idea states that the individually optimal actions undertaken by the agents may result in socially undesirable outcomes. In fact, we may relate it to a story that combines the general idea of the fallacy of aggregation and stresses the importance of *expectations* regarding others' behavior in interdependent situations. Imagine a number of firms that have to simultaneously decide on their investment programs. Their investments signify increased demand for others' products (directly, or indirectly because of increased purchasing power of the workers employed). In that case, a decision where all invest may be profitable for all. If, on the other hand, only some invest, their spending may not be profitable because the lack of investment by others can signify an overall demand that is not high enough to lead to an amortization of the investment spending undertaken. In short, if enough companies invest, everyone's investment will be worthwhile. If not enough firms invest, those who did will lose money, even as they produce a positive effect for all firms who profit from the additional demand that is created by the investment spending.

Depending on the relative strength of the effects involved, we may imagine the situation as a coordination or a dilemma problem. Either, it will become worthwhile to invest if enough other companies invest (their increased demand may necessitate additional production capacities to satisfy it), or a company may be unequivocally better off not investing, while still preferring all others would engage in investment programs and profiting from the additional demand this would create. If additional demand can be met by increasing the degree of utilization of existing production structures (as would be the case in a recession), the second case becomes more likely. However, if the scenario is true for all companies, none will invest, and the overall result is worse than it would have been if every firm had invested.

The degree of conflict thus differs depending on the overall problem structure that agents face. It has become clear that there is a *continuum of problem structures* beyond the individually easily solvable case of rational decisions resulting in a Pareto-optimum. In the case of coordination problems, expectations regarding others' behavior are crucial, whereas dilemma problems cannot be optimally solved by rational individualistic agents. In the case described, a fiscal program to stimulate demand and possibly transform the dilemma problem into a coordination problem may be a way out. More generally, an easy way out may be to call for enforcing socially optimal behavior, which, however, is problematic for a number of economic and political as well as social reasons. An endogenous solution that is attained and can be maintained by the agents themselves is clearly preferable. How such solutions may be developed will be taken up in Chapters 2 and 3 below.

1.3 UNCERTAINTY, STRATEGIC UNCERTAINTY, AND BOUNDED RATIONALITY

Uncertainty (sometimes also strong or true uncertainty) describes a situation in which agents do not know about future states of a system. This can manifest in different ways, as they may not know in which different states the system may be in the future or they may know about the different states, however, without being able to put probabilities on them and on that basis calculate risk (or, it may be a mixture of both). Economic situations are generally characterized by such uncertainty, and increasingly so, the longer the time horizon adopted.

In situations characterized by direct interdependence, we can also introduce the concept of *strategic uncertainty* (or initial strong strategic uncertainty). This term specifically captures the notion of not knowing how other agents will behave. As the results agents can achieve depend on the behavior of others, they will form expectations about these others and make their own choice based on these expectations. But being able to form expectations about the behavior of others presumes that agents have some knowledge, or at least can formulate some assumptions, about the others' motivations. The less they know, or the less sure they can be about the assumptions they have made, the higher is the *degree of uncertainty* under which agents take their own decisions.

If agents were not able to change that situation, it would mean the end of our analysis. There would be no regularities in behavior we could observe, at least no systematic ones, and hence there would be no foundation from which an analysis could be developed. But obviously there are *behavioral patterns* that are regularly repeated, that are observed, and that thereby allow agents to form expectations regarding future choices of behavior by others. These regularities are the reflections of *social rules* and *social institutions* that guide agents' behaviors, concepts to which we will momentarily return.

Another aspect that presents problems for agents when taking decisions is that they cannot handle the amount of data available in any given moment. When we assume rationality of the agents, but concede their *limited cognitive* capacities, we speak of *boundedly rational* agents in our analyses. They would however have to be able to handle all available data in any given moment in order to optimally inform their decisions. Hence, there is no reason to suspect that the decisions eventually taken would in any structured way lead to optimal results for them. This argument is independent of a possible interdependence of agents so far. We merely concede that agents' capacities are limited. Even if they were to make purely rational decisions on the basis of a strict cost-benefit analysis based on the information they have, they might end up with any kind of result. They may have taken the best possible decision given the information they had, but some crucial piece may still have been missing. Of course they can *learn* and *adapt their behavior*, but, again, they have limited capacities and therefore cannot continuously analyze and possibly upgrade all of their decisions frequently, an aspect that becomes all the more important once we recognize that the environment they are moving in may be changing over time. Furthermore, they do not face all relevant situations on a frequent basis, but some decisions have to be taken only occasionally. An upgrading of decision-rules based on earlier experiences is obviously difficult in this case. Such decision-rules are embodied in the social rules and social institutions that structure interactions in groups. We return to these below and in Chapter 8.

1.4 PATH DEPENDENCE AND NON-ERGODICITY IN PROCESSES OF CHANGE

Change is a constitutive element of economic systems. Environmental changes, technological development, adaptations of rules to allow for better results to be achieved, and other influences combine to create an economic sphere that is constantly in flux. We can employ the concept of *path dependence* for capturing some of the principal dynamics in these processes (see also Chapter 8 for a model of such dynamics). Another characteristic that economic systems show is the *non-ergodicity* of processes of change they undergo.

The state of a system depends on the path the system followed to that moment. The shape of this path is not predetermined, however. As can be appreciated from what has been said until here, influences from a number of sources can have an impact on the path taken and the shape of a situation that results from it in a given moment. Learning capacities of agents and the solutions to collective problems employed in a group can differ, for instance, and are likely to have an influence on future developments in their specific group and circumstances. At the same time, *random shocks, stochastic events*, or *accidents of history* influence the development an economic system undergoes.

Such influences and the resulting reactions and developments are typically not reversible in complex social and economic systems. We use 'complex' to describe situations that involve a number of heterogeneous agents having different behavioral options to choose from possibly pursuing different objectives. Even a number of individually minor incidents may combine to have a significant influence on the overall dynamic of such a system as behavioral decisions reinforce one another in a *cumulative process*. Accordingly, there will be no predetermined endpoint for the development either, no equilibrium at which it comes to rest. Rather, economic structures are reflections of ongoing processes, of which change is a constitutive characteristic. Such processes are called non-ergodic, if the systems governed by them do not return to prior states in a sufficiently long time interval. Non-ergodicity is a characteristic of processes in the economic sphere, and approaches based on a given equilibrium assumption, or even multiple possible equilibria, can therefore at best only serve as first approximations to an enhanced understanding of problems in that sphere (for such models, see Chapters 4, 5, and 6 below).

1.5   SOCIAL RULES AND SOCIAL INSTITUTIONS AS INFORMATIONAL DEVICES

If we know some agents from a group, we will increasingly be able to formulate assumptions about other members of this group. This is because behavior in groups follows social rules. Such rules serve a dual function. On the one hand, they make decisions easier for individual agents because there exist rules that agents can orient their decision on. In fact such rules are necessary for individuals because of the vast amounts of data available to them in every moment, from which they have to filter information that has to be analyzed in order to take a decision. If you have a rule to guide you, that process is much easier to go through. In fact, as the sheer amounts of data available are substantially beyond individuals' capacity to process, we need to have constructs that support us and facilitate the taking of decisions for us.

Here, social rules help by providing guidelines that agents can automatically follow and apply in their decisions. As long as the outcome is satisfactory (meets the *aspiration level* of an agent), such *satisficing* behavior is not in need of further changes. The formation of the aspiration level in turn depends on the environment in which agents are moving, as this shapes the reference frame on which agents draw. Here, we can already identify a first *feedback* cycle among behavior and outcomes that is mediated through the social rules followed and will have an impact on changes of these rules in the future.

On the other hand, social rules also help to form expectations about other agents' behavior. Therefore, such social rules have to be *common knowledge* in the groups in which they apply. They help to *reduce* the *uncertainty* surrounding the possible choices of other agents. This is a crucial function in situations that are characterized by a direct interdependence of agents, in which ones' results depend on the others' behaviors. Our expectations regarding others' behavior matter for our own choice of behavior in such situations, and the formation of expectations is facilitated by a common knowledge of rules governing social situations.

The existence of social rules and common knowledge regarding such rules allows agents to interact in a purposeful manner. As you will have realized, the existence of such rules does not imply their optimality for given situations. They facilitate agents' decision-making by reducing uncertainty in situations characterized by their direct interdependence. There is no reason to suspect that the outcome for the agents that results should be in any way optimal for them, alone or as a group, especially if we assume satisficing behavior under bounded capacities to be a more appropriate approximation to agents' decision-making. But the rules allow reaching some outcome, instead of letting agents face situations that they cannot solve at all. By reducing the options available to the agents in the first place, and thereby reducing complexity, social rules thus make situations accessible to the agents and only thereby permit them to reach a result. For many situations, thus, what may appear as a constraint on behavioral options in the form of social rules is in fact a necessary first step *enabling* agents to reach a decision at all, or help them attain a superior outcome relative to the situation without.

Additionally, we can point to the fact that there is no reason to suspect that different groups would have developed the same rules for solving their collective problems. On the contrary, different groups most likely have developed different sets of rules (cultures) for addressing the relevant problems that they have been facing in their possibly specific environment and over time. Finally, as groups apply numerous rules for a broad range of problem sets, and these rules are linked to one another (aligned with the broader 'world view' prevailing in a group), the transfer of selected ones from one group to another can prove difficult, and lead to results that were not anticipated nor desired, if they do not integrate with the prevailing set there. As rules are *learned* and over time *habituated*, and therefore applied without every time undergoing a rigorous process of consideration and evaluation, it is on the other hand likewise difficult to impossible to simply mandate the change of broader sets of rules. This does not mean change would not happen, though. It does mean that there is no single direction into which systems move and that could be identified based on universally valid axioms. Rather, they develop path-dependently.

1.6 SOCIAL RULES AND SOCIAL INSTITUTIONS AS SOLUTIONS TO COORDINATION AND DILEMMA PROBLEMS

Observing social situations in general more closely has shown us that the degree of a conflict of interests between the agents involved differs depending on the problem structure they face. For a group to be able to sustain situations and some degree of social cohesion, we can recognize that different situations require different kinds of rules, depending on the underlying problem structure that they serve to solve. As different groups can be expected to have developed different sets of rules over time, their ability to collectively confront economic situations and problems can be expected to differ.

For different problem structures, different social rules are needed for the agents if they are to reach a Pareto-optimal result. For coordinating on a Pareto-optimal outcome a social rule suffices. Achieving a Pareto-optimal result in a dilemma situation is more complicated.

The complication results from the problem structure and individually optimal behavior therein. This signifies that even in the socially optimal situation agents have an incentive to change their behavior (in terms of the above, choose B instead of A). How to incentivize the individuals not to do so is thus a necessary consideration when attempting to *structure policies* in order to improve the economic situation for a group. Within the group social institutions fulfill the role of *stabilizing* socially preferable behavior patterns and thus of *sustaining the socially preferable situation* that agents can profit from in the longer term. Agents thus have to be *socially embedded* such that the temptation to opt for a short-term advantage does not overturn the longer-term perspective and the social institution that is reaffirmed by the behavioral choices of the agents is kept alive.

If agents opt for the individually optimal behavior, the others can follow suit, and the overall result is the Pareto-inferior outcome, which also leads to a reduction of the payoff attainable by the individual agent who first opted for the short-term gain. We call the achieving of the Pareto-optimal result in a dilemma situation the result of *cooperation*. Cooperation is defined as *coordination plus sacrifice*. The social institution that contains the behavior leading to this outcome is accordingly defined as a *social rule plus sanction mechanism*. How this can be represented formally and how and why the threat of a sanction is credible will be taken up below, once game-theoretic methods have been introduced.

The sacrifice that is involved in adhering to the social institution is based on the resistance to the temptation of applying the individually rational behavior under a short-run perspective to the detriment of the individual and the group's longer term results, at the same time that agents put themselves in the position of potentially suffering from such behavior by others who might not act based on the social institution. But if the situation can be structured to include an endogenous sanction, there may be a way to stabilize the Pareto-optimal result. As we will see in the game-theoretic analyses that follow, such mechanisms can be built into games that are played repeatedly relatively easily. A longer time horizon of interactions is thus a very basic mechanism that can help to bring about improvements in the results agents in groups can achieve. Arguing for the adoption of a *longer time horizon* is easiest basing it on *learning* by the agents. This is important insofar as the ability to learn differentiates these agents from the ones in a number of economic models, where it is posited that all agents have all necessary information at the outset. We will take this aspect up in Chapter 3.

The sacrifice of a short-term advantage that may be individually realizable, if the others generally obey the rule embodied in the institution, may be seen as the *opportunity cost* of the long-term improved result. An opportunity cost describes the gains that another alternative would provide although this option is not pursued. If you buy good I, and then do not have enough money for good II, the unit of good II you do not buy is the opportunity cost of acquiring good I. The outcome that an agent does not realize because she opts for another kind of behavior is the opportunity cost of the outcome realized. The opportunity cost is a relevant decision variable in fact – if it is higher than the gain promised from the option realized, another decision should be taken by the agent. In directly interdependent decision situations such calculation is more complicated, because expectations about the reaction of other agents have to play a part in the considerations of the agents, as these shape the true costs of as well as benefits from decisions.

Behaviors and institutions are especially important when exchanges are concerned that are not executed simultaneously, but where some agents have to get active first, and have to rely on others to follow suit and honor commitments they may have entered into in order for long-term projects to become viable (think of research and development activities that run for long periods and rely on sequential contributions by the involved agents). *Reciprocity* and *trust* become necessary ingredients in order to bridge over time. The necessity to put trust into the interaction partners is aggravated as *contracts* are necessarily *incomplete*. They cannot contain provisions for every contingency. Therefore, they can support long-term exchanges (that do not coincide in time and/or place) but may not provide sufficient certainty and hence may not restructure a situation so that all potential problems for agents are provided with a solution mechanism. To strengthen the foundation for a relation, an alteration of the nature of the underlying problem structure is going to be helpful, or even required. And, again, some degree of trust is going to have to be invested, especially at the beginning of a new partnership.

If we develop the analyses of social problem-structures based on narrowly rational agents, we have to be aware that we have to involve some kind of transformation of the original dilemma situation, as a dilemma is a problem that an individualistic and rational agent will not be able to solve. As long as we build our analyses on agents that we assume to be rational in the economics understanding, we have to alter the situation they face, for a superior outcome to be systematically realizable. As you will see, the solution concepts employed in game-theoretic analyses and the tools developed for other methodological approaches to economic questions require rationality of the agents to work. We can later introduce behavioral motivations that are not strictly rational, but a first baseline and reference point can be the 'rational' individualistic agent. Finding mechanisms that allow even these types of agents to solve specific problem structures, such as dilemmas, without having to fall back on an external enforcer suggests that a strong solution mechanism may have been found.

1.7   PUBLIC GOOD CHARACTER AND POSITIVE EXTERNAL EFFECTS OF SOCIAL RULES AND SOCIAL INSTITUTIONS

We can understand social rules and social institutions as the collective solutions to a common problem. We have seen that they increase the problem-solving capacities of agents by offering behavioral guidelines and reducing uncertainty in the formulation of expectations about other agents' behavior. When social rules and institutions exist, they thereby have the character of what is called a *public good*. That means, they are *non-rival* and *non-exclusive* in consumption. Non-rivalry signifies that one agent's use of a good does not reduce or prevent its use or usefulness by and to others. Non-excludability signifies that once the good is in existence, agents cannot normally be stopped from using it.

Goods that are rival and exclusive are so-called *private goods*, in contrast. Rivalry means that one agent's consuming of a good means that others cannot consume it. Excludability in turn means that agents can be excluded from utilizing the good (through provisions defining the transfer of rights of ownership and assorted other rights). Given these dimensions for categorizing goods, we can additionally distinguish two other types, namely, *club goods* that are characterized by excludability and non-rivalry, and *commons* that are characterized by non-excludability and rivalry.

Different groups of agents have found different arrangements structuring their treatment of goods that are characterized by their non-excludability, so-called *collective goods*. As will be taken up below, a number of problems result here, regarding production in the case of public goods and exploitation and consumption in the case of commons (as these already exist). Depending on how a group's approach to the collective sphere is defined and formed, the consequences and the relative success in the economic sphere will differ between groups, as the relation to and treatment of non-excludable goods bears significantly on the overall economic structures and success groups realize.

When agents follow social rules and social institutions to inform their behavioral decisions, they create a positive effect on other agents, as these can take better-informed behavioral decisions themselves. There are, therefore, so-called *positive external effects* in the application of social rules and social institutions (or simply rules, in what follows). These positive external effects in the case under consideration here coincide with *positive net externalities*, because one agent's application of a rule does not only provide positive effects on the other agents, but because additionally the usefulness of rules increases with the number of agents applying them in their decision-making processes. The other way around: If a rule is not followed by a sufficient number of agents, so that there is not a sufficient coherence in behavior, any given rule fails to reduce uncertainty sufficiently, leading to a reduction of problem-solving capacities of the agents in a group. What constitutes a sufficient number of agents may depend on the problem in question.

Agents always have the choice of contributing to the collective good social institution, or of not contributing, which would result in its weakening, and potentially even its deterioration and eventual breakdown. Agents have to contribute to the institution's maintenance and reproduction, they affirm it through their behavior. The breakdown of the institution would signify a worsening of the results achievable by the agents in a group. We thus find negative external effects of not contributing, and positive external effects of contributing to the maintenance of the social institution by adhering to its prescriptions on this level of social relations as well. The positive external effects of the rules and institutions are derived from the positive external effects of the concurrent behavior patterns on the results achievable by other agents.

Related concepts are *economies of scale* and *returns to scale*. Economies of scale is the term used for describing falling average costs as a result of increasing production volumes or numbers. The more a firm produces of a good, the cheaper every single unit becomes. To expand production is thus a generally advantageous strategy to pursue in this case because it purports a potential cost advantage over other producers in a similar market segment. Returns to scale are derived from production technologies and refer to the proportionality of output changes following changes in all inputs. If output increases over-proportionally following an equal increase in all inputs, we refer to this as increasing returns (with constant and decreasing returns as the equivalent categories for proportional and under-proportional increases; see Chapter 5). Economies of scale are a consequence of increasing returns to scale.

The application of a rule shows a similar characteristic to that of economies of scale in the number of times it has been used by agents. The more often agents apply a rule, the less they have to invest in the taking of decisions in similar situations any longer, as they can simply apply a rule in a certain situation without further reflection. Thereby they also reduce the necessary effort level for other agents, because those increasingly know what to expect from their peers. The more often a rule has been applied, the less costly its application becomes.

However, that may mean that the rule itself is in use long after its problem-solving capacity has started to diminish. A change in the environment may lead to results that are increasingly far from what would be attainable if different behavioral options were chosen. The diminishing cost of applying the rule may simply make the cost of switching to a new rule (or even set of rules) seem prohibitive to the agents. They might profit if the new rule were established (though they do not necessarily know that, especially as they act under uncertainty). But the initial cost of switching may prevent them from doing so, even as that reduces their long-term economic results. The network effects related to the characteristics of social rules may prevent their adaptation to newly arising challenges, or the adaptation of newly emerging opportunities.

Still, social rules and social institutions are not natural laws. They do change eventually. And at times some drastic changes in the overall framework of rules structuring groups' interactions occur. Consider that it is a mere two-hundred years since the organization of economic exchanges in markets as we understand them as particular sets of social rules and social institutions has started to dominate in Western societies, concurrent to the radical reinterpretation of the role of the individual in society. And since then, the institutional structures of markets have undergone substantial changes as well.

1.8   INSTRUMENTAL AND CEREMONIAL DIMENSIONS OF SOCIAL INSTITUTIONS

Originally, social rules and social institutions are assumed here to emerge as problem-solving devices enabling agents to solve common and collective problems. This function is described by their so-called *instrumental* dimension. Rules may, however, eventually appear to the individual agent as *norms*, prescriptive behavioral requests. This introduces a change in the motivation for maintaining the rule as well. The normative aspect can be considered as an additional dimension of the rule, a dimension in which the original problem-solving character is no longer consciously present. A *ceremonial* dimension becomes part of the overall character of the rule. Over time, all rules acquire an increasingly pronounced ceremonial dimension.

In more detail, the typical 'life-cycle' of a rule contains a number of stages. Being established as an instrumental rule, it eventually acquires a normative dimension, becoming a, still instrumental, norm. Once the normative character is thus established, it turns into an abstract norm over time. As that stage is reached, the ceremonial dimension is established.

The increasing dominance of the ceremonial aspect of rules derives from status and distinction, power and hierarchy considerations of agents. The ceremonial is thus a *value-dimension* in which differential power and status are the dominating influence factors. They have their roots in feelings of identity and belonging, as well as a desire for leadership that together reduce individuals' fears under conditions of uncertainty. The social stratification that emerges in groups is reinforced by accordingly defined acceptable behavioral patterns of individuals, depending on their rank in the group. The resulting structure is strengthened by narratives that combine to form an ideological framework that justifies the hierarchical structures in place. In turn, individuals are further emotionally conditioned to accepting prevailing hierarchical structures by sets of ritualized behaviors and rites that reinforce their attachment to the system in place.

Changes in the environment reduce a rule's usefulness in a new situation. So, over time a reduction in a rule's problem-solving, instrumental capacity comes about. However, related to the emergence of rules' ceremonial dimension, the original problem-solving motivation for maintaining rules is driven to the background, and increasingly replaced by ceremonial considerations regarding their preservation. The stronger these considerations are, the more petrified a group's social structure has become, the more difficult it gets to change rules according to instrumental needs and considerations. The situation is *locked-in* (the concept of a lock-in will be explained in more detail below, in Chapter 8).

We can additionally point to the cost factor mentioned above contributing to the conservation of rules beyond their instrumental usefulness and justification. The cost-reduction per application reduces the attractiveness of establishing a new rule that is more costly to follow at first. Establishing a new way of coordinating agents' behaviors may be difficult to formulate and may also be difficult to organize if larger numbers of agents are involved.

We have to note, though, that even a strongly ceremonially dominated rule is not without problem-solving capacity. This capacity is merely reduced, possibly substantially reduced, relative to that of other possible behavioral patterns in certain circumstances. But it still allows the coordination of agents and hence the achieving of some coordinated outcome, where without any rule no such outcome might be feasible. But the result is not as good as it could be under different rules given the circumstances. We can thereby appreciate that different sets of rules will result in different levels of problem-solving capacities by groups. There will also be a dynamical component to this, as, at least periodically, some general sets of rules or some environments may be more conducive to change than others.

1.9   REAL-WORLD MICROECONOMICS

We have seen that agents' limited cognitive capacities and the uncertainty they face make the establishment of behavioral rules necessary to support them in their decision-making processes. Such rules serve a dual purpose.

They facilitate the reaching of decisions by agents, by limiting the effort necessary for them to orient themselves in certain situations. They also reduce the strategic uncertainty of agents in directly interdependent situations. As a result they enable agents to realize superior outcomes.

Depending on the problem-structure faced, different rules or institutions are needed for facilitating the solution of common and collective problems. As sets of rules develop over time, different groups show different problem-solving capacities. At the same time, the transfer of selected rules from one group to another is unlikely to be successful, as rules have developed in complex path-dependent processes and are structured in complementary sets.

Rules undergo changes over time in reaction to but also contributing to changing environments. Their problem-solving, instrumental component is reduced as a function of two related phenomena. The first is the fact that the repeated application of a rule leads to its habituation. An effect of such habituation is a reduction in the cost of applying a rule. New, potentially better suited rules may then be difficult to establish, as they signify elevated costs or effort during the process of their establishment. The second conserving force is related to the fact that the motivation for maintaining rules changes over time. The original problem-solving objective behind them may be pushed to the background by ceremonial considerations that have developed for a given set of rules. Some agents profit within given structures and gain due to the social position they have reached. Keeping this social position may be a strong motivation for maintaining given rules, even if their change might promise economic improvements. Others may simply be unwilling to give up their established patterns of thought, and 'world-view', even if they could gain thereby (economically, but also for instance politically).

Finally, we have seen that interdependent problem structures can be characterized according to the degree of conflict of interests among the agents facing the problem in question. Different rules, or institutions, depending on the specific problems, allow solutions to be reached, that can be differentiated by their overall economic effectiveness. The better suited a set of rules is for solving collective problems, the more successful the group in question is likely going to be.

We can appreciate here that all behavior is institutionally embedded, and that therefore an understanding of institutional structures and the functions these fulfill is a necessary component of analyzing economic structures and problems.

In fact, the principal focus of much of microeconomic theory, the 'market', is a construction, a set of institutions, serving to resolve some societal conflicts, namely the distribution of available resources. This construct has developed over time, and has been shaped by earlier conditions that find their reflections in current structures. Depending on how earlier conditions and power-distributions have been shaped in detail, current *'market' arrangements will differ*, thus offering different solutions to the same general problem structures in different groups. To suspect a commonly applicable set of axioms could enhance our understanding of market arrangements seems rather optimistic under these circumstances. An understanding of the rules surrounding the interactions in markets and any other form of coordination, cooperation, allocation or organization can on the other hand significantly enhance our understanding of the problems involved and the solutions reached, stressing the different problem-solving abilities of different groups.

When observing economically relevant behavior, we see the solutions that are implemented by groups of agents. The objective of analyzing such situations and solutions is to understand the underlying problem structures, be they markets, hierarchies, networks, informal systems, or states. Only thereby can we understand basic problems and processes in economic matters and eventually arrive at statements regarding the desirability of change and the potential for improvement that may have been identified. The first step towards an analysis of different social situations is the acquisition of *tools* and *methods* for understanding different problem-structures so as to be able to recognize them and then be able to devise adequate proposals for how to deal with them in the second step.

All these considerations are additionally relevant as many social situations involve some kind of structure that can be understood in terms of a social dilemma in the background. Understanding how dilemmas have been solved, which structures and processes have contributed to their solution and what may be crucial factors helping to achieve such solutions is what modern microeconomics is about. Microeconomics thus becomes the science of complex coordination, cooperation, and organization among individual agents in processes under conditions of direct interdependence and uncertainty. Different tools for approaching questions related to these aspects will be explained in what follows in Chapter 2.

FURTHER READING

For an annotated list of a range of selected micro-textbooks, some selected monographs on evolutionary, institutional, and applied game-theoretic economics of interactive economies, and for some selected article references, see the textbook website at www.microeconomics.us.

2. Methods for Analyzing Interactive Economies: An Introduction to Game Theory

2.1 INTRODUCTION

Game theory is a field of mathematics closely related to economic considerations of preference relations and the effects of direct interdependence on individual 'utility' yielding interactive strategic behavior. The field has emerged since the 1940s notably with John von Neumann and Oscar Morgenstern's theory of utility presented in their groundbreaking monograph 'Theory of Games and Economic Behavior' (von Neumann and Morgenstern, 1944) and was subsequently complemented by the introduction of concepts of decision making and stable states in interactive situations, in turn allowing the prediction of likely outcomes. Early game theory received notable contributions by John Nash (equilibrium and dominance concepts), John Harsanyi, Robert Aumann (mixed strategy equilibrium concepts), John Maynard Smith, Stephen Jay Gould (evolutionary game theory), Reinhard Selten, Roger Myerson and Robert Axelrod (strategies in repeated games).

While game theory allows to model far from equilibrium situations, including axioms and analyses entirely different from orthodox neoclassical economic theory, it still requires the assumption of a universal and well defined rationality of the economic agents. This has been heavily criticized by psychological, experimental, and behavioral economists, who were able to show systematic biases in human decision making (Tversky and Kahneman, 1973). While economic game theory adapted itself to the criticism by considering different kinds of bounded rationality (Simon, 1956) and investigating possible empirically measurable decision heuristics in human decision making (Experimental Economics, Fehr et. al., 2002) the original approach of game theory may be seen as both inspired and limited by the scientific spirit of the mid 20th century, the endeavor to analyze, reproduce, measure and predict anything with however limited methods (Hargreaves-Heap and Varoufakis, 2004, p.3). Bounded rationality is a usual assumption in multi-agent models in game theory. In evolutionary game theory, the focus shifts from individual rational decision making to the dynamic performance of strategies thus relaxing the assumption of universal rationality (e.g. Nelson and Winter, 1982; Axelrod, 1984).

Notwithstanding its limitations, game theory has helped economics and other fields of research to achieve a better understanding of a vast variety of phenomena in socio-economic systems. It has not only provided a multiplicity of instructive models it has also inspired the development of more sophisticated methods both within and beyond the scope of traditional game theory. It might be justified to argue that game theory has been and continues to be for economics what the theory of dynamic systems has been for physics: An area of applied mathematics fitting the needs and developed with the assistance of the academic field it is to be applied to.

2.2   FORMAL CONCEPTS

2.2.1   Invisible Hand and Fallacy of Aggregation again

In the first chapter we introduced the general concepts of economic modeling, the invisible hand and the fallacy of aggregation and the invisible hand. Both tell illustrative stories of the direct interaction of rational agents. The invisible hand describes a situation where every agent chooses the socially optimal option out of her incentive to maximize individually. Say, every agent has an option to contribute (costs: 1) or not to contribute (zero cost) to a public good and receives three times her own contribution (benefit: 2 or 0 respectively) and twice the contribution of the other player(s) (2 or zero respectively); see Figure 2.1.

		Player B	
		Strategy 1	Strategy 2
Player A	Strategy 1	4 4	2 2
	Strategy 2	2 2	0 0

Figure 2.1   Social Optimum Game

The concept of optimality in interactive situations, specifically the *Pareto optimum* has been introduced in Chapter 1. It is easy to see that the game will arrive at the socially optimal (and single Pareto-optimal) point (4,4). Consequently, this model justifies ignoring the micro-level of direct interactions (since everyone chooses equivalently and optimally). A different story is told by the *fallacy of aggregation.*

| | | Player B | |
		Strategy 1	Strategy 2
Player A	Strategy 1	1 1	2 -1
	Strategy 2	-1 2	0 0

Figure 2.2   Prisoners' Dilemma Game

Say, as before, the agents choose whether to contribute or not, but this time, they only receive twice the payoff of their opponents. We can see that the second strategy seems to be strictly better (strictly dominant) against the first one, the most likely outcome would therefore be $(0, 0)$ which of course is *Pareto inferior* compared to $(1, 1)$; see Figure 2.2. The message conveyed by this metaphor is that it is possible that agents choose a socially suboptimal situation. Social interactions may take the form of an extensive continuum of games with different properties and great attention has to be given to the modeling of the micro-structure of an economy along the lines of different games, different concepts of decision making and social interaction. To quote from one of the most important recent game theoretic textbooks, Hargreaves-Heap and Varoufakis: 'One is hard put to find a social phenomenon that cannot be so described [as a strategic game.]' (2004, p. 3).

The game given as an example for the metaphor of the invisible hand is called a Social Optimum Game; it is symmetric and for both players the first strategy is preferable to the second no matter what the opponent does (a *strictly dominant strategy*). Both players choosing this strategy leads to a situation where neither of the players has an incentive to unilaterally deviate from this outcome which brings stability to this result and justifies it being called an equilibrium – specifically a Nash equilibrium. This property (no incentive for unilateral deviation) does not hold for any of the alternative three possible outcomes; the Nash equilibrium is thus unique and it is furthermore the only Pareto-optimal outcome. The game discussed for the fallacy of aggregation is a *Prisoners' Dilemma*; it is a *symmetric* game as well, it too contains a *strictly dominant* strategy for both players, leading to the single Nash equilibrium. However, this time the Nash equilibrium is the only outcome that is not Pareto-optimal.

Thus far, both games are 2-person, 2-strategy normal form games; however, the same two games may be defined as n-person games with the same results. All n agents choose a strategy s_i. For convenience and in accordance with other game theory textbooks we define the vector of the strategies of the other players

$$s_{-i} = (s_j)_{j \neq i},$$

$-i$ being the index for all strategies other than s_i, thus $-i = 1, \dots, i-1, i+1, \dots, n$. For the social optimum game with (as above) $s_i \in \{0, 1\}$ the payoff in the social optimum game is

$$\Pi_i = 2s_i + 2 \sum_{-i} s_{-i}.$$

It is easily seen that the second term is equal for both strategies, while the payoffs depend positively on the first term – the own contribution of the agent s_i – making her highest possible contribution her strictly best strategy. For the Prisoners' Dilemma, again with $s_i \in \{0, 1\}$ the payoff computes as

$$\Pi_i = -s_i + 2 \sum_{-i} s_{-i}.$$

Here, the payoffs depend negatively on the own contribution while the term for the contribution of the other players is again equal for all strategies s_i. It is obviously the best possible strategy to contribute as little as possible. Hence, provided that all agents are sufficiently informed and act rationally we can predict that a social optimum game will result in all agents contributing as much as possible, while a game of the Prisoners' Dilemma type will prevent rational agents from contributing at all. As mentioned, the two games reflect two different if not oppositional economic principles, the invisible hand, which for more than two centuries has guided classical and neoclassical thought, and the fallacy of aggregation, that describes a more complex, conflictive and interdependent setting.

2.2.2 Games

To provide a more structured approach to game theory, this section will provide definitions, clarify assumptions and introduce commonly used notations.

A *strategic game* (or just game) is an abstract model of the interaction of directly interdependent subjects (humans, or more generally *agents*). A game is properly described if

1. the set of rules of the game,
2. the set of agents in the game,
3. the set of *strategies* of the agents and
4. the set of *information* available to each agent

are defined.

The set of rules is usually implied in the description of the game as belonging to a particular type of games. For the moment it is sufficient to define the type of normal form games (further types such as evolutionary games will be introduced later). A *normal form game* is a game with a defined (finite or infinite) number of agents each of which chooses between (not necessarily identical) strategies with given payoffs for each agent for each possible *combination of strategies*. Any combination of strategies contains one strategy for each agent participating in the game. The number of strategies per agent may also be finite or infinite. Many concepts, however, do not apply for infinite numbers of agents and strategies; the usual approach that will also be taken in this chapter is that of the number of agents and strategies both being finite. The agents choose their strategies simultaneously, implying that at the time of choosing they are not informed about the choice of their opponents.

Consider a normal form game with n agents. Let s_i denote abstractly any particular (pure) strategy of the i-th agent and S_i the set of all (pure) strategies of the agent i. Further let S be the set of the sets of strategies of all agents in the game,

$$S = \{S_i\} \qquad i = 1, \dots, n.$$

Let s be any particular feasible configuration of strategies, containing one strategy for each agent, let a particular strategy of agent i be called s_i, and let the strategies of all other agents be written as $s_{-i} = \left(s_j\right)_{j \neq i}$, $s = \{s_i, s_{-i}\}$.

The set of all sets of strategies S implies the set of all feasible combinations of strategies s. Therefore the *set of payoffs* of an agent i resulting from all possible combinations of strategies can be written as

$$\Pi_i (S) = \left(\Pi_i (s)\right)_{\forall s} = \left(\Pi_i (s_i, s_{-i})\right)_{\forall s_i \forall s_{-i}}.$$

A normal form game G with n agents is written as

$$G = \{S_i; \Pi_i(S), I_i\} \qquad i = 1, \dots, n$$

where I_i denotes the set of information of the *i*-th agent. A *2-person normal form game* is a normal form game with $n = 2$; thus

$$G = \{S_1, S_2; \Pi_1(S), \Pi_2(S); I_1, I_2\}.$$

This special type of normal form games is the most widely known and used type of strategic games. In addition to this *formal notation*, it may be written in *matrix notation* (Figure 2.3)

		Player B	
		Strategy 1	Strategy 2
Player A	Strategy 1	$\Pi_B (s_{A1}, s_{B1})$ $\Pi_A (s_{A1}, s_{B1})$	$\Pi_B (s_{A1}, s_{B2})$ $\Pi_A (s_{A1}, s_{B2})$
	Strategy 2	$\Pi_B (s_{A2}, s_{B1})$ $\Pi_A (s_{A2}, s_{B1})$	$\Pi_B (s_{A2}, s_{B2})$ $\Pi_A (s_{A2}, s_{B2})$

Figure 2.3   Normal form game in matrix notation (general form)

2.2.3   Agents and Decision Making

With the game, the strategies, the payoffs, and the information set thus defined, what remains to be explained in order to predict strategy choices and payoffs of the game, are the properties of the agent. In the above example we assumed that rational agents would, if possible, always choose strategies to award themselves the highest possible payoff. This is something that must be assumed, since it does not follow from an ex-ante logic nor is it always empirically measurable in human behavior. In fact, it has been firmly criticized by a number of scholars (see the introduction to this chapter). Nevertheless, some kind of regularly predictable decision making has to be assumed in order to derive solutions and predictions. Standard game theory thus requires agents

1. to derive their choices using *well defined preference orderings*, that is their *preferences* for *bundles of goods* must be
   a. *complete*: $a \succ b$ or $a \sim b$ or $a \prec b$,
   b. *reflexive*: $a \succ b \Leftrightarrow b \prec a$, and
   c. *transitive*: $a \succ b$ and $b \succ c \Rightarrow a \succ c$.
   If this holds, one may derive an *ordinal payoff measure* Π for any game no matter what kinds of goods the game is originally about;
2. to be aware of common rationality (*CKR* - *common knowledge of rationality*). That is, agents do not only fulfill condition (1) but are also

aware that all other agents fulfill condition (1) as well. Further they are aware that all other agents are aware that all agents are rational; etc.

Note that the agents are neither *envious* nor *benevolent*, i.e. they neither work to decrease nor to increase the payoffs of other agents. They are truly indifferent towards the payoffs of each other. However, CKR (condition (2)) enables agents to anticipate decisions of other agents and react accordingly. In fact, without CKR they were left without any reasonable assumptions about their opponents' behavior and would have to neglect the outcome of other agents completely. In this case the game is equivalent to an ordinary non-interdependent decision problem – an important point to start with when considering game theory.

2.3　SOLUTIONS OF NORMAL FORM GAMES

2.3.1　Dominance of Strategies

As we can see from the introductory examples, the Social Optimum Game and the Prisoners' Dilemma, individually rational decision making on the part of the agents can lead to socially unfavorable outcomes. The structure of the problems as interdependent decision situations, however, defies traditional methods of non-interdependent optimization. Further, using methods of non-interdependent decision theory would also lead to systematic errors as they are unable to take reactions of an 'intelligent' opponent into account. A more appropriate course of action is to systematically identify superior and inferior strategies and derive solution concepts from this taking advantage of the (by definition) guaranteed rationality of all players.

　　The general definition of *dominance* with respect to the set of strategies S_i of an agent i in a normal form game G is as follows: A strategy $s_i^* \in S_i$ is said to *dominate* another strategy $s_i^{\sim} \in S_i$ if, and only if,

$$\Pi_i(s_i^*, s_{-i}) \geq \Pi_i(s_i^{\sim}, s_{-i}) \forall s_{-i}$$

and

$$\exists s_{-i}: \Pi_i(s_i^*, s_{-i}) > \Pi_i(s_i^{\sim}, s_{-i}).$$

$s_i^{\sim}$ is in this case said to be *dominated* (by s_i^*).

　　s_{-i} is any possible combination of the strategies of all other agents. That is, the product of the number of strategies per agent (except for agent i) is the number of combinations contained by the set s_{-i}. The inequalities essentially state, that for any possible combination of actions of all other agents, the strategy s_i^* must be at least as good (the payoffs for i at least as high) as $s_i^{\sim}$ and for at least one combination s_i^* must be strictly better (the payoffs for i strictly higher) than the strategy $s_i^{\sim}$. For 2-person 2-strategy normal form games, this formula becomes much simpler.

Player B

		s_{B1}	s_{B2}
Player A	s_{A1}	a_A $\quad a_B$	d_A $\quad b_B$
	s_{A2}	b_A $\quad d_B$	c_A $\quad c_B$

Figure 2.4   Normal form game in matrix notation (simple general form)

The payoffs of agent A when choosing her dominating strategy s^* for any possible strategy of agent B (s_{B1} or s_{B2}) must be at least as high as the payoffs resulting from her dominated strategy $s^{\sim}$. More specifically (s_{A1} being the dominating strategy), $a_A \geq b_A$, $d_A \geq c_A$. Further, for at least one possible strategy of B (s_{B1} or s_{B2}), A's dominating strategy must perform strictly better, that is $a_A > b_A$ or $d_A > c_A$.

The stronger form of the dominance criterion is obtained by demanding strictly higher payoffs for any possible combination of the strategies of all other agents. A strategy s_i^* of an agent i in a normal form game G is said to be *strictly dominating* another strategy $s_i^{\sim}$ if, and only if,

$$\Pi_i(s_i^*, s_{-i}) > \Pi_i(s_i^{\sim}, s_{-i}) \ \forall \ s_{-i}.$$

$s_i^{\sim}$ is in this case said to be *strictly dominated* (by s_i^*). In terms of the 2-person 2-strategy variant of normal form games it is again much easier: s^* is said to dominate $s^{\sim}$ strictly, if $a_A > b_A$ and $c_A > d_A$.

We can now proceed to predict, that strictly dominated strategies will always be abandoned in favor of the respectively dominating strategies. No rational agent will ever choose a dominated strategy, meaning that any dominated strategy is irrelevant for the outcome of the game. This in turn enables us to safely remove any strictly dominated strategy $s_i^{\sim}$ (of any agent i) from a normal form game G (obtaining a reduced game G1) without affecting the outcome of the game. With CKR, we can further say that the opponent is informed as well that the first player will never play that strictly dominated strategy. In turn, she also uses game $G1$. The process may be repeated successively for both players which is a solution concept commonly referred to as *successive elimination of strictly dominated strategies (SESDS)*. This yields a finite sequence $G, G1, G2 \ldots Gm$ which ends with a game Gm that does not contain any strictly dominated strategies and thus terminates the process. If Gm contains only (and exactly) one strategy s_i^* for every agent i, the combination of these strategies

$$s^* = \{s_1^*, \ldots s_n^*\}$$

constitutes a unique solution of G. In this case the game G (and all games of the series $G1, G2, \ldots$) are called solvable by SESDS. Rational agents will always reach this combination of strategies when playing G.

2.3.2   Nash Equilibrium

While SESDS is a feasible and reliable method to predict a unique rational outcome of games it does not always yield a solution since not every game has a unique best combination of strategies or more technically not every game contains strictly dominated strategies. Consider as examples the structures known as *Coordination Game* (Figure 2.5) and *Hawk-Dove Game* or *Chicken Game* (Figure 2.6).

		Player B	
		s_{B1}	s_{B2}
Player A	s_{A1}	2 2	0 0
	s_{A2}	0 0	2 2

Figure 2.5   Coordination Game

		Player B	
		s_{B1}	s_{B2}
Player A	s_{A1}	2 2	3 1
	s_{A2}	1 3	0 0

Figure 2.6   Hawk-Dove Game (also called Chicken Game)

In both games, by using SESDS we cannot predict anything – none of the strategies is strictly dominated. One way to deal with this is simply to accept the fact that rational actors may play both strategies and none of the possibilities can be ruled out – which is a solution of some kind as well. However, it is clear that some of the payoffs are undesirable and even avoidable by simply letting the respective agents choose another strategy. This argument is not per se a valid one since the choices are by definition made at the same time and without knowledge of the action of the other players. Still, we can assume that even rational agents have beliefs about what others will do. Given such beliefs, and thus neglecting any element of uncertainty, the agents have perfect best answer strategies. Any strategy combination that is exclusively composed of best answers offers no incentive to any of the players to reconsider her choice. These mutual best answers or *Nash equilibria* can reasonably be considered more likely outcomes than other combinations of strategies (even more so of course if the game is repeated).

More formally, a Nash equilibrium is any combination of strategies

$$s^* = \{s_1^*, \dots, s_n^*\}$$

in a normal form game G such that

$$\Pi_i(s_i^*, s_{-i}^*) \geq \Pi_i(s_i, s_{-i}^*) \qquad \forall\, s_i \in S_i \,\forall\, i.$$

There may be more than one Nash equilibrium in G (consider the above Coordination and Hawk-Dove Games as examples). Even in finite games (requiring the number of strategies s_i for all agents i to be finite) the best answer structure in the game takes a circular form, it is possible that G does not contain a Nash equilibrium in pure strategies at all. For example, in a 2-person game strategy s_{A1} of player 1 is the only best answer to s_{B1} of player 2, s_{B1} is the only best answer to s_{A2} of player 1 which is the only best answer to s_{B2} of agent 2. s_{B2} in turn is the only best answer to s_{A1}. The most simple example of this is the *Matching Pennies Game* (Figure 2.7).

		Player B	
		s_{B1}	s_{B2}
Player A	s_{A1}	-1 / 1	1 / -1
	s_{A2}	1 / -1	-1 / 1

Figure 2.7   Matching Pennies Game

2.3.3   Mixed Strategies

We have seen that not every normal form game has a solution in terms of dominance (SESDS), nor in terms of Nash equilibria in pure strategies. Returning to the matching pennies game introduced above we may therefore ask how rational agents will decide in this situation and by extension if a rational decision is possible in this and similar situations. Another example is the well known *Rock-Paper-Scissors Game* (Figure 2.8).

		Player B		
		Rock	Paper	Scissors
Player A	Rock	0 0	1 -1	-1 1
	Paper	-1 1	0 0	1 -1
	Scissors	1 -1	-1 1	0 0

Figure 2.8   Rock-Paper-Scissors Game

Of course, a rational decision is possible. However, the *pure strategies* rock, paper, and scissors are no good candidates: All of them are exploitable by another pure strategy. Humans engaging in this game will therefore never decide to always play the same pure strategy but try to be as incomputable as possible. And so do rational agents; the game theory concept is called mixed strategies.

Let a *mixed strategy* formally be defined as a vector of probabilities. Any available pure strategy is assigned a probability with which the agent will play this strategy; hence the number of elements the vector is composed of must equal the number of pure strategies of the underlying game. Hence, formally, a mixed strategy σ_i of player i contains any probabilistic combination of all x available pure strategies weighted with probabilities $p_1, p_2, \ldots, p_x$ to play these pure strategies. For the 2-strategy case (i.e. two pure strategies), the mixed strategy is thus

$$\sigma_i = \begin{pmatrix} p \\ 1 - p \end{pmatrix}.$$

2.3.4   Nash Equilibrium in Mixed Strategies

A Nash equilibrium in mixed strategies σ^* is a configuration of mixed strategies for all n players $\sigma^* = \{\sigma_1^*, \sigma_2^*, \dots, \sigma_n^*\}$ such that

$$\Pi_i(\sigma_i^*, \sigma_{-i}^*) \geq \Pi_i(\sigma_i, \sigma_{-i}^*) \qquad \forall \sigma_i \forall i.$$

Lemma (1): A mixed Nash equilibrium strategy σ_i^* can never yield a higher expected payoff (against all other agent's corresponding mixed Nash equilibrium strategies σ_{-i}^*) than any of player i's pure strategies $s_{i,j}$ played with a positive probability $p_j > 0$ in the mixed strategy Nash equilibrium

$$\sigma_i^* = \begin{pmatrix} p_1 \\ \vdots \\ p_j \\ \vdots \\ p_x \end{pmatrix}$$

thus,

$$\Pi_i(\sigma_i^*, \sigma_{-i}^*) = \Pi_i(s_{i,j}, \sigma_{-i}^*) \qquad \forall j: p_j > 0.$$

Proof: Assume the Lemma did not hold, hence

$$\Pi_i(\sigma_i^*, \sigma_{-i}^*) > \Pi_i(s_{i,j}, \sigma_{-i}^*).$$

The expected payoff Π_i computes as

$$\Pi_i(\sigma_i^*, \sigma_{-i}^*) = (p_1 \cdots p_j \cdots p_x) \begin{pmatrix} \Pi_i(s_{i,1}, \sigma_{-i}^*) \\ \vdots \\ \Pi_i(s_{i,j}, \sigma_{-i}^*) \\ \vdots \\ \Pi_i(s_{i,x}, \sigma_{-i}^*) \end{pmatrix}$$

$$= p_1 \Pi_i(s_{i,1}, \sigma_{-i}^*) + \cdots + p_j \Pi_i(s_{i,j}, \sigma_{-i}^*) + \cdots + p_x \Pi_i(s_{i,x}, \sigma_{-i}^*).$$

The expected value of the jth pure strategy of this term is smaller than the overall result. Hence a combination of the remaining strategies (the weight relation among them remaining equal) without strategy $s_{i,j}$, thus a mixed strategy

$$\sigma_i^{\sim} = \frac{1}{(1-p_j)} \begin{pmatrix} p_1 \\ \vdots \\ p_{j-1} \\ 0 \\ p_{j+1} \\ \vdots \\ p_x \end{pmatrix}$$

must yield a better payoff than σ_i^* (note that the factor $\frac{1}{(1-p_j)} > 1$)

$$\Pi_i(\sigma_i^{\sim}, \sigma_{-i}^*) > \Pi_i(\sigma_i^*, \sigma_{-i}^*).$$

σ_i^* is in this case strictly dominated by $\sigma_i^{\sim}$ and can therefore not be the best answer to σ_{-i}^*, $\sigma_i^{\sim}$. This proves the above assumption wrong.

Further, this must hold for any positive element p_j of a mixed Nash equilibrium strategy where $s_{i,j}$ shall be the set of pure strategies played with positive probability as a part of the mixed Nash equilibrium strategy by player i. Consequently it follows that

$$\Pi_i(\sigma_i^*, \sigma_{-i}^*) = \Pi_i\left(s_{i,j}, \sigma_{-i}^*\right) \qquad \forall j : p_j > 0$$

and even that all possible mixed strategy combinations of the j strategies $s_{i,j}$ yield the same payoff.   ∎

Lemma (2): Every finite n-person normal form game G (with a finite number of strategies for each of the n players) has at least one Nash–equilibrium in pure or mixed strategies.

Outline of proof: Either G does have a Nash equilibrium in pure strategies or it does not. In the first case, Lemma (2) is always true; therefore it remains to be shown, that for games G that do not have a Nash equilibrium in pure strategies, there is always at least one in mixed strategies. We proceed by eliminating any strategy $s^{\sim}$ in G that does not constitute a best answer to any of the remaining players' strategy configurations s_{-i} to construct a modified game G' (which is a subgame of G) and repeat the process until no $s^{\sim}$ is left to be eliminated in G'. Further we eliminate all players with only one strategy left as their choice does not affect the outcome of the game and they do obviously have only one strategy they can rationally play in G or any of its subgames G'. Call the resulting game G'', n the number of players in G'' and the number of strategies player has in G''. Since no best answer strategy has been effected, mutual best answers (Nash equilibria) in pure strategies cannot exist in G'' either as they did not in G. However, all players will now rationally play all of their remaining strategies s_i with positive probability if all combinations of strategies of the other players s_{-i} occur with positive probability. This condition is fulfilled exactly if all players play all remaining strategies with positive probability. The expected payoff for any of the strategy configurations of the remaining players σ_{-i} and player i using her mixed strategy $\sigma_i = \begin{pmatrix} p_1 \\ \cdots \\ p_{x_i} \end{pmatrix}$ is

$$\Pi_i(\sigma_i, \sigma_{-i}) = p_1 \Pi_i(s_1, \sigma_{-i}) + p_2 \Pi_i(s_2, \sigma_{-i}) + \cdots + p_{x_i} \Pi_i(s_{x_i}, \sigma_{-i}).$$

It follows that for each agent i there is a combination of mixed strategies for all other players σ_{-i} such that

$$\Pi_i(s_1, \sigma_{-i}) = \Pi_i(s_2, \sigma_{-i}) = \cdots = \Pi_i(s_{x_i}, \sigma_{-i})$$

in which case i is indifferent between all possible mixed (and pure) strategies in G''. This is possible if there are different best answers for each combination s_{-i}, that is $\Pi_i(s_j, \sigma_{-i})$ is the sum of both low and high payoffs resulting from strategy s_j weighted with the mixed strategy probability values of the other players. This follows from the nature of G'' without dominant strategies as analyzed above, therefore there are valid solutions for each agent. Now, we have the solutions that fulfill the above condition for all agents simultaneously. This results in a system of n equations (one for each remaining agent) to assert

$$\Pi_i(s_1, \sigma_{-i}) = \Pi_i(s_2, \sigma_{-i}) = \cdots = \Pi_i(s_{x_i}, \sigma_{-i})$$

for all agents. The equations contain $\sum_i x_i - n \geq n$ independent variables - the probabilities of the mixed strategy vector for each agent minus one to fulfill the condition that the probabilities sum up to 1. As the number of equations is at most the number of independent variables there is at least one solution with

$$\Pi_i(s_1, \sigma_{-i}) = \Pi_i(s_2, \sigma_{-i}) = \cdots = \Pi_i(s_{x_i}, \sigma_{-i}) \qquad \forall i$$

in G''. That is, a combination of mixed strategies σ^* exists to which any mixed or pure strategy of any agent is a best answer in G'' including the mixed strategies that are part of the combination σ^*. Hence, σ^* is a combination of mutual best answers and thus a Nash equilibrium in G''. Since the strategies that are additionally part of G (but not of G''; those removed above) do not add best responses, they do not affect the structure of Nash equilibria and σ^* must also be a Nash equilibrium in G.

Note that there is a more elegant proof by Nash (1950) using the so-called fixed point theorem of Kakutani. Showing that the space of mixed strategies in G is convex (any linear combination of two mixed strategies is also a mixed strategy) and compact (the space is bounded and closed (between 0 and 1 for any probability to play a pure strategy as part of a mixed strategy)) the proof proceeds to demonstrate that the global best answer function (the combination of best answer functions of all players) is quasi-concave. Kakutani's fixed point theorem applied to this yields that the global best answer function must have a fixed point. In other words, there must be a subset of the strategy combinations for which the global best answer function maps the strategy combination into itself (that is, the strategy combination is a best answer to itself.)

2.4   REPEATED GAMES

Consider the coordination game above in the normal form specification. You are to choose one of two options; if your choice matches that of your opponent, you win, otherwise you lose. What choice do you make? How would you rate the likelihood winning given that the opponent does not have a dominant strategy and no way to predict your choice either? Note that the setting is a *one-shot game*: The players choose their strategies simultaneously and only once. There is no opportunity for corrections or reactions to the opponent's choice. Once the decisions are made, the game is over – for the better or for the worse of the agents.

From the viewpoint of game-theoretic modeling with the purpose to explain real world phenomena, the answer is simple: You will not have a chance significantly surpassing 0.5 to successfully coordinate in a one-shot coordination game. One-shot games, however, are arguably relatively rare in real world systems. The one-shot Nash equilibrium considerations for instance are better perceived as practical simplifications of specific repeated games. Hence, the agents get the opportunity to reconsider their strategy and thus to coordinate and settle on a common choice. Once the strategy of the opponent is revealed decision making becomes much easier and coordination is easily accomplished. The eventual solution will be one of the Nash equilibria of the one-shot game as the repeated setting matches the condition for a Nash equilibrium: No agent must have an incentive to unilaterally deviate from the Nash equilibrium.

To briefly clarify the notation, a repeated normal form game G is considered a *sequence of repetitions* of the same one-shot game G. Agents are able to retain their memory for at least the last few interactions but usually (and if not specified otherwise) perfectly from the beginning of the interactions to their eventual end (if there is one). We call G a *supergame*. Supergames may be finite or infinite.

Why then do we not generally consider repeated games if it is so obviously more appropriate as a modeling framework of the phenomena we want to deal with? For infinitely repeated games, the now unrestricted set of strategies is incredibly large and incredibly rich. In fact, a single strategy itself could contain an infinite number of instructions, for instance one for each repetition. Strategies can further take the history of the game into account, thus reacting to past interactions. In short, the situation is far more complex than for one-shot games. For a finitely repeated supergame G, the number of possible strategies is of course finite as well, restricted by the number of iterations, say T, and the number of strategy combinations (including the strategies of all involved agents) possible in each state, say $|S|$. As the game is not an irregular sequential game but rather a repeated normal form game, it follows that the number of possible distinguishable states of the game is

$$V = \sum_{t=1}^{T} |S|^t$$

out of which

$$V_{nf} = \sum_{t=1}^{T-1} |S|^t$$

are non-final distinguishable states, that is, states in which the agents have to make a decision. (Distinguishable means in this case that the starting points of the decisions of individual agents in the same interaction are not counted separately.) The maximum possible number of strategies of an individual agent i is the number of states in which she has to make a decision (V_{nf}) times the number of options (strategies) among which she can choose, $|s_i|$.

$$\left|s_i^G\right| = V_{nf} |s_i|.$$

This is more easily understood when written in extensive form; however, it comes down to the sum over the number of strategies i can choose at each time she has to make a decision, namely T times. Those in turn are greater in a repeated game than in a single-shot game as the history of the game, namely, the prior decisions may be taken into account and multiplied by the number of options. The number of prior decisions at a time t is $|S|^t$.

In repeated games and *sequential games* in general, the information set differs from that of normal form games as agents may react to their opponent's strategy choices in subsequent rounds. However, for finite sequential games, there is a last period in which this option does not exist. Agents may in this period choose as if it were a simple non-repeated game. Since agents in the second-to-last period are perfectly able to predict which choices rational opponents will make in the last period, they can choose as if the second-to-last period was the last one. This argument also applies to all prior periods until the first period is reached. This method allows perfectly rational behavior in finite sequential games; it is known as *backward induction*.

Finite supergames are conveniently solved by backward induction and are in no way different from other finite sequential games. For infinite supergames, this is not valid. Usually the payoffs of infinite supergames are discounted because they would otherwise, if positive, say a value $a > 0$ with each interaction, sum up to ∞ no matter the exact value of a. For the same sequence, discounting with a rate δ generates the finite present value of

$$\Pi = a + \delta a + \delta^2 a + \cdots = \frac{a}{1 - \delta}.$$

Generally, the discounted payoffs of rational players of an infinite supergame $\mathcal{G}$ can never be less than the infinite sum of the discounted maximin payoffs $a_{Maximin}$ of the underlying one-shot game G. This is because any agent can ensure $a_{Maximin}$ for each interaction. If a strategy s_i of G that leads to at least $a_{Maximin}$ can further inflict damage on an opponent (reducing her payoffs for all possible strategies), $s_{i,Maximin}$ can be used to construct a *trigger strategy* $s_{trigger}^{\mathcal{G}}$ in the supergame $\mathcal{G}$. The maximin property guarantees that the trigger strategy is *subgame perfect*, that is, the strategy stays a rational (not dominated) option at any point in time no matter how the game evolved to this point (i.e. any *subgame*). Threatening to employ $s_{trigger}^{\mathcal{G}}$ if a specific expectation was not matched by the opponent and employing it often enough to strip the opponent of any gains she might have made by deviating from the expectation is a called a *credible threat*. That is, it must be rational (not dominated) to exercise the punishment when an opponent deviated from the expected behavior (i.e. the threat did not work), which is a specific subgame of $\mathcal{G}$. A trigger strategy can be used to force the opponent to accept mutually beneficial agreements that do not constitute a Nash equilibrium in a one-shot game (the so-called '*folk theorem*'). For example in the Prisoners' Dilemma, to defect satisfies the property required for $s_{i,Maximin}$ as it ensures $a_{Maximin}$

(the payoff of mutual defection for the Prisoners' Dilemma) and reduces the payoffs of the opponent no matter what her strategy is. As an example, consider the trigger strategy *tit-for-tat* (for a detailed discussion of this strategy, see Chapter 3) that starts with cooperation and then adheres to the rule

$$s^{\mathcal{G}}_{trigger} = \begin{cases} \text{cooperate} & \text{if -i cooperates} \\ \text{defect } (s_{i,Maximin}) & \text{if -i deviates from cooperation.} \end{cases}$$

As for the opponent $-i$ not conforming to the expected behavior (cooperation), thus defecting, is no best answer to $s^{\mathcal{G}}_{trigger}$ (tit-for-tat), while $s^{\mathcal{G}}_{trigger}$ is a best answer to itself, so mutually playing $s^{\mathcal{G}}_{trigger}$ is a Nash equilibrium in the supergame $\mathcal{G}$. The infinitely repeated Prisoners' Dilemma has two types of Nash equilibria, the first being mutual defection $(s_{i,Maximin})$ in all periods, the other mutually playing trigger strategies like tit-for-tat. For details on the repeated Prisoners' Dilemma, see Chapters 3 and 8 or (Axelrod, 1984); for details on trigger strategies, the maximin strategies in repeated games, see (Rubinstein, 1979).

   Trigger strategies are not possible in finite games. From the point on at which the time of the end of the game is known they are dominated by the backward induction considerations – known in game theory as *endgame effect*.

2.5   POPULATION PERSPECTIVES AND EVOLUTIONARY GAMES

2.5.1   Evolutionary Approaches to Game Theory

The most important goal of game theory is the modeling of social interactive situations. It is convenient, as in the concepts discussed so far, to simplify reality to obtain a single game (one-shot or repeated) with the interaction rules, players, and information sets specified and proceed analyzing this game. Depending on the number of actors, the repeatedness, information sets etc. even these approaches may lead to overly complex mathematical problems. Still, they may be considered insufficient in their scope as they are unable to cover the dynamics present at a larger scale. How are social interactions related in a dynamic population? What can game theory contribute to the prediction of population dynamics if single interactions are modeled as games? Applying game theory to population settings enables the branch to take the step from a distinctly microeconomic technique to a generalized method. It becomes possible to consider the meso- and macro-levels and most importantly to offer a convenient bridge between different scales, to gain an integrated view of complex socio-economic problems including their micro, macro and intermediate aspects, to provide macro-economic theories with proper micro foundations, an old dream of especially neoclassical economics that the general equilibrium theories were never able to fulfill (see Chapters 5 and 6).

As seen in the previous sections, game theory is able to predict rational behavior in interactive situations whether repeated or non-repeated, whether between two agents or in large groups (an n-person game), whether with perfect or imperfect information. Assuming that all agents in a population are strictly rational, it follows that the whole population will, if possible, play dominant strategies or at least Nash equilibrium strategies (or strategies leading to Nash equilibria). For repeated games, as discussed in Section 2.4, we may also assume that the population will eventually arrive at a Nash equilibrium even if there is more than one. However, this is merely the application of the solution concepts of a single game to another setting reasoning that what is impossible at the small scale (irrational behavior) will not occur at the large scale either.

There is another somewhat different approach to games in populations, *evolutionary game theory*. This approach involves some further assumptions:

1. the population consists of a number of distinguishable and specified types of agents
2. the composition of the population (of agents of the various types) develops according to the performance of these types in games played in this population.

It is convenient to explicitly specify this evolutionary performance of a type of agents as a variable, usually called the *evolutionary fitness f_i* of type i. Note that it is not necessary to measure this quantity or even to specify it explicitly for the model to function, it is merely a concept adopted from evolutionary biology that may be helpful for predictions. Also note that the evolutionary fitness may (and usually does) change with the composition of the population which is also analogous to evolutionary biology.

The three most important solution concepts for evolutionary game theory will be discussed in this textbook (two of them in this section, the third, simulation, in Chapter 7):

1. *Evolutionary stability* (developed by Maynard Smith and Price, 1973) is a refinement of the Nash equilibrium to evolutionary settings. A population of n agents playing *symmetric (usually 2-person) normal form one-shot*

games is considered. The agents are matched randomly; the possible types of agents correspond to the mixed strategies of the underlying game the types are playing. As evolutionary stability as a general game theoretic solution concept must be a general property of the strategies (thus the types) it is independent of any specific composition of the population. Rather, it considers which strategies (that is, which types) are generally able to prevail in the population.

2. *Replicator dynamics* is a mathematical specification of the dynamic development of a population of n agents playing *sequential n-person games*. Dynamic processes may or may not contain equilibrium points with various properties with respect to stability, a question addressed with methods of *dynamic systems theory*.

3. *Simulation of dynamic populations in evolutionary game theory* is the computational study of well-specified dynamical systems representing population settings of evolutionary game theory of various kinds. Simulation is not an exact mathematical method (which is a major disadvantage); however it is a very flexible and powerful technique to conveniently analyze systems of great complexity. The idea is to study the behavior of a dynamic system for a broad range of possible initial states in order to identify regular patterns in its development. Simulation is most attractive for the most complex settings, in game theory especially those with heterogeneous agents, in which case the situation is modeled to represent each individual agent separately (*agent-based modeling*). For details see Chapter 7.

2.5.2 Evolutionary Stability

The standard Nash equilibrium is – by definition – the combination of mutual best answers. We may be inclined to deduce that Nash equilibria are also stable states in population settings: As the dynamic development of the players of a Nash equilibrium strategy (that is, a strategy leading to the Nash equilibrium) follows their performance in the underlying game against the rest of the population, it should be the best possible performance against a population of actors aiming at the same Nash equilibrium. However, there are two major issues with this intuition. Firstly, in order to apply to both the population and the single game, a Nash equilibrium should involve only one strategy that in turn is the best answer to itself. These are the Nash equilibria located on the main diagonal in the game matrices, other Nash equilibria would imply a configuration of two (for 2-person games) strategies with the specific shares of the strategies not defined. Secondly, the application to population dynamics requires a robust analysis of stability for any equilibrium concept.

As a refinement of the Nash equilibrium for population settings the concept of evolutionary stability formulated by Maynard Smith and Price (Maynard Smith and Price, 1973) is used. A strategy σ^* is called evolutionary stable if a population dominated by σ^* is not invadable by any other strategy $\sigma^\sim$. That implies that once the population is dominated by σ^* this situation will remain stable. It does not explain how the population comes to be dominated by σ^*. Note that while both the Nash equilibrium and the evolutionary stable strategies are equilibrium concepts, the Nash equilibrium refers to a combination of strategies in a game while the evolutionary stable strategy refers to a particular strategy or rather a stable situation in a population (which is, the population is completely dominated by the evolutionary stable strategy).

Let $\mathcal{P}_{\mathcal{EV}}$ be an evolutionary population setting with the underlying one-shot normal form game $G_{\mathcal{EV}}$. $G_{\mathcal{EV}}$ shall be a symmetric game, that is, all players face the same options of strategy choice including the same payoffs and information sets. The game may be represented as a matrix $\mathcal{A}$ containing the payoffs of just one of the (identical) players – most intuitively the row player; an example is given below. Note that expected payoffs are again computed as a simple matrix multiplication of the form

$$\Pi_{\sigma_1/\sigma_2} = \sigma_1^T \mathcal{A} \sigma_2,$$

in this case computing the expected payoff of a strategy σ_1 against σ_2. The agents are matched randomly to play $G_{\mathcal{EV}}$ employing their pre-defined strategies, in turn represented as mixed strategies σ. According to their performance the composition of the population changes which may be seen as forced switching of strategies in case of poor performance or – to put it more cruelly – as a birth-death process. The population is assumed to be large and – in the limit – infinitely divisible.

To formalize the above description of evolutionary stability, consider the strategy σ^* in a population primarily composed of σ^*-players with a small invading group playing a strategy $\sigma^\sim \neq \sigma^*$. Call the share of invaders ε; ε being arbitrarily small. A share $1 - \varepsilon$, close to encompassing the total population continues playing σ^* resulting in an expected composition of the population (in terms of the shares of pure strategies expected to be played)

$$(1 - \varepsilon)\sigma^* + \varepsilon\sigma^\sim$$

where σ^* is evolutionary stable if and only if it yields a higher expected payoff in this population than the invading strategy $\sigma^\sim$, thus

$$\sigma^{*T}\mathcal{A}\big((1 - \varepsilon)\sigma^* + \varepsilon\sigma^\sim\big) > \sigma^{\sim T}\mathcal{A}\big((1 - \varepsilon)\sigma^* + \varepsilon\sigma^\sim\big)$$

$$\sigma^{*T}\mathcal{A}(1-\varepsilon)\sigma^* + \sigma^{*T}\mathcal{A}\varepsilon\sigma^\sim > \sigma^{\sim T}\mathcal{A}(1-\varepsilon)\sigma^* + \sigma^{\sim T}\mathcal{A}\varepsilon\sigma^\sim. \quad (2.1)$$

As ε is arbitrarily small, the inequality must also hold for $\varepsilon \to 0$ which yields the *first condition of evolutionary stability* (though it does not necessarily have to hold strictly, thus replacing the 'greater than' with a 'greater or equal')

$$\sigma^{*T}\mathcal{A}\sigma^* + 0 \geq \sigma^{\sim T}\mathcal{A}\sigma^* + 0.$$

Indeed, this means that σ^* must be a best answer to itself in turn requiring the strategy configuration composed of σ^* for every player, in the 2-person case (σ^*, σ^*), to be a symmetric Nash equilibrium of the underlying game $G_{\mathcal{E}\mathcal{V}}$.

The first condition as stated above is a necessary condition for evolutionary stability; as ε is arbitrarily small, however, it is not just the necessary but also the sufficient condition if it holds strictly.

$$\sigma^{*T}\mathcal{A}\sigma^* > \sigma^{\sim T}\mathcal{A}\sigma^*.$$

If it does not, however, that is if

$$\sigma^{*T}\mathcal{A}\sigma^* = \sigma^{\sim T}\mathcal{A}\sigma^*$$

we may substitute $\sigma^{\sim T}\mathcal{A}\sigma^*$ with $\sigma^{*T}\mathcal{A}\sigma^*$ in Equation 2.1, resulting in

$$(1-\varepsilon)\sigma^{*T}\mathcal{A}\sigma^* + \varepsilon\sigma^{*T}\mathcal{A}\sigma^\sim > (1-\varepsilon)\sigma^{*T}\mathcal{A}\sigma^* + \varepsilon\sigma^{\sim T}\mathcal{A}\sigma^\sim$$

$$\varepsilon\sigma^{*T}\mathcal{A}\sigma^\sim > \varepsilon\sigma^{\sim T}\mathcal{A}\sigma^\sim$$

$$\sigma^{*T}\mathcal{A}\sigma^\sim > \sigma^{\sim T}\mathcal{A}\sigma^\sim,$$

which is the *second condition of evolutionary stability*. Note that the second condition is to be considered only if the first condition holds with equality.

As an example consider a population setting with the following Hawk-Dove game $G_{\mathcal{H}\mathcal{D}}$ as the underlying game-theoretic structure as given in Figure 2.6. As explained above, the game may be completely represented by a game matrix

$$\mathcal{A} = \begin{pmatrix} 2 & 1 \\ 3 & 0 \end{pmatrix}$$

containing only the payoffs of the row player (player 1) since it is a symmetric game.

Using the first condition of evolutionary stability, we know that only Nash equilibrium strategies may be evolutionary stable. The game $G_{\mathcal{H}D}$ has three Nash equilibria, in pure strategies (H, D) and (D, H) and in mixed strategies $(M, M) = \left(\begin{pmatrix} 0.5 \\ 0.5 \end{pmatrix}, \begin{pmatrix} 0.5 \\ 0.5 \end{pmatrix} \right)$. Hence, we have three strategies that may be evolutionary stable, $D = \begin{pmatrix} 1 \\ 0 \end{pmatrix}$, $H = \begin{pmatrix} 0 \\ 1 \end{pmatrix}$, and $M = \begin{pmatrix} 0.5 \\ 0.5 \end{pmatrix}$.

Testing H and D against each other, we can easily show that they fail to fulfill the first condition, for H

$$H^T \mathcal{A} H < D^T \mathcal{A} H$$
$$(0 \quad 1) \begin{pmatrix} 2 & 1 \\ 3 & 0 \end{pmatrix} \begin{pmatrix} 0 \\ 1 \end{pmatrix} < (1 \quad 0) \begin{pmatrix} 2 & 1 \\ 3 & 0 \end{pmatrix} \begin{pmatrix} 0 \\ 1 \end{pmatrix}$$
$$0 < 1$$

and for D

$$D^T \mathcal{A} D < H^T \mathcal{A} D$$
$$(1 \quad 0) \begin{pmatrix} 2 & 1 \\ 3 & 0 \end{pmatrix} \begin{pmatrix} 1 \\ 0 \end{pmatrix} < (0 \quad 1) \begin{pmatrix} 2 & 1 \\ 3 & 0 \end{pmatrix} \begin{pmatrix} 1 \\ 0 \end{pmatrix}$$
$$2 < 3.$$

What remains to be tested is the mixed strategy M. In order to prove M evolutionary stable it must be shown that no mixed or pure strategy $M^{\sim} = \begin{pmatrix} m \\ 1 - m \end{pmatrix}$ with $m \neq 0.5$ (that would be M itself) that would be able to invade M does exist.

$$M^T \mathcal{A} M = M^{\sim T} \mathcal{A} M$$
$$(0.5 \quad 0.5) \begin{pmatrix} 2 & 1 \\ 3 & 0 \end{pmatrix} \begin{pmatrix} 0.5 \\ 0.5 \end{pmatrix} = (m \quad 1 - m) \begin{pmatrix} 2 & 1 \\ 3 & 0 \end{pmatrix} \begin{pmatrix} 0.5 \\ 0.5 \end{pmatrix}$$
$$1.5 = (3 - m \quad m) \begin{pmatrix} 0.5 \\ 0.5 \end{pmatrix}$$
$$1.5 = 1.5.$$

Thus the first condition holds. All possible strategies perform equally against M. Proceed with the second condition

$$M^T \mathcal{A} M^{\sim} > M^{\sim T} \mathcal{A} M^{\sim}$$
$$(0.5 \quad 0.5) \begin{pmatrix} 2 & 1 \\ 3 & 0 \end{pmatrix} \begin{pmatrix} m \\ 1 - m \end{pmatrix} > (m \quad 1 - m) \begin{pmatrix} 2 & 1 \\ 3 & 0 \end{pmatrix} \begin{pmatrix} m \\ 1 - m \end{pmatrix}$$
$$(2.5 \quad 0.5) \begin{pmatrix} m \\ 1 - m \end{pmatrix} > (3 - m \quad m) \begin{pmatrix} m \\ 1 - m \end{pmatrix}$$
$$2m + 0.5 > 4m - 2m^2$$
$$m^2 - m + 0.25 > 0.$$

Except for the point $m = 0.5$ the function $m^2 - m + 0.25$ is indeed always larger than 0. Thus M must be evolutionary stable.

Note that alternatively it could also be shown that the two conditions for evolutionary stability hold for M against the pure strategies D and H. With this proven, and keeping in mind that M is the strategy against which both pure and all mixed strategies perform the same, it can be seen that the expected payoffs of any mixed strategy other than M would be a combination of the expected payoffs of M and a pure strategy, the former equal to the performance of M, the latter worse. Hence, showing that the conditions of evolutionary stability hold against H and D would also prove M evolutionary stable. Testing M against D yields

$$M^T \mathcal{A} M = D^T \mathcal{A} M$$
$$(0.5 \quad 0.5)\begin{pmatrix} 2 & 1 \\ 3 & 0 \end{pmatrix}\begin{pmatrix} 0.5 \\ 0.5 \end{pmatrix} = (1 \quad 0)\begin{pmatrix} 2 & 1 \\ 3 & 0 \end{pmatrix}\begin{pmatrix} 0.5 \\ 0.5 \end{pmatrix}$$
$$1.5 = 1.5.$$

Thus, the second condition must be tested and proves to hold as well.

$$M^T \mathcal{A} D > D^T \mathcal{A} D$$
$$(0.5 \quad 0.5)\begin{pmatrix} 2 & 1 \\ 3 & 0 \end{pmatrix}\begin{pmatrix} 1 \\ 0 \end{pmatrix} > (1 \quad 0)\begin{pmatrix} 2 & 1 \\ 3 & 0 \end{pmatrix}\begin{pmatrix} 1 \\ 0 \end{pmatrix}$$
$$2.5 > 2.$$

Testing M again with H as opponent gives similar results:

$$M^T \mathcal{A} M = H^T \mathcal{A} M$$
$$(0.5 \quad 0.5)\begin{pmatrix} 2 & 1 \\ 3 & 0 \end{pmatrix}\begin{pmatrix} 0.5 \\ 0.5 \end{pmatrix} = (0 \quad 1)\begin{pmatrix} 2 & 1 \\ 3 & 0 \end{pmatrix}\begin{pmatrix} 0.5 \\ 0.5 \end{pmatrix}$$
$$1.5 = 1.5$$

$$M^T \mathcal{A} H > H^T \mathcal{A} H$$
$$(0.5 \quad 0.5)\begin{pmatrix} 2 & 1 \\ 3 & 0 \end{pmatrix}\begin{pmatrix} 0 \\ 1 \end{pmatrix} > (0 \quad 1)\begin{pmatrix} 2 & 1 \\ 3 & 0 \end{pmatrix}\begin{pmatrix} 0 \\ 1 \end{pmatrix}$$
$$0.5 > 0.$$

2.5.3 Replicator Dynamics

Contrary to evolutionary stability, replicator dynamics does not envisage the abstract stability properties of a strategy but rather the development of the population as a dynamic system. Dynamic systems are discussed in more detail in Chapter 9; for now, it shall be sufficient to say that dynamic systems generally describe the development of a set of z state variables in time. Assume the state variables written as a vector

$$\theta_t = \begin{pmatrix} \theta_{1,t} \\ \theta_{2,t} \\ \dots \\ \theta_{z,t} \end{pmatrix} = \left(\theta_{i,t} \right)_{i=1,\dots,z}.$$

The development is independent of the time the system is initialized, t_0. For the sake of simplicity, let us however assume the nomenclature $t_0 = 0$, in other words the system starts at time index 0. Though the development is independent from t_0 it does depend on the initial values of the state variables θ_0 and, of course, the (system of) development equations, which in turn are either difference equations of the form

$$\theta_{t+1} = F_{\widetilde{D}}(\theta_t)$$

(where $F_{\widetilde{D}}(\sim)$ is a function) or differential equations of the form

$$\frac{\partial \theta(t)}{\partial t} = F_{\widetilde{d}}(\theta(t)).$$

Specifically in the case of replicator dynamics, the state variables are the shares of specific types of agents $i = 1, \dots, z$ in the population, hence

$$\sum_i \theta_{i,t} = 1 \; \forall t.$$

According to the agent types' evolutionary potential, described above as evolutionary fitness $f_{i,t}$, the share of the population increases or decreases over time. Note, however, that models of replicator dynamics have nothing to do with misanthropic ideologies of the so-called 'social Darwinism'. In fact, there are a number of different evolutionary mechanisms apart from the 'survival of the fittest' which is an extreme special case (for a detailed discussion see Nowak, 2006, Chapter 2). Further the example considered below shows that evolutionary systems (both biological and other) are much more complicated with the global state of the system (the ecology, so to speak) having a profound impact on the individual fitness values and with the globally stable state the system converges to being a combination of different populations (types of agents in the system). From the individual fitness values it is straightforward to define an average fitness of the population

$$\phi_t = \sum_i \theta_{i,t} f_{i,t}.$$

As evolutionary performance of the agent types is determined by the relation of their individual fitness and the average fitness in the population, the development equation functions ($F_{\widetilde{D}}(\sim)$ and $F_{\widetilde{a}}(\sim)$) may be specified more conveniently to include $f_{i,t}$ and ϕ_t to yield

$$\theta_{i,t+1} = F_D(\theta_{i,t}, f_{i,t}, \phi_t)$$

or respectively as a differential equation

$$\frac{\partial \theta_i(t)}{\partial t} = F_a(\theta_i(t), f_i(t), \phi(t)).$$

The central question of replicator dynamics is which situations (state variable configurations $(\theta_{i,t})_{i=1,...,z}$) are equilibria and which of these are stable. Of course, an equilibrium θ^* is any state from which the system does not change any more, in other words the development equation maps the state into itself and if the equilibrium is reached at time t', then the state of the system is at this equilibrium point for all times after t', hence

$$\theta_t = \theta^* \quad \forall t \geq t'.$$

For difference equation systems the equilibrium condition is

$$\theta_{t+1}^* = F_D(\theta_t^*, f_{i,t}, \phi_t)$$

and for differential equation systems it is

$$\frac{\partial \theta_i^*(t)}{\partial t} = F_a(\theta_i^*(t), f_i(t), \phi(t)) = 0.$$

Compared to other methods of game theory, it is rather easy to assess the stability properties of these solutions (equilibria) since they are determined by continuous functions, the development equations. Specifically, we have to consider the eigenvalues λ and determine whether the dynamic process is contractive in the neighborhood of the equilibria. For systems of difference equations, this is the case if the dominant eigenvalue, the eigenvalue with the largest absolute value, is smaller than 1, which means that all eigenvalues are smaller than one, $|\lambda| < 1$. In the case of differential equations, the dominant eigenvalue, here the eigenvalue with the largest real (as opposed to imaginary) part, is negative, hence all eigenvalues are negative $Re(\lambda) < 0$. (For details on eigenvalues, see Chapter 9, Box 9.1.) The systems of replicator dynamics we investigate in this section do not usually have constant eigenvalues; the eigenvalues depend on the position in the phase space (the state variables). Hence we have the eigenvalues typically as functions of the type

$$\lambda = \lambda(\theta_t).$$

For a more detailed discussion of replicator dynamics see Nowak (2006); for an assessment of the role of models of replicator dynamics for microeconomic theory, see Kirman (1997).

Consider the following case as an example: Two types of enterprises offer mobile phone contracts in an economy (or region). Every agent maintains her own mobile phone network in which calls are offered at marginal costs, thus without profits. Their profits result entirely from intra network communication, where both involved networks share the profits. One type of enterprise (D) offers equal sharing of profits, while the other type (H) tries to exploit other networks by charging higher network access costs. Suppose that the network access costs between two H-type networks are prohibitive for the customers, hence no profits are generated, while otherwise there are revenues of 4 monetary units per customer. The allocation of these profits follows the scheme given in Figure 2.6.

Further, the agents are matched randomly a large number of times such that the distribution of opponents each agent meets is representative for the composition of the population. The payoffs are normalized to those in the matrix above (thus divided by the number of encounters), yielding payoffs for type D and H of

$$\Pi_D = \begin{pmatrix} 1 & 0 \end{pmatrix} \begin{pmatrix} 2 & 1 \\ 3 & 0 \end{pmatrix} \begin{pmatrix} \theta_D \\ \theta_H \end{pmatrix} = \begin{pmatrix} 1 & 0 \end{pmatrix} \begin{pmatrix} 2 & 1 \\ 3 & 0 \end{pmatrix} \begin{pmatrix} \theta_D \\ 1 - \theta_D \end{pmatrix}$$
$$= \begin{pmatrix} 2 & 1 \end{pmatrix} \begin{pmatrix} \theta_D \\ 1 - \theta_D \end{pmatrix} = \theta_D + 1$$

$$\Pi_H = \begin{pmatrix} 0 & 1 \end{pmatrix} \begin{pmatrix} 2 & 1 \\ 3 & 0 \end{pmatrix} \begin{pmatrix} \theta_D \\ \theta_H \end{pmatrix} = \begin{pmatrix} 0 & 1 \end{pmatrix} \begin{pmatrix} 2 & 1 \\ 3 & 0 \end{pmatrix} \begin{pmatrix} \theta_D \\ 1 - \theta_D \end{pmatrix}$$
$$= \begin{pmatrix} 3 & 0 \end{pmatrix} \begin{pmatrix} \theta_D \\ 1 - \theta_D \end{pmatrix} = 3\theta_D$$

respectively. Assume the payoffs to be the individual fitness

$$f_D = \Pi_D = \theta_D + 1$$

$$f_H = \Pi_H = 3\theta_D$$

and the development equation to be the following differential equation

$$\frac{\partial \theta_i(t)}{\partial t} = \theta_i(t) \left(f_i(t) - \phi(t) \right) \qquad i = D, H.$$

As the state vector has just two elements, one of them depending on the other due to the requirement that shares sum up to one $(1 - \theta_D = \theta_H)$, it is sufficient to consider just one development equation (for example that of θ_D)

$$\frac{\partial \theta_D(t)}{\partial} = \theta_D \left(f_D - (\theta_D f_D + (1 - \theta_D) f_H) \right) = \theta_D \left(1 - \theta_D \right) (f_D - f_H).$$

Proceeding to substitute the fitness values in the development equation yields

$$\frac{\partial \theta_D(t)}{\partial t} = \theta_D \left(1 - \theta_D \right) (-2\theta_D + 1) = 2\theta_D^3 - 3\theta_D^2 + \theta_D.$$

There are three equilibria:

$$\theta_{D,1}^* = 0$$
$$\theta_{D,2}^* = 0.5$$
$$\theta_{D,3}^* = 1.$$

The eigenvalue of this one-dimensional system (system of only one equation) is the first derivative of the development equation with respect to the state variable. (For larger systems the eigenvalues would have to be computed using the Jacobi matrix J of the development equations to fulfill $\lambda J = \lambda v$ as explained in Chapter 9, Box 9.1.)

$$\lambda = \frac{\partial^2 \theta_D(t)}{\partial t \partial \theta_D} = 6\theta_D^2 - 6\theta_D + 1$$

Consequently the eigenvalue assumes for the fixed points the values

$$\lambda\left(\theta_{D,1}^*\right) = \lambda(0) = 1$$
$$\lambda\left(\theta_{D,2}^*\right) = \lambda(0.5) = -0.5$$
$$\lambda\left(\theta_{D,3}^*\right) = \lambda(1) = 1.$$

It follows that $\theta_{D,2}^* = 0.5$ is the only stable equilibrium. This is not surprising as the game used to construct this population setting is a Hawk-Dove Game. In fact, it is the very Hawk-Dove Game used as an example in the section on evolutionary stability and $\theta_{D,2}^*$ corresponds to the evolutionary stable mixed strategy M computed there.

2.6   RATIONALITY IN GAME THEORY

Before getting to the conclusions, a few words about conceptions of rationality in game theory are in order. As mentioned in the context of formal concepts of game theory, agents are required to be perfectly rational in order to apply game theory concepts. This may seem an unrealistically heroic assumption not unlike those used in neoclassical theory, especially in the light of empirical findings from behavioral and experimental economics (see, for instance Tversky and Kahneman, 1973). However – in contrast to neoclassical theory – game theory allows for imperfect and incomplete information (the information set available to the agent is modified, see Chapter 1) and with certain extensions also for bounded rationality, i.e. the agents apply a heuristic as considered for instance in evolutionary game theory (see Chapter 1). It is impractical to drop every concept of rationality; this would lead to the impossibility to predict anything. Any heuristic approach will again make the assumption that agents adhere to the defined heuristic, that is, in effect, they are rational within the limits of the setting under investigation. Reality is complex and real agents (humans) do not have the processing capacity to be perfectly rational (and do not even try to be); for some approaches that explicitly include complex modeling, see Chapters 7 and 9.

2.7   CONCLUSIONS

This section provided a formal introduction to game theory drawing on the basic game theoretic concepts already introduced in Chapter 1 as well as on the extensive discussion of the context which makes game theory a necessary and valuable tool for microeconomics. The current section added the formal conventions of notation and a discussion of the basic solution concepts of game theory (the Nash equilibrium and dominant strategies). Further, several extensions to both the setting and the solution concepts have been discussed, including mixed strategies and repeated games. These extensions are among many others especially valuable to push the extent to which game theory is able to approximate real world systems. Finally, the last part of the section introduced basic conceptions of evolutionary game theory which in turn forms the basis for many of the models discussed in Chapters 3, 4, 8, and 9.

In short, game theory provides a rich toolkit for economics that leads to important insights both for analyzing the models and predictions of neoclassical general equilibrium theory (which will be discussed in detail in Chapter 5), assessing their explanatory scope and constructing a different kind of models. Many authors have analyzed game theory representations of neoclassical perfect market systems (Albin and Foley, 1992; Kirman, 1997) with the result that the neoclassical world is possible – as a limit case of a large variety of systems with very different results. (However to go into detail about these discussions, especially that presented by Albin and Foley, an extensive discussion of graph theory and the theory of games on networks would be required. For an introduction on this topic, see Easley and Kleinberg, 2010.) As Chen (2002) describes it, neoclassic theory works by defining heterogeneity away – using the argument of general rationality – and arriving at a one-body problem. Evolutionary models (with a game theory micro foundation) however allow heterogeneity and construct multi-body problems, while physics taught us that three-body problems may already be sufficiently complex to lead to deterministic chaos and make predictions very difficult. However, certain mechanisms (discussed in more detail in Chapter 9), e.g. emergence, may still lead to stable patterns being produced in complex systems. Arguably, evolutionary game theory explains some of the most important and powerful mechanisms of emergent stability. It is this field microeconomic theory should turn to in order to find more plausible explanations for the many phenomena of a complex world. In fact, many of the models discussed in Chapter 8 are part of this tradition.

FURTHER READING

For an annotated list of dedicated game theory textbooks and for selected other references see the textbook website at www.microeconomics.us.

3. Problem Structures and Processes of Interactive Economies

The first and second chapters have introduced you to the basic conditions that agents face in real-world economic decision-situations and basic tools for representing and analyzing these. In this chapter, we will in more detail introduce you to the variety of problem structures agents have to deal with and to solution mechanisms for these problems that we can derive with the help of the game-theoretic methods you have learned about.

3.1 A CONTINUUM OF SOCIAL PROBLEM STRUCTURES

As explained in Chapter 1, the fact that agents face situations characterized by their direct interdependence leading to direct interactions results in various types of problem structures. Depending on the type, these are solved more easily or with more difficulty, if at all. A solution here means the achieving of a Pareto-optimal outcome. The difficulty of achieving such an outcome depends on the basic problem structure. These problem structures can be represented by games.

If individually optimal strategy choices lead to a Pareto-optimal outcome, the problem is minor (non-existent, in fact, in the game-theoretic set-ups we consider here). The *coordination problems* we have mentioned in Chapter 1, however, do not involve an ex-ante optimal strategy, as the optimal choice for an agent depends on the choices of the other agents in the game. We will see different types of coordination problems exist with differing degrees of *asymmetric interests* of the agents regarding which outcome exactly to coordinate on, as a consequence of asymmetric payoffs in the coordinated outcomes. Finally, there are *dilemma problems*. As we will see, the basic problem is such that it cannot be solved by 'rational' agents. Still, there are solutions to a dilemma, as we will also see, as the underlying situation can at times be transformed and thus offer chances for the agents to improve their results.

We will use *normal-form games*, introduced to you in Chapter 2, to describe these basic problem structures in more detail than in the brief reference to them we have offered in Chapter 1. As the basic outline of the problems is captured by *2x2* games, we use these for purpose of presentation. It must not be forgotten, however, that usually more agents and more behavioral options, strategies, are involved, making problems potentially much more difficult to solve than may appear from a *2x2* normal-form game.

		Player B	
		Strategy 1	Strategy 2
	Strategy 1	3 3	2 2
Player A			
	Strategy 2	2 2	1 1

Figure 3.1   Social Optimum Game

Figure 3.1 shows a *social optimum game*. As you see, each agent's first strategy is strictly dominant and therefore their only sensible choice. When facing such situations, the agents achieve a socially optimal outcome simply by following their individually optimal behavioral pattern. There is no conflict of interests between the agents, and as long as no one makes a mistake in the execution of her strategy (an extension of analyses that we do not integrate here), the Pareto-optimal outcome is reached.

Coordination problems can be understood as problems in which strategies are best answers to themselves (strategy *1* of one player is the best answer to strategy *1* of another player, and so on; a distinction between these games and others, in which strategy *1* may be the best answer to strategy *2* becomes important in the context of evolutionary game theory, as has been explained in Chapter 2) and in which at least one of the resulting pure-strategy Nash equilibria is Pareto-optimal. In contrast to the social optimum games, there are no strictly dominant strategies in coordination games.

Regarding coordination problems, we can distinguish a number of gradually distinct types. The distinction is based on two different aspects. The first is whether all Nash equilibria are Pareto-optimal or only some, or even only one, of them. The other is whether the payoffs in the Nash equilibria are the same for all agents, or whether some profit more than others in certain Nash outcomes.

Figure 3.2 shows a *basic coordination problem*. There are two Nash equilibria, in the upper left and lower right cell of the matrix. If both agents choose their first strategy, or both choose their second strategy, they end up in a Pareto-optimal situation. As both agents get the same payoff within a Nash equilibrium, and the same payoff in either Nash equilibrium, they have no preference regarding which one they reach, as long as they can coordinate on one of them (drive on the right- or left-hand side of a street; use one communication technology or another, etc.).

		Player B	
		Strategy 1	Strategy 2
Player A	Strategy 1	2 2	1 1
	Strategy 2	1 1	2 2

Figure 3.2   Basic Coordination Game

A variant of this problem is one in which only one of the two Nash equilibria is Pareto-optimal. Such a problem is depicted in Figure 3.3. It is called a *stag hunt game*, adapted from a story told by Jean-Jacques Rousseau. Two agents go hunting. If they both focus their efforts on a stag (strategy 1) they will catch it. They have to coordinate their efforts though. If one deviates and tries to catch a hare (strategy 2), she can do that alone, but the result attainable is smaller than her share of the stag would be. Should the other player, however, make that decision, she could not catch the stag on her own. If the players cannot communicate during the hunt, the temptation to change strategies and switch to unilaterally hunting a hare may increase over time. A switch of strategies may then appear increasingly favorable, be it only to insure against a change of mind of the other player(s).

		Player B	
		Strategy 1	Strategy 2
Player A	Strategy 1	3 3	1 2
	Strategy 2	2 1	2 2

Figure 3.3   Stag Hunt Game

In addition to the general problem of a coordination of strategies, there is a *second problem involved* here therefore. As you can see, the payoff for strategy 2 is the same independently of the other player's choice of strategy.

It can be seen as the safe option. As long as you are sure that the other agent will choose strategy 1, there is no reason for you not to do so either. As soon as you have doubts, though, the *safe strategy* may be the better option for you. Choosing it, you can be sure to avoid the loss that you would face in case of a strategy-switch by the other player. Such games allow a Pareto-optimal outcome to be reached, and there is no reason why players would not want to try and do that. But if they cannot communicate (which by assumption they cannot), or maybe fear a mistake may happen to the other player in deciding on her strategy, or simply assume the other is so distrustful or simply fearful as to rather choose the safe option for herself, they have no choice but to do the same. Their expectations regarding the motivations of the other player(s) in the game matter greatly now. Depending on how they assess the other(s), one or the other strategy is their best choice. That includes how they assume they are perceived by the other(s), as their choice depends on what they expect, etc. *Rules supporting agents* in their choice of the strategy make it easier for agents to take the risk of losing out through their strategy choice, by *signaling* that everyone is expected to make a certain choice and thus reducing the risk of other choices within a given group.

Another variant is a coordination problem in which the agents profit from coordinating, but to different degrees. In such a case we speak of asymmetric interests among the players. See Figure 3.4 for an example of such games. These are called *battle of the sexes games*. As an example for a situation that may be captured by a simple coordination game, we had referred to coordinating on the application of a given communication technology. Here, we may assume that companies have invested in developing such technologies, and have thus incurred costs (technology 1 being developed by player 1, and technology 2 by player 2). For effectively communicating, they both need to use the same technology, however, meaning one has to switch to the other's technology, incurring additional costs.

		Player B	
		Strategy 1	Strategy 2
Player A	Strategy 1	4 3	2 2
	Strategy 2	1 1	3 4

Figure 3.4   Battle of the Sexes Game

As said, the players prefer being coordinated to not being coordinated, but both have different preferences regarding which Nash equilibrium to reach.

There is no way to determine at the outset which result may be achieved. For addressing that question, we'd have to leave the narrow game setting and analyze the wider situation, so as to understand whether one player might influence the other in a way, or whether the players may be able to negotiate a solution for the situation.

In more general terms, this may become easier if they play repeatedly, in which case they may opt simply to alternate strategy choices. As both prefer being coordinated to being uncoordinated, there is no reason to expect the agents not to follow a rule describing how to achieve coordination. Once such a rule has come into existence it can be expected to be stable. There are a number of possibilities for such rules, but whether it allows agents in turn to reach their best result (for instance, through alternating between the Nash equilibria), or whether it permanently gives an advantage to one (group of) player(s) cannot be answered within this set-up. We can say, however, that a rule establishing a coordinated outcome in the game will improve the situation of all players as compared to an uncoordinated outcome.

Another interesting variant of coordination games are the *hawk-dove games* (that are called *anti-coordination games*, as the Nash equilibria result from players choosing different strategies). As you can see in Figure 3.5, the two Nash equilibria in pure strategies (upper right and lower left) are Pareto-optimal. There is a third Pareto-optimum, though, in the upper left. Even though one player gains with respect to that third Pareto-optimum in a Nash equilibrium, the other one loses.

		Player B	
		Strategy 1	Strategy 2
Player A	Strategy 1	3 3	4 2
	Strategy 2	2 4	1 1

Figure 3.5   Hawk-Dove Game

There are relatively strong asymmetric interests in such a set-up. But without knowing about broader structures that this particular game may be embedded in, there is, as in the battle of the sexes games, no way of knowing in which equilibrium the players will find themselves. Still, even though one of the players may feel exploited by the other, there is no reason to change her strategy choice, once the coordination on one Nash equilibrium is established. The outcome is stable. A strategy change by the player who is worse off in the Nash equilibrium would lead both to the worst possible result in the game. We will take up this kind of games again below and analyze them from an evolutionary game-theoretic perspective as well.

Finally, in this continuum of games describing problem structures in directly interdependent decision situations, there are dilemma problems. These are characterized by the fact that the strictly dominant strategies of the players lead them to an outcome that is not Pareto-optimal. Figure 3.6 shows such a game. The Nash equilibrium is located in the lower right cell. The other three results are Pareto-optimal.

		Player B	
		Strategy 1	Strategy 2
Player A	Strategy 1	3 3	4 1
	Strategy 2	1 4	2 2

Figure 3.6   Dilemma Game

You can see that both players would be better off if they both chose their dominated strategy. But in that case, they face the threat of exploitation by the other player. And as 'rational' players, they have to expect that the other tries that exploitation (maximizing her payoff); just as the opponent has to expect that of you. For rational players of the kind assumed in game theory, there is no way of solving such a dilemma problem. They are doomed to playing their strictly dominant strategies, even as that takes them to the relatively bad result. Note the difference to the hawk-dove game where the exploiting situation is stable, as a Pareto-optimal Nash equilibrium (that may serve as a reminder that the Pareto-criterion does not include any specific notion of fairness).

In Chapter 1, we had referred to dilemma problems agents may face in relation to *collective goods*, public goods or commons. Regarding *public goods* the dilemma results in the provision of these goods. Recall that public goods are characterized by non-excludability (as well as non-rivalry) in consumption. Once they exist, no one can be excluded from using them. If resources are needed for their production, that means that every agent has an incentive not to contribute to the production of the good (strategy *2*). If the other(s) do(es), the agent can utilize the public good and has all her resources available for private consumption. If she contributes (strategy *1*) some of her resources will be utilized in the production of the public good, and thus not available for her private consumption. And if the other player chooses not to contribute, the contributing player has to carry the efforts alone. Not contributing is the dominant strategy in this case. The public good, from which both would profit when compared to the situation in which it is not produced (strategy *2* / strategy *2*) is not produced, then.

This problem structure results if a public good is to be produced by the members of a group. If it is a company considering whether to produce a good with public good-character, or not, the problem is a different one: A private company has no incentive to produce a public good because the non-excludable character of the good means that it cannot charge agents using it once it is in place. It would therefore not have a chance of recovering its investment. In both cases, public goods would not be produced by private agents, though. The provision of public goods is hence a classical economic problem, and often seen as the principal task of government in economic matters. As we will see below, though, there are solutions to dilemma problems which offer ways in which private agents, as a group, can be supported in efforts to contribute to the production of a good with public-good character.

The second group of collective goods are the *commons*. Here, the problem results from the use of an already existing resource. If non-excludability is given in the use of resources that may mean that agents have an incentive to utilize it beyond its sustainable limits (strategy *2*), eventually depleting it. For ensuring its long-term availability, a group needs institutions governing the use of such resources if their depletion is to be avoided (strategy *1*). Historically, different groups have had different degrees of success in the development of such institutions, and therefore different degrees of economic success.

In the following section, we will introduce ways that allow even 'rational' agents to improve their results in situations that developed from dilemma problems. Once such solution mechanisms have been explained in the following sections, we will adopt a broader perspective, and address the function of institutions as well.

3.2   SOLUTIONS TO SOCIAL DILEMMA PROBLEMS

If agents are to realize a Pareto-superior outcome in a dilemma situation, a transformation of the problem structure or additional capabilities of the agents are necessary because the basic dilemma cannot be solved by the agents as conceived in basic game theory. In this section we will introduce you to some basic possibilities that allow dealing with dilemma problems in a way so that agents can improve the results they can achieve.

3.2.1   Transformation of the Problem Structure: Supergames and Single-Shot Solution

As the players cannot solve the dilemma problem as such, one possibility is to try and change the underlying problem-structure. The way to do this is to move *beyond the one-shot game* considered above, and allow agents to meet *repeatedly*. As we will momentarily see, if certain conditions are met, then a *transformation* of the game *into a stag hunt-type coordination game* is feasible. Such a transformation opens the possibility for agents to improve their results if they can coordinate on the now existing Pareto-optimal Nash equilibrium.

This may, remember, still involve considerable problems in an *N*-person setting, especially if those that attempt to switch to the new Nash equilibrium have to fear losses in case not enough others make the same attempt. In fact, a second aspect that we will explain in the next section is what minimum share of agents in a group has to switch strategies, or what minimum share has to generally emerge in a population for the strategy leading to the Pareto-optimal new Nash equilibrium to become the then preferred option in a population of agents.

As you remember, a *supergame* is a repeated game. Here, the same underlying game is played by the agents in *indefinite or infinite repetition*. As they play the same basic game every time, we can sum up the payoffs over the duration of the interactions. As this is undetermined, we can make use of the infinite geometrical series for expressing the interactions' expected value in the current period (Chapter 2).

		Player B	
		Strategy 1	Strategy 2
	Strategy 1	a a	b d
Player A	Strategy 2	d b	c c

Figure 3.7   Dilemma Game: b>a>c>d

Figure 3.7 shows a dilemma game again, this time in general form. The relations between the payoffs to arrive at a dilemma situation is $b > a > c > d$. You see that the first strategy of the agents is strictly dominated, the second strategy is strictly dominant, leading them to the non-optimal Nash equilibrium. As agents could improve the result for both themselves and the others, if they chose their strictly dominated strategy, we call this strategy *cooperation*, and the second strategy *defection*. The choice in the one-shot game is to defect, no matter what the other player may be expected to do. Now, if agents meet repeatedly, a change is introduced to the strategic situation they find themselves in. The repetition allows them to take *prior strategy choices of other players into account* in their own strategy choice.

This said, when approaching such a problem using game-theoretic analytical methods we have to formulate agents' strategies at the outset of their playing the supergame. When analyzing the situation we do not let agents reconsider their choices after every interaction (every move within the supergame). Rather, they have to formulate a *game-plan at the outset*, and then have to follow it until the supergame (the round) is completed. This game-plan can include contingencies for the other players' earlier choices. An easy strategy to build our illustration on is called *tit-for-tat* (TFT). It is nevertheless a good choice for introducing a number of the basic issues involved and, in fact, a simple representative of a generally quite successful type of strategies in repeated dilemma-games, as we will see in Chapter 8.

The game-plan for a player choosing TFT is, start with cooperation and then mirror your opponent's prior choice in all subsequent interactions. Should two TFT players meet, they will choose cooperation in every interaction, therefore, as they will both have started cooperating and then choose what the other one did in the preceding interaction.

For a discussion of whether the transformation of the dilemma game into a coordination game can succeed, and under what conditions, we can draw on TFT as one component of the strategy set of the agents. The other will be to choose defection in every interaction (All-D). The payoffs that result if two players meet that can choose either TFT or All-D are shown in Figure 3.8.

		Player B	
		TFT	All-D
Player A	TFT	$\dfrac{a}{1-\delta}$ (upper right) $\dfrac{a}{1-\delta}$ (lower left)	$b - c + \dfrac{c}{1-\delta}$ (upper right) $d - c + \dfrac{c}{1-\delta}$ (lower left)
	All-D	$d - c + \dfrac{c}{1-\delta}$ (upper right) $b - c + \dfrac{c}{1-\delta}$ (lower left)	$\dfrac{c}{1-\delta}$ (upper right) $\dfrac{c}{1-\delta}$ (lower left)

Figure 3.8   Dilemma-based Supergame (TFT and All-D)

TFT/TFT in the upper left cell is equivalent to the result achievable if two agents choose the cooperative strategy in the underlying game in every move. But, it does so in a way that takes into account the prior choices of the opposing player. As opposed to a strategy that would simply say always cooperate, TFT involves a mechanism to punish an agent who chooses defection. Following the defection of the other player, the TFT player likewise defects in their next interaction. This reduces the payoff in the future round; possibly in all future rounds, depending on the game-plan(s) of the other player(s).

Now, whether this threat of punishment can really discipline the players depends on the overall payoffs achievable, because these determine whether the threat is credible or not. In a set-up such as this, where agents only decide based on payoffs, a threat's credibility depends on the related payoffs. We will return to this point momentarily.

As $a > c$ continues to be given, the result in the upper left cell continues to be superior to the result in the lower right. But as we can see, the TFT game-plan means that the payoffs in the upper right (TFT/All-D) and lower left (All-D/TFT) have not changed proportionally to the underlying dilemma game (and vice versa for the row player). In the first interaction of the supergame, the players receive payoffs b and d, respectively. Afterwards, they get c in each interaction. Therefore, the c can be treated as being received infinitely often from the second interaction onward, leading to the overall expected payoffs shown in the payoff-matrix. The series contains one c that has not been received, namely the first interaction's payoff, and which therefore has to be subtracted. Now, if

$$b - c + \frac{c}{1 - \delta} > \frac{a}{1 - \delta}$$

holds, then All-D strictly dominates TFT as a strategy, and the Pareto-superior result (as compared to the Nash equilibrium) in the TFT/TFT combination is unattainable for 'rational' players. If the relation does not hold, if the inequality is reversed, however, there is no longer a strictly dominant strategy in the supergame. If

$$\frac{a}{1 - \delta} > b - c + \frac{c}{1 - \delta}$$

TFT becomes a best answer to itself, and the outcome in the upper left hence a Nash equilibrium. The strategy combination leading to the result in the lower right continues to be a Nash equilibrium as well. In the resulting game, we therefore see two Nash equilibria, one of which Pareto-dominates the other. This is a version of a stag hunt-type game. The dilemma problem is transformed into a coordination problem and hence a problem that the agents can solve.

The payoffs are given in the game. Jointly, they constitute the problem-structure. What we have to ask ourselves then, is what *value of δ* is sufficient for the transformation of the problem structure from dilemma to coordination? A quick manipulation of the above condition, that TFT/TFT >! All-D/TFT gives us the so-called single-shot condition,

$$\delta > ! \frac{b - a}{b - c}.$$

The discount factor δ is usually a simple expression given by *$1/(1+r)$* where *r* is a market interest rate that is assumed to be equal to the discount rate employed by the agent in the discounting of future payoffs in the formulation of the supergame. To allow for indefinite instead of infinite games, we formulate it as *$p/(1+r)$*, though. For a *$p=1$*, the assumption is that the game continues infinitely, for a *$p<1$*, there is an endpoint; however, that endpoint cannot be known by the agents, as it is a stochastic event. The game is indefinite, and endgame effects cannot occur. There is always the possibility that there will be further interactions in which behavior can be sanctioned.

The single-shot condition shows us that the less likely a *common future*, meaning the lower the value of *p* and hence δ, the less likely it is that the transformation into a coordination game succeeds. Conversely, we can say, the longer the time horizon agents adopt (reflected in increasing values of p), the more likely it becomes that they can solve a dilemma problem by transforming it into a coordination problem. The threshold value of δ depends on the payoff structure. For a given *b*, the larger *a* is relative to *c*, the more likely it becomes, that the problem can be transformed. Accordingly, the lower the value of *b* is for given *a* and *c*, the more likely it becomes that the transformation succeeds. If you think in terms of *policy*, how to *strengthen relations between agents* and thereby *extend the time-horizon* under which they operate can be a valuable guiding question in a number of problematic fields (such as R&D cooperation, for instance, but also in approaching public good contributions or commons exploitation).

The next step would be the actual solution of the new problem structure, a rule that establishes the changes in behavior patterns that lead to the Pareto-optimal Nash equilibrium TFT/TFT being realized. In the set-up considered up to this moment, a rule suffices, because the problem now is one of coordination. We will return to this point in a moment.

When the single-shot condition is fulfilled, the threat embodied in the TFT strategy becomes a credible one – the strategy says, if you defect on me, I will defect on you in the future. And this is in fact worthwhile for me to do, because in those circumstances, once you have defected, defecting is the least bad option amongst the ones open to me. You, as the first to defect, however, will see your payoff reduced subsequently, and end up worse than in a situation of common cooperation. Expressed with the help of the payoffs that means because

$$d - c + \frac{c}{1 - \delta} > \frac{d}{1 - \delta}$$

that is by definition of the underlying game always fulfilled, as it can be rewritten as

$$\frac{\delta}{1 - \delta} c > \frac{\delta}{1 - \delta} d$$

it pays to defect against a defector. Once you meet someone who defects against you, you are better off defecting yourself. That makes the threat of switching from cooperation to defection in subsequent interactions credible. The defector, on the other hand, faces the payoff relations

$$b - c + \frac{c}{1 - \delta} < \frac{a}{1 - \delta} < \frac{b}{1 - \delta}$$

as soon as the threat of a strategy switch in reaction to her choice, as embodied in the TFT game-plan, is made. Defecting, she may hope to continuously exploit the other player(s), always receiving *b*. The TFT strategy, however, prescribes to choose defection in reaction to such a move in the following interaction in the supergame. This worsens the result that the defector can achieve. And it reduces it below the level of return achievable if she sticks to choosing cooperation in every interaction. Therefore, it is effective as a punishment.

When the single-shot solution is fulfilled, that means we have the believable announcement of a strategy change in case of being faced with defective behavior, combined with an effective punishment that results from this strategy change. This leads to a *credible threat* players can make once they have achieved the coordination on the Pareto-superior Nash equilibrium to keep others from deviating from it.

In fact, in more general terms, this result has been known for a long time among game theorists as the *folk theorem*. It tells us that any result from individually rational decisions can be sustained as an equilibrium in a supergame with a finite number of players and a finite number of strategies.

A decision is individually rational if the expected resulting payoff is at least as large as the maximin payoff for a player in the game. Which one of the possible Nash equilibria will result in the end cannot be determined on this basis, however (see also Section 2.4 on folk theorem and trigger strategies).

The construction of the single-shot game relies on the infinite or indefinite repetition of the game to ensure that there is no defined endpoint (we may also imagine this as a situation with an endpoint beyond the planning horizon of agents). If there was a defined endpoint, endgame effects would result and backward induction would lead agents to defect in every round. We stress this to underline that in every interaction agents still face a dilemma-structure. For the rational agent who decides on a game-plan today and sticks to it until infinity, this is irrelevant. But if we move beyond the game-theoretic analysis and approach real-world agents, we have to be aware that these do have a choice in every interaction. What the single-shot solution allows us is to show that a dilemma-problem may be altered in a way that allows the individual agents to find a solution to it. How this solution is stabilized in real-world situations is not described therein. For real-world agents, we in fact need the institutionalization of behavior, in semi-conscious behavioral decisions. We will take this point up in more detail in Section 3.2.4.

3.2.2   The Population Perspective

As you have seen, if the single-shot condition is fulfilled, there are two Nash equilibria (TFT/TFT and All-D/All-D) in the supergame we have looked at in the previous section. The best strategy choice for an agent depends on the choice by the player she meets in the game. Broadening the perspective now, we can imagine a population, in which players are randomly matched to play these supergames. The overall size of the group is given by n, the TFT players in the group are given by k. In this case, the expected payoffs for the players change insofar as they have to include the probabilities that their opponent chooses All-D or TFT. As the best choice for a player depends on the choice of her opponent, both are viable strategy choices. The expected payoff when choosing TFT is given by

$$\pi^e_{TFT} = \frac{k}{n}\frac{a}{1-\delta} + \frac{n-k}{n}\left(d - c + \frac{c}{1-\delta}\right)$$

the expected All-D payoff is,

$$\pi^e_{All-D} = \frac{k}{n}\left(b - c + \frac{c}{1-\delta}\right) + \frac{n-k}{n}\frac{c}{1-\delta}.$$

As the single-shot condition is assumed to be fulfilled, we know that for some population share the expected payoff for TFT has to be higher than that for All-D because both are best answers to themselves in the underlying game. A graphical representation of the payoff schedules for this case is shown in Figure 3.9.

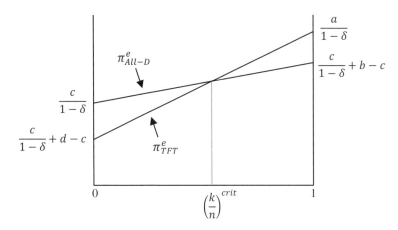

Figure 3.9   TFT and All-D-payoff schedules in a population

The point at which the two payoff-schedules intersect gives the population share from which the expected payoff from choosing TFT becomes higher than that of choosing All-D for increasing TFT-shares (an increasing number k in a given population of size n). We call this the *minimum critical mass* of TFT-players that have to be present in a population for the Pareto-superior Nash equilibrium to become viable. The share depends on the payoff structure, including the discount factor. The larger δ, the further to the left lies the intersection, meaning the smaller the minimum critical mass.

If the agents know about the respective shares in the population, they will decide accordingly and choose the strategy with the higher expected payoff; if they form expectations about the shares, it depends on what these expectations look like. As long as the agents know about the shares of strategies in the population, they have a strictly preferred choice, namely the strategy with the higher expected payoff. In that case, they will all end up choosing the same strategy, and every agent plays either All-D or TFT in every round she enters. At that point there is no mechanism within the set-up of the game to let them change strategies and lead the agents in the population to choosing the other strategy.

This is of course especially interesting in case of a group in which every agent plays All-D because in that case a switch would promise a Pareto-superior result. But unless for some reason enough players switch strategies to reach a minimum critical mass, that Pareto-superior result is not attainable. As said, within the game there is no mechanism that might lead to such a minimum critical mass forming. We may take this as a first hint at the increasing difficulty involved in solving even coordination problems in larger groups. Even though the agents are still matched in pairs of two in the supergames they play, changing their expectations regarding others' choices becomes more difficult as they have to be assured that a sufficiently large number of other players will adopt the overall preferable strategy as well.

In order to be able to argue for why a group of agents that has been playing All-D might eventually manage to switch to a TFT outcome, we have to resort to a broader *process story*, for which we have to relax some of the assumptions about the agents. Relaxing those assumptions may allow us to introduce feelings such as frustration from the continued unattractive result obtained (*c* instead of the also possible *a*), learning effects, experimentation due to curiosity, or other motivations that the perfectly informed and rational agent at the heart of the above explained situations cannot experience.

3.2.3   Agency Mechanisms

The transformation of the problem structure (the single-shot solution) is one way that allows agents to improve the results from their interactions. For another possible solution of the dilemma, we have to alter assumptions about the agents. Assume that agents are able to *monitor* other agents and that they have a certain *memory* period over which they can remember others' behavior. Also, they may be able to gain information about other players through third parties, in which case players can build a *reputation*. Additionally, assume that players can *use the information* that is available to them through these different channels and *reject* entering into *interactions* with other agents and so at least to some degree select their interaction partners. In that case, the probability for a TFT-player to interact with another TFT-player is presumably larger than their share in the population, the probability of an All-D player interacting with a TFT-player is accordingly lower than the TFT-share of the population. The changes in expected payoffs can be written as:

$$\pi^e_{TFT} = \left(\frac{k}{n}\right)^\alpha \frac{a}{1-\delta} + \left(1 - \left(\frac{k}{n}\right)^\alpha\right)\left(d - c + \frac{c}{1-\delta}\right)$$

$$\pi^e_{All-D} = \left(\frac{k}{n}\right)^{\frac{1}{\alpha}}\left(b - c + \frac{c}{1-\delta}\right) + \left(1 - \left(\frac{k}{n}\right)^{\frac{1}{\alpha}}\right)\frac{c}{1-\delta}.$$

In order to introduce the difference between the share of cooperators in a population and the probability of playing against a cooperator in the following supergame, we have added the exponent α. For $0 < α < 1$, the probability of playing with a cooperator is larger than their share in the population for another TFT-player. Accordingly, the probability for an All-D player to interact with a TFT-player is lower than the TFT-share in the population. Thus, we can formulate a mathematical representation of agency mechanisms.

Represented graphically, the schedules delineating expected payoffs (payoff schedules in the following text) then change as shown in Figure 3.10 (for the payoff schedules' shape, check the derivatives of the expected payoffs, that will give you $π^e(k/n)' > 0$ and $π^e(k/n)'' < 0$ for TFT-players and $π^e(k/n)' > 0$ and $π^e(k/n)'' > 0$ for All-D-players). Note that in this approach the underlying dilemma still exists as in this approach the single-shot condition is assumed not to be fulfilled (if it was, the minimum critical mass would simply be further reduced). As you can see, in this set-up there result two intersections of the payoff schedules. The population share of co-operators is presented on the horizontal axis, again. In this case, a population in which both types of strategies continue to be played is one stable outcome, the other is the whole population playing All-D.

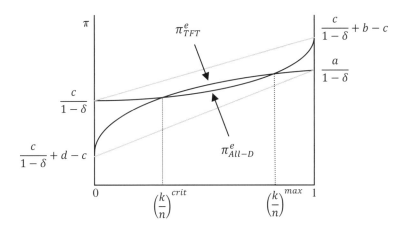

Figure 3.10   Payoffs in a population with agency capacities by the agents

To the left of the first intersection, the expected payoff for All-D is higher than that for choosing TFT. No single player has an incentive to choose TFT, hence, the share of these players stays at zero. To the right of the first intersection, the expected payoff for TFT is larger than that for All-D. Hence, agents switch to choosing TFT, the share of TFT players in the population increases. To the right of the second intersection, the expected payoff for choosing All-D is higher than that for the TFT-choice. It pays to switch to All-D therefore, and the share of TFT would be reduced. The second intersection, a *mixed population*, is therefore also a *stable outcome* in this set-up.

The exact intersections of the payoff schedules depend on the payoffs in the underlying game, the time horizon as mirrored in the discount factor, and, in difference to the set-up without agency mechanisms, the strength of these mechanisms as represented by the parameter α, where agency mechanisms are stronger the smaller α. Also, the smaller α is, the steeper the slope of the TFT payoff schedule for low shares of cooperators in the population. We may interpret it as saying that the stronger agency mechanisms are, the easier it is for TFT-players to identify and interact with one another. As the share of cooperators can be expected to increase once the first intersection has been crossed, for a given incentive structure, as a consequence, the stronger the agency mechanisms, the smaller the initial share of TFT-players (minimum critical mass) necessary for leading the system to the stable mixed population equilibrium. Note that this is basically a verbal description of what a replicator would show us in quantitative terms, with payoffs as the fitness-indicator.

3.2.4   Institutionalization of Cooperative Behavior

As we have explained in Chapter 1 and briefly referred to in Section 3.2.1, assuming strict 'rationality' of agents can only be a first approximation to understanding problem structures and possible solutions. The representation of problem structures as strictly 'rational' agents would perceive and approach them is a helpful analytical approach, and solutions for specific problem structures, especially dilemma situations, that can be derived in such a set-up are very promising for informing policy suggestions. But some questions can only tentatively be answered on this basis.

For instance, in the derivation of the single-shot solution we assume interactions of pairs of agents. These may be able to coordinate on behavior patterns that lead to Pareto-superior results, given that the time horizon of their interaction is sufficiently long to make this worthwhile. This does, however, only tell us about two agents being able to transform the problem they face, not about the establishing of a cooperative culture in a group of agents, where interactions may be short-lived.

Adopting a population perspective allows us to extend the set-up. Now, expectations about others' behavior, as expressed by the (expected) probability of meeting cooperative partners are introduced into the set-up. As we have seen, in the simple framework allowing for two strategies, this will lead to a situation in which either everyone chooses TFT, and hence de facto cooperates in every interaction, or everyone chooses All-D. However, the basic condition for this situation to become possible is still that the single-shot condition is fulfilled, and therefore that agents can expect to play many interactions with one another once they enter into a relation. Transferring this analytical set-up to real-world situations, agents have to ignore the fact that in every interaction they still face a dilemma-problem. Institutions, as social rules plus sanction mechanism (Chapter 1), that establish a rule under which agents abstain from trying to gain a short-term advantage over others are the tool enabling agents in groups to nevertheless show behavior allowing the realization of a cooperative outcome. So, a rule would suffice under single-shot conditions, as it enables agents to solve the coordination problem they face there, but, when transferring our results to real-world situations, we have to be more cautious. In order to establish the coordination problem, a transfer of the underlying dilemma problem-structure is necessary. A longer time horizon supports this transformation, but it necessitates an institution for stabilizing it. So, the at least latent dilemma structure in the background requires additional mechanisms enabling a stable cooperative environment.

Allowing for agency mechanisms permits the introduction of another way for establishing a cooperative environment. Agency mechanisms change the expected payoff of agents as a function of the share of cooperators in a population. Expected payoffs for TFT-players increase relative to a situation without agency, whereas those for All-D-players are reduced. As a result of the changed payoff schedules, the resulting population will be a mixed one, in which both types of agents coexist. Here, the single-shot condition is not fulfilled; we solve the dilemma in a different way. Still, the resulting mixed population-shares are determined by the underlying incentive structure, and are given by the point where both payoff schedules intersect, where the expected payoff for both strategies is the same.

The problem in this set-up may be seen as more pronounced again, as even in the supergames, the dilemma structure is kept in place. Thinking in terms of a real-world agent again, as information is never perfect, we may assume that the temptation to try and exploit others may increase again, compared to a set-up in which the single-shot condition is fulfilled. Transferring the analytical set-up to real-world problems, we can recognize that further support for the agents, enabling them to maintain cooperative behavior patterns, is going to be a very helpful, even necessary, addition. This support is gained from the institutional structure. Every group interacts under a set of rules and institutions. An institution's rule that is reaffirmed in semiconscious behaviors, in a habitual application, can lead agents to show cooperative behavior, even where the basic conditions would lead us to suspect that no such behavior would be observed.

These considerations also allow us to address a further question: Why extend cooperation to people you do not know about, in a generalized culture of cooperation? If agents face an underlying dilemma structure, and their time horizon is short, meaning they do not expect many interactions with the person they are facing at the moment, or if they do not know about that person, why should they still opt for a cooperative kind of behavior? Within the different set-ups utilized so far, there is no answer to this question; in fact, the agents we have utilized for the explanations so far would not make such a choice. What we might argue is that following the behavioral rule of the institution is based on the understanding that the maintenance of the institution (that may have emerged in a set-up involving smaller groups) benefits the (larger) group in the long run. However, here some defecting agents may, conceivably relatively quickly, lead to the breakdown of the institution (low δ), or at least prevent an extension of it being applied in the larger group as well. Remember that the only thing keeping it alive is agents following it. As long as they do, the individually rational incentive to defect in a dilemma situation can be kept in check by generally accepted behavioral rules. If the only reason for them to follow an institution is the long-term benefit of the group this may lead to, we need a very pronounced understanding of this possible long-term development, and a very pronounced check on desires of distinguishing oneself within the group through enhancing one's economic potential in order to limit the temptation of giving in to trying to exploit other players.

An institution provides this. And more *stability* results if cooperation is understood as the result of *habitual behavior* that is enabled by and embodied in social institutions. As also explained, limited cognitive capacities make such behavioral rules necessary, because agents cannot make conscious decisions in every moment and situation they face. Furthermore, such institutions serve to reduce the degree of uncertainty that agents face by informing them about socially acceptable behavior patterns and hence about what generally to expect from counterparts in a given situation.

Once we give up the assumption of strictly (boundedly or not) 'rational' agents, decisions are no longer purely informed by achievable payoffs. As in the case of an institution that embodies cooperative behavior in a dilemma situation, patterns may emerge that are not strictly 'rational' from an individual point of view; the time horizon is short, the single-shot condition therefore not satisfied, and defection the strictly dominant choice, but still cooperation is observed. Other factors shaping behaviors have to play a role here.

A social institution directs agents to play cooperatively even in a dilemma situation. Once it is in place, it may eventually be accepted without the connection to the agents who may have developed it, as a general norm in situations where the dilemma structure is in place (the single-shot condition is not fulfilled) and agency mechanisms play no important role (as agents from different peer groups interact, for instance). The institution has in that case become detached from any specific relations, and constitutes a generally accepted code of behavior. Agents accept these behavioral rules independently of the exchange relation they are about to enter as a generally applicable norm. This effect is called *reconstitutive downward causation* as it involves an institution that has emerged and is now established on the aggregate ('macro') level affecting individual agents' choices, their behavior on the micro level.

But, you still have to believe in another person adhering to the institution, even if for her that means *sacrificing* the potential gain from another possible behavioral option. For a cooperative outcome to become possible, you have to believe the other person to be willing to forego the short-term gain that defection promises, even if you do not expect to have a long-term relation with the person; what is more, the other person has to come to the same assessment, as otherwise she may defect in order to protect herself from being exploited, and not even from the desire to try and exploit you.

This connects to another aspect of relations between agents that can be included in our considerations, namely, *trust*. When referring to trust, we usually imply that agents have faith in others to make choices that do not harm them, even though the others have the possibility to do so (for their own gain). A functioning institutional frame supporting cooperative behavior can then lead to the constitution of a more trustful environment based on a broader kind of trust, detached from personal relations and transferred to less familiar acquaintances or even strangers, that is embedded in the institutional framework that has emerged over time.

Once a generally cooperative environment has emerged, it may be more easily sustained as agents do not consciously decide on whether they think other players follow the institutional rule or not, but simply habitually take a certain decision in a given moment. Once the behaviors and results have repeatedly been reaffirmed there is no reason for further continued questioning of behavioral decisions. Individual agents simply habitually apply certain behavior patterns in this case. Only once they are caught by surprise when others start not to act in accordance with the institution might they be forced to reconsider their behaviors. In that case the emergence of a new behavioral pattern can result, that may, however, take time, as the coordination on a new pattern may not be easily achieved.

3.3   AN INEFFICIENT EQUILIBRIUM: THE HAWK-DOVE GAME IN AN EVOLUTIONARY PERSPECTIVE

In this final section of this chapter we will return to the hawk-dove game introduced above already as a situation of stable exploitation in the two-player version, this time from an evolutionary game-theoretic perspective, though.

The players in the game have two strategies when they meet and decide about the distribution of a resource they have access to. The overall value of the resource is given by v. When deciding the distribution, agents can behave aggressively (as a *hawk*) or peacefully (as a *dove*). When two doves meet, the resource is evenly distributed between them, both receive half of it. If a dove meets a hawk, the dove withdraws from the competition for the resource and the hawk receives it in its entirety. When two hawks meet, they incur costs from their aggressive behavior. The amount of these costs is given by c. For a hawk-dove game to emerge, $c > v$ has to hold (if $0 < c < v$ were to hold, the players would face a dilemma game). Figure 3.11 depicts a general version of the underlying normal-form game.

		Player B	
		Dove	Hawk
	Dove	$v/2$ $v/2$	0 v
Player A	Hawk	v 0	$(v-c)/2$ $(v-c)/2$

Figure 3.11   Hawk-Dove Game

Calculating the mixed-strategy Nash equilibrium gives us $p = v/c$, with p as the share of the first strategy therein. In an evolutionary perspective, we find that the *pure strategies* are *not evolutionarily stable*, but that the mixed one, $(v/c, 1 - v/c)$, is. As shown in Chapter 2, both pure strategies can be *invaded*, only the mixed one cannot be. We may interpret this as every player applying the mixed strategy, or as a mixed population, in which the shares of the pure strategies correspond to those of the probabilities for them in the mixed strategy.

The heading of the section indicates that this result from an evolutionary process was inefficient. This inefficiency here is taken to mean that for the population as a whole, a better result was achievable. The inefficiency results from the fact that in the evolutionarily stable situation, hawks will play against hawks at times. This introduces the cost of them fighting over the resource's distribution. If only doves were to play against one another, and/or hawks always played against doves, no such costs would arise. There would be distributional issues, but not efficiency issues. As players are randomly matched under the perspective adopted, or stochastically choose their pure strategy in any given interaction, however, the cost of hawks fighting cannot be avoided. This reduces the overall payoff achieved in the group. Still, it is the equilibrium outcome in an evolutionary process given this kind of problem structure. This shows us that there is no reason to suspect that a stable equilibrium is efficient, even if it does exist at all.

In fact, you have already seen above, in Section 3.2.2, that evolutionarily stable outcomes need not be 'efficient', when we were explaining the transfer of a dilemma game into a stag hunt-type coordination game in a population perspective. The outcome in which all players choose All-D is evolutionarily stable therein as well. (The minimum critical mass referred to signifies a substantial share of the population, whereas we test the capacity to resist an invasion from an arbitrarily small group under the perspective of evolutionary stability.) Imagine the group being at the unstable, mixed, equilibrium. A random shock would lead the agents towards one of the corner solutions, with everyone either playing TFT or All-D. There is no reason to suspect that All-D might not result as an outcome in such a case. It does not have to, of course; but it might. Again, the possibility exists that the evolutionary process would lead to an overall 'inefficient' result for the population; one that it would not be able to leave again in the basic set-up of evolutionary game theory. We will return to processes and the results in dynamic systems in Chapter 9.

FURTHER READING

For a list of selected references on interactive economies, including institutional economics and applied game theory, see the textbook website at www.microeconomics.us.

4. Real-World Markets: Hierarchy, Size, Power, and Direct Interdependence

4.1 REAL-WORLD PHENOMENA AND THE GLOBAL CORPORATE ECONOMY

Real-world markets exist in geographical space of overlapping size on different levels (sub-local, local, regional, interregional, national, international, continental, global) and are nets of directly interdependent agents. Situations of direct interdependence are genuinely complex, and cause highly non-trivial coordination problems as we have explained in the previous chapters.

Real-world markets have undergone radical structural changes during the last decades. With 'neoliberalism', in many developed countries a deregulation policy took place, which in fact enhanced the complexity of the socio-economic environment. The development and use of new information and communication technologies contributed to a

- decentralized and fragmented,
- digitized, net-based and tele-communicating,
- clustered and networking

character of the global economy. Furthermore, the growing importance of financial markets, with their crises and crashes, heralds the start of a turbulent era.

These developments intensified the effects of the direct interdependence of economic agents. Thus, the information required to form expectations and to effectively coordinate agents becomes more difficult to acquire. Hence, markets have become even less effective in solving the complexity challenge. This increasing complexity forces powerful corporate hierarchies to try and increase their power even more and even faster to keep control over their socio-economic environment and, thus, the global system has increasingly become a power-based entity.

The global corporate economy has responded to arising challenges:

1. through individualist strategies to deal with complexity and turbulence by gaining more control through size and power, to purchase and merge with other firms, to collude and cartelize, combine with financial agents, and differentiate their products and make them more non-transparent in order to create separate sub-markets for their products (*monopolistic competition* – see Section 4.6 below), and other forms of power-strategies like rent-seeking, lobbying and gaining subsidies, government contracts and property-rights protection, privatization of public assets, public-private partnerships, and so forth,
2. through efforts for and battles around setting the (technological and behavioral) standards, but also
3. through new efforts to coordinate and establish cooperation and networks among independent firms,
4. through using repeated interaction and more stability based on spatial and cultural proximity, thus forming culturally more embedded regional clusters and networks,
5. and finally, through the combination of net structures and power by large corporations forming global-sourcing structures as hub & spoke networks, in this way gaining control over global sourcing, labor, and perhaps customers, distributors, and consumers.

In this chapter, we start with a short introduction to the main reasons why a decentralized spontaneous 'market' system inherently tends to degenerate into a system with agents of large size and great power – rather than into an (ideally competitive) system of no power. Real-world markets tend to be competitive systems among few agents, thus an oligopoly is the typical market structure rather than polypolistic (close to 'perfect') competition among many small entities that are not in a position of influencing each other and each others' results. We present oligopoly models for increasing the understanding of particular problem-structures companies face in markets and, before them, a model of a monopoly market that establishes one of the typical benchmark-models of microeconomic theory. Taking up the problems identified for companies in oligopolistic markets we then present some of the strategies that companies have developed for solving these problems.

4.2   FACTORS EXPLAINING SIZE, POWER, AND A SMALL NUMBER OF INTERDEPENDENT SUPPLIERS

There is an inherent tendency of real-world markets towards increasing market concentration. In what follows we summarize the set of factors that are working in the real world that endogenously lead to this phenomenon:

1. Real-world markets mostly exist in limited geographical, industrial, or commodities spaces. Thus, they are nets of limited sets of directly interdependent agents at local, regional, national, interregional, international, and global spaces.
2. Firms tend to grow in size due to economies of scale (cost benefits of large firms, reflected in falling average costs) and economies of scope (cost benefits of joint production of two or more products) in the production and cost functions, a supply-side push in favor of size (see Chapter 1 and Chapter 5).
3. Being few, firms tend to avoid competition through informal *collusion* or formal *cartelization*, as this often reduces profits and may lead to fierce rivalry and ruinous price-competition.
4. They tend to actively restrict or deter entry through threats, if entry is not difficult anyway due to the high fixed investment that technology may require.
5. Given ubiquitous net technologies, there is another powerful force supporting the trend towards few large suppliers dominating the markets: *Network effects*. These indicate that the benefit of a service or a product becomes more valuable as more people use it resulting in a cumulative effect that lets customers/users/consumers join the largest net (see Chapter 8).
6. They tend to connect with financial corporations (banks, financial investment dealers, private equity funds, etc.) in order to gain a financial advantage over their competitors, and to acquire, or merge with, other firms.
7. Other well-known cumulative factors in favor of size, power, and small numbers are *first-mover advantages* and learning curves, both connected to cumulative effects such as economies of scale and net externalities, as well as high initial fixed costs in specialized technology and large buildings, machinery and other hardware, representing sunk costs that cannot easily be liquidized or reconverted later. Like increasing returns, the latter allow for decreasing average costs over time.

Thus, a variety of factors, dominating the reality of production, demand, and markets, tend to make firms gain and exert power over others agents, allowing them to set prices and conditions, thereby redistributing/transferring profit into their own pockets and commanding global hub & spoke supplier and sales networks (for more detailed approaches on cooperation for high prices and 'joint dominance', see, e.g., Mischel, 1998; Vatiero, 2009).

4.3   PURE MONOPOLY

In this section we examine the effect of large corporations with great power on market outcomes and overall welfare. For that purpose we introduce an ideal-type monopoly model. One firm is selling a good to numerous buyers for which there is no close substitute. The sole seller faces a downward-sloping *demand function* $q = q(p)$, which indicates that the quantity q demanded by consumers declines as the price p rises (and vice versa). In the static market under consideration, the threat of entry by potential competitors is not an issue at this stage. Customers buy the quantity of the good that is indicated by the demand function that describes their aggregate decision. There is no direct interdependence in this model.

This market structure gives the monopolist *market power*. She can change the quantity she offers, and thus determine the price of her product. In what follows, we explain the decision of the monopolist. Profits are given by $\pi(q) = R(q) - C(q)$, where $R(q)$ is the monopolist's revenue function, defined as demanded output times price and $C(q)$ is the monopolist's cost function, which relates the cost of production to the level of output. The monopolist chooses the quantity q she produces and maximizes profits:

$$\max_q \pi(q) = R(q) - C(q).$$

The first order condition (FOC) for this problem is given by:

$$\frac{d\pi}{dq} = \frac{dR}{dq} - \frac{dC}{dq} = !\, 0.$$

Here, $dR/dq = MR$ is the *marginal revenue* function of the monopolist and $dC/dq = MC$ is its *marginal cost* function. MR gives the change in total revenue resulting from the sale of an additional unit of output. MC indicates the change in cost from producing one additional unit of output. The FOC says that a profit-maximizing firm will produce a quantity for which MR equals MC:

$$MR = \frac{dR}{dq} = \frac{dC}{dq} = MC.$$

This optimality condition holds for all profit-maximizing firms, independently of the market structure assumed. As we will momentarily see, however, marginal revenue develops differently, depending on the market structure assumed.

We had said that the monopoly model serves as one of the benchmark-models of neoclassical economic theory. The other is the perfect market model that we will explain in detail in Chapter 5 but briefly refer to here as a point of comparison for the monopoly-results. In the model of a perfect market, a homogeneous good is produced by many firms, none of which can dramatically alter market supply through a change in its production. As a consequence, supply-changes by any single company have no effect on the market-price, which is therefore treated as a given for every single company. Because the price for a single firm is given, the only way to maximize profit is to determine the optimal quantity to supply. The revenue function for a firm in a competitive market takes the form: $R^{PC} = \bar{p}q$. Thus the marginal revenue of a firm is given by the market price: $MR = p$. Hence the optimality condition for a firm in a competitive market takes the form: $p = MC$. This means that a firm will produce the quantity at which market price and marginal costs are equal.

Box 4.1   Elasticities

As you have already seen briefly, and will be introduced to in more detail in Chapter 5, in many instances economics assumes that agents' behaviors can be modeled by choosing appropriate mathematical formulations. These typically describe how a change in an independent variable affects the observed outcome in economically relevant situations. An example would be, 'an increase in the price of the good increases the quantity demanded of that good'.

If we work with a specified function, we can determine the elasticities related to them. Elasticity describes the relative change in a dependent variable in relation to a relative change in an independent variable. Assuming that the quantity demanded q (the dependent variable) can be described as a function of the price p (the independent variable), we get $q = q(p)$. The price elasticity of demand would then be given by

$$\varepsilon_{q,p} = \frac{dq/q}{dp/p}.$$

If this price elasticity of demand is larger than 1, we speak of elastic demand; if it is less than 1, we speak of inelastic demand. Only few functions are of a form that leads to constant elasticities over the whole range for which they are defined. Rather, normally, there are elastic and inelastic ranges (see Figure 4.1).

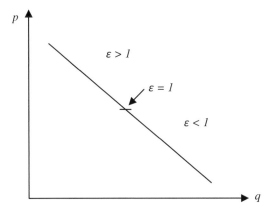

Figure 4.1   Elastic and inelastic demand ranges

Consequently, there are price ranges for which a change in the price will result in a change in quantity that is relatively larger than the price change (increasing (reducing) overall revenue following a reduction (increase) in the price asked), and areas where the overall change in revenue will be relatively lower than the price change (reducing (increasing) overall revenue following a reduction (increase) in the price asked).

   An idea regarding the expected magnitude of demand changes is important information for companies structuring their price policies; but also, for instance, for governments when deciding tax structure. In taxation we can distinguish between taxes aiming at steering behavior (where the demand change is elastic) and taxes that aim at revenue (where demand is relatively inelastic).

   Other elasticities offering information about the economic sphere are the income elasticities of demand

$$\eta_{y,q} = \frac{dq/q}{dy/y},$$

which allows goods to be characterized, depending on the change in demand that can be expected following a change in income. 'Normal' goods are those that see an increase in the quantity demanded following increases in income (these are the goods that are usually used for analyzing markets). Among goods that are increasingly demanded following a price increase one can distinguish between Giffen goods (or inferior goods - those that cover basic needs and are demanded more frequently when an income constraint gets more pronounced, meaning that price increases have a noticeable impact on real income levels; potatoes having been a typical example) and Veblen goods (or luxury goods - that are consumed for the purpose of signaling economic potency, as a status symbol, and thereby an example of invidious consumption, as one instance of the more general concept of invidious distinction).

Finally, we want to mention the cross-price elasticity of demand, that describes how demand for good 1 may be affected by changes in prices for good 2, as

$$\varepsilon_{q1,p2} = \frac{dq_1/q_1}{dp_2/p_2},$$

If demand for good 1 increases following an increase of the price for good 2, we speak of substitutes (tea and coffee being a typical example). If demand for good 1 falls following an increase in the price of good 2, we speak of complements (coffee and coffee-filters, for instance).

In a monopoly market the producer faces a downward sloping market demand curve $q(p)$, that tells her how many units of the commodity can be sold at any given price. Inverting the demand curve to $p(q)$, the inverse demand function shows the price the market is willing to pay for any given quantity of a good. The quantity supplied has an impact on the market price, conversely, if the company decided to set a price this would determine the quantity it would be able to sell. The revenue that the monopolist can expect to receive if she produces q units of output is $R^M(q) = p(q)q$. Using the product rule of differentiation, the monopolist's marginal revenue can be expressed as

$$MR(q) = \frac{dR}{dq} = \frac{dp(q)q}{dq} = p + \frac{dp}{dq}q.$$

The optimality condition for a monopolist is thus given by

$$MR = p + \frac{dp}{dq}q = MC.$$

This optimality condition states that a monopolist will supply a quantity of a good where the marginal revenue of the last unit sold is equal to its marginal cost. As the monopolist influences the price for all units sold by changing the quantity offered in a market, marginal revenue changes because it includes not only the change in units sold, but also the change in the price of each of these units. In the perfect market benchmark, marginal revenue is constant as firms are assumed to not affect the market price through their decisions. The FOC can be rewritten as follows:

$$p + \frac{dp}{dq}q = p\left(1 + \frac{dp}{dq}\frac{q}{p}\right) = p\left[1 + \frac{1}{(dq/dp)(p/q)}\right] = p\left(1 + \frac{1}{\varepsilon}\right) = MC.$$

Here ε is the price elasticity of demand, which tells us the percentage by which quantity demanded falls as the price increases by 1%. Since we assume a downward sloping demand function ε will always be negative. Hence the equation can be rewritten as:

$$p\left(1 - \frac{1}{|\varepsilon|}\right) = MC \leftrightarrow p = \frac{MC}{\left(1 - \frac{1}{|\varepsilon|}\right)}. \tag{4.1}$$

The relation between the price elasticity of demand, marginal costs and price in Equation 4.1 is called the *Amoroso-Robinson-Relation*. This relation shows that the monopoly price exceeds the competitive price (=*MC*) to a degree that is inversely related to the elasticity of demand a company faces. Generally, this degree indicates a firm's market power, and may also be drawn upon for gaining an idea of its position in an oligopolistic market. This market power can be measured through the *Lerner-index* that we can deduce by rearranging Equation 4.1:

$$\frac{p - MC}{p} = \frac{1}{|\varepsilon|}.$$

The index ranges between 0 and 1 (as presumably no company would produce a quantity, where $MC > p$, as here every additional unit would reduce profits). The higher its value, the higher the degree of market power a firm enjoys, or, the higher the *degree of monopoly* in the market.

After examining the price- and quantity-setting policies of a monopolist, in what follows we will evaluate the welfare effects this market power induces. The question is whether monopoly-behavior results in an outcome that can be characterized as optimal from a social point of view. In order to evaluate the outcome we have to introduce a measure of *welfare*. We define welfare as the sum of *consumer surplus* and *producer surplus*.

The consumer surplus is defined as the monetary difference between what consumers are willing to pay and the price they actually pay for the quantity of good purchased. Since the market demand curve states the unit price consumers are willing to pay given the quantity on offer we can measure the consumer surplus by determining the area under the market inverse demand curve minus the area given by market price times quantity (for an illustration see Figure 4.2 below):

$$CS = \int_0^{q^*} p(q^*)dq - pq^*.$$

Given the monopoly price p^M in Figure 4.2 the consumer surplus depicts the area circumscribed by points E, D and F.

The producer surplus measures the benefit a producer gains by selling a product as the difference between cost of production and sales-price. The producer surplus gained for selling an amount q at a price p can be measured by summing up this difference over all units produced:

$$PS = pq - \int_0^q \frac{dC}{dq} dq. \tag{4.2}$$

The marginal cost reflects the amount by which a firm's cost changes if the firm produces one more unit of output; since only variable costs change with output we can define marginal cost as the change in variable cost from a small increase in output. Hence the sum of all marginal costs, which is equal to the area under the marginal cost curve, must equal the sum of the firm's variable costs. Equation 4.2 can be rewritten as:

$$PS = pq^* - \int_0^{q^*} \frac{dC_v}{dq} dq = pq^* - C_v(q^*).$$

Given the monopoly price p^M in Figure 4.2 the producer surplus depicts the area circumscribed by points A, B, D and E.

A socially optimal price-quantity combination is one that maximizes welfare, defined as the sum of producer surplus and consumer surplus.

$$\max_q W = CS + PS = \int_0^{q^*} p(q^*)dq - C_v(q^*).$$

The FOC for this problem implies:

$$p(q) = \frac{dC_v}{dq} = MC.$$

In a competitive market this condition holds by assumption. In a monopoly market, it does not.

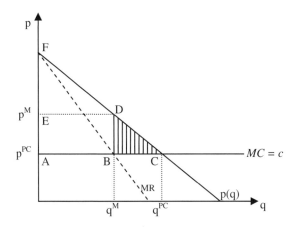

Figure 4.2   Price-output combinations in a monopoly market and in a market under perfect competition

The result of the monopolist's decision is a 'deadweight welfare loss' which is formally given by

$$\int_{q^M}^{q^{PC}} [p(q) - c] \, dq > 0$$

and is illustrated in Figure 4.2 as the area circumscribed by points B, C and D. C gives the efficient solution, where price is equal to marginal costs (so that in a market under perfect competition, the consumer surplus is given by the area A-C-F). B is the point where price equals marginal revenue. D, finally, shows the Cournot point, the profit maximizing price-quantity combination in a monopoly market.

4.4   OLIGOPOLY

In oligopoly markets there is only a small number of firms, serving a particular market. By assumption, they are hence in a position to set quantities (or prices) which means they exercise market power. As a result, as is the case in the monopoly market, the equilibrium price will generally be higher than it would be under perfect competition, and the quantity supplied will generally be lower than it would be under perfect competition. As already mentioned above, oligopolistic markets open up some room for strategic interaction.

There are three standard oligopoly models, Cournot, Bertrand, and Stackelberg. The models are similar in that they are static and considering only one period, excluding repeated interactions. The firms offer one homogeneous good. In the Cournot and Bertrand models firms make their choices simultaneously while in the Stackelberg model firms make their choices sequentially. In the Cournot model, firms compete by choosing the quantities and prices then adjust in order to clear the market. In the Stackelberg model, it is also quantities that are chosen. As choices are made sequentially, this allows the first mover to gain a larger market share than that of the competitor firm. Finally, in the Bertrand model, firms compete by choosing prices and quantities adjust in order to clear the market. The Bertrand model differs in its result since it predicts that two firms competing in prices are sufficient in order to arrive at the outcome that the perfect market model shows as well.

For didactic reasons we present the oligopoly models with only two competing firms, hence we speak of 'duopoly'. All three duopoly models, however, can be extended to more than two firms without changing the main results.

4.4.1   Cournot (Cournot–Nash) Oligopoly

Assume there are two firms (A and B) who simultaneously decide on how much of a *homogeneous good*, q_A and q_B respectively, to produce. The firms face a downward-sloping demand function and it is assumed that the price adjusts in order to clear the market. Thus, the larger the quantity supplied by both firms, $q = q_A + q_B$, the lower the price will be. Formally, this means that the price is a function of output whose first derivative is negative. This function is the inverse demand function $p = p(q)$, with $p'(q) < 0$ for all $q \geq 0$ and, by assumption, $p(0) > c$.

Assume that marginal costs, c, for both firms are identical and constant (both firms utilize the same technology). Firm A's profit maximization problem can then be written as

$$\max_{q_A \geq 0} \pi_A = p(q_A + \bar{q}_B)q_A - cq_A.$$

Here, $\bar{q}_B$ indicates that firm A takes firm B's quantity as given. Deriving the first-order-condition (FOC) we get

$$p'(q_A + \bar{q}_B)q_A + p(q_A + \bar{q}_B) \leq c, \tag{4.3a}$$

where the left-hand side corresponds to firm A's marginal revenue and the right-hand-side to marginal cost. The FOC holds with equality if firm A supplies a positive amount of the good, i.e. $q_A > 0$. Firm B engages in the same reasoning so that, given the assumptions made, we can write firm B's FOC as follows:

$$p'(\bar{q}_A + q_B)q_A + p(\bar{q}_A + q_B) \leq c. \tag{4.3b}$$

Since a Nash equilibrium is an equilibrium in choices and beliefs every firm's belief about the other firm's output is correct, i.e. $q_A = \bar{q}_A = q_A^*$ and $q_B = \bar{q}_B = q_B^*$ where the asterisk denotes a firm's optimal choice of output level. As the goods are homogeneous and both firms utilize the same technology, we further know that $q_A^* = q_B^*$. Adding Equations 4.3a and 4.3b we arrive at the following condition that has to hold in the Nash equilibrium:

$$p'(q_A^* + q_B^*)\left(\frac{q_A^* + q_B^*}{2}\right) + p(q_A^* + q_B^*) = c. \tag{4.4}$$

Equation 4.4 implies that firms are making positive profit since they are charging a price larger than marginal cost (remember that $p' < 0$). Also, the quantity supplied is lower than the socially optimal level. We know this since the demand curve is downward sloping and prices and quantities are therefore negatively related (higher prices meaning lower quantities).

Let us consider an example. For simplicity we assume that firms are producing with a constant-returns-to-scale technology and face a linear inverse demand function given by

$$p(q) = a - bq. \tag{4.5}$$

In Equation 4.5 a and b are positive constants. We know that in the perfect competition (PC) market the price equals marginal cost, $p^{PC} = c$. Output at p^{PC} will be $q = \frac{a-c}{b}$. Using the same functions for the monopoly model explained in the previous section, we would get $p^M = \frac{a+c}{2}$ and $q^M = \frac{a-c}{2b}$

respectively, indicating the higher price (as by assumption $a > c$) and lower quantity (half the perfect market amount in this example).

In the oligopolistic situation firms interact strategically. Equations 4.6 and 4.7 state firm A's profit maximization problem and the FOC:

$$\max_{q_A \geq 0} \left(a - b(q_A + \bar{q}_B)\right)q_A - cq_A \tag{4.6}$$

$$a - 2bq_A - b\bar{q}_B = c \tag{4.7}$$

We now derive firm A's best-response-function q_A^{BR} which is the FOC solved for q_A. We see that firm A's optimal output is inversely related to q_B:

$$q_A^{BR}(q_B) = \frac{1}{2}\left(\frac{a-c}{b} - q_B\right). \tag{4.8a}$$

Since both firms are identical firm B's best-response-function is given by

$$q_B^{BR}(q_A) = \frac{1}{2}\left(\frac{a-c}{b} - q_A\right). \tag{4.8b}$$

Figure 4.3 depicts both best-response functions graphically. The Nash–equilibrium is given by the intersection of those functions. It can be derived by substituting Equations 4.8a in 4.8b. Output at equilibrium is:

$$q_A = q_B = \frac{1}{3}\left(\frac{a-c}{b}\right).$$

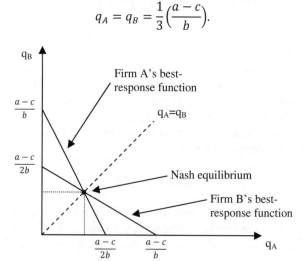

Figure 4.3   Best-Response Functions and Cournot–Nash Equilibrium

Substituting into Equation 4.5 we get the oligopoly price $p^C = \frac{a}{3} + \frac{2c}{3}$. In the Cournot oligopoly total quantity supplied is smaller than at the social optimum, but larger than the quantity in the market if it were a monopoly:

$$\underbrace{\frac{1}{2}\left(\frac{a-c}{b}\right)}_{q^M} < \underbrace{\frac{2}{3}\left(\frac{a-c}{b}\right)}_{q^C} < \underbrace{\left(\frac{a-c}{b}\right)}_{q^{PC}}.$$

If the possibility of collusion is considered, the Cournot model becomes a Prisoners' Dilemma. As above, we assume that both firms are identical. Collusion means that the firms behave as if they were a monopolist and split quantities and profits equally. The Prisoners' Dilemma structure results from the fact that half the monopoly profit is larger than the profit generated in the Nash equilibrium on the one hand, and the fact that with unilateral deviation from the agreed quantities, companies can increase their profits above half the monopoly profits, on the other.

To illustrate this, we resort to a numerical example. Assume that parameters *a* and *b* are given by *a = 14* and *b = 1*. Further assume that constant marginal costs *c* are given by *MC = 2*. We know that profit is maximized where marginal revenue is equal to marginal cost. Here, marginal revenue is given as *MR = 14 − 2q*. The monopolist's profit-maximizing quantity is consequently $q^M = 6$ which corresponds to a price of $p^M = 8$. Total profits in this case are *36*. Two firms colluding would therefore produce *3* units of output each, generating profits of *18* for every company. Contrast this with the mutual best replies in the Cournot duopoly case. Here, each company would supply *4* units of the good produced, the corresponding price would be $p^C = 6$. We see that, compared to collusion, Cournot competition results in a lower price and higher quantities. Also, profits would be lower in Cournot competition, namely *16*. Thus, it is in the interest of both firms to achieve collusion. But will collusion be stable?

		Firm B	
		Collusion / Cartel	Deviation from Cartel Agreement
Firm A	Collusion / Cartel	18 18	20.25 13.5
	Deviation from Cartel Agreement	13.5 20.25	16 16

Figure 4.4   The Cournot–Nash Oligopoly as a PD – numerical example

As can be seen in Figure 4.4, in the one-shot game under consideration at the moment, it will not be. We arrive at this result assuming that one company sticks to the agreement, and then calculate the other firm's best response. The collusion quantity for each company is *3* units. We plug these into one of the best response functions and see that the best answer in that case is to produce *4.5* units. The deviating company would see its profits increase to *20.25*, whereas the profits of the company sticking to the agreement fall to *13.5*. Therefore, the rational choice would be for both to deviate. But if both firms deviate from collusion and play their Nash-strategies, they will end up at the Cournot equilibrium. If profits are interpreted as payoffs, ·this situation corresponds to a PD.

4.4.2   Bertrand Oligopoly

As in the Cournot duopoly model, for the presentation of the Bertrand duopoly (Bertrand, 1883), we assume a downward-sloping continuous demand function $q(p)$ and a constant-returns-to-scale technology for both firms. We assume that $q(c)$ is positive and finite, i.e. if price equals marginal cost a positive and finite quantity of the good is demanded.

In contrast to the Cournot duopoly, competition takes a different form. In the Bertrand duopoly model firms *simultaneously set prices* and supply adjusts in order to clear the market. The firm that chooses the lowest price captures 100 percent of the demand. If both firms choose the same price each firm gets 50 percent of demand:

$$q_A(p_A, p_B) = \begin{cases} q(p_A) & if \;\; p_A < p_B \\ 0.5q(p_A) & if \;\; p_A = p_B \\ 0 & if \;\; p_A > p_B. \end{cases}$$

Firms produce to order, meaning that they produce only what they can sell in the market. For firm A profits are given by

$$\pi_A = (p_A - c)q_A(p_A, p_B).$$

The Bertrand duopoly model is a simultaneous move game. In the following we will derive the Nash equilibrium. We will show that at the equilibrium prices are equal to marginal cost and each firm captures 50 percent of the market share.

Consider the situation where both firms set their prices according to $p_A^* = p_B^* = c$. The firms will divide the market equally and each firm makes zero profits. To show that this is a Nash equilibrium we consider what happens when one firm changes its strategy while the other firm keeps its strategy. If a firm raises its price it will sell nothing, so profits will be zero. No firm can gain by raising its price. If a firm lowers its price and charges a price below costs its market share will rise to 100 percent but the firm makes negative profits. Hence $p_A^* = p_B^* = c$ is a Nash equilibrium since no firm can gain by deviating from its strategy.

Next we check if there is another strategy that could be a Nash equilibrium. If the firm which charges the lowest price charges a price below cost, it will incur losses. It will always be rational to charge a price of c or higher because by behaving this way the firm will make no losses. Hence in a Nash equilibrium firms won't charge a price below c.

What about the following situation in which both firms charge a price above costs? Consider firm A charging a price $p_A > c$ and firm B charging $p_B > p_A$. This is not a Nash equilibrium since firm B can gain by lowering its price and charging a new price p_B' with $p_A > p_B' > c$. Now firm B sells to the entire market earning a positive profit while firm A earns zero profits, but we are not at a Nash equilibrium yet. Firm A can lower its price to p_A' with $p_B' > p_A' > c$. In this new situation firm A sells to the entire market, but again, this is not a Nash equilibrium. The general point is that at prices above costs the firm charging the highest price can always increase its profits by undercutting the other firm's price. Competition will drive down prices to the Pareto optimum characterized by $p_A^* = p_B^* = c$.

Lastly, we consider the situation in which one firm charges a price equal to costs ($p_A = c$) and the other firm charges a price above that ($p_B > p_A$). Both firms make zero profit. Such a situation is not a Nash equilibrium since firm A can increase its price slightly to p_A' with $p_B > p_A' > c$, thereby increasing its profits. But then we are back in the case that we discussed in the preceding paragraph. Hence we conclude that $p_A^* = p_B^* = c$ is the unique Nash equilibrium in the Bertrand duopoly model.

In case of constant marginal costs we get the same result as in perfect competition, completely independent of the number of participating companies. This is known as the 'Bertrand Paradox'.

As one of the possible extensions of the basic Bertrand model, we briefly consider the case of different cost-structures for the producers (other variations include extending the time-period to increase the attractiveness of collusion, price-fixing in this case, capacity constraints, or switching costs, as in the other models discussed here as well).

Consider two firms (A and B) with different marginal costs $c_A < c_B$. In this case, the company with higher marginal cost (B) cannot remain in the market, since it would be undercut by the cost leader (A). The cost leader would monopolize the market by charging a price below c_B, i.e., $p_A < c_B$. Whether company A can actually charge the monopoly price p_A^M depends on the marginal costs c_B. If the monopoly price is lower than the marginal costs of the competitor $(c_A < p_A^M < c_B)$ the Bertrand–Nash–equilibrium is given by: $(p_A^*, p_B^*) = (p_A^M, c_B)$. The cost leader A can set her monopoly price without fearing a market entry by a competitor.

If the monopoly price p_A^M is higher than the marginal cost of company B $(c_A < c_B < p_A^M)$ the monopoly price would lead to the market entry of company B. To prevent the market entry the cost leader will charge a price just below the marginal cost of B. The Bertrand-Nash equilibrium in this case is thus: $(p_A^*, p_B^*) = (c_B - v, c_B)$, with v the smallest monetary unit. The price that provides for entry deterrence is also called the limit price. The potential competition has a disciplining effect on company A. Despite its monopolistic position, the price set and the profits gained are lower than in the pure monopoly model. To sum up, the cost leader will set her price according to the equation below:

$$p_A = \begin{cases} p_A^M & if \ c_A < p_A^M < c_B \\ c_B - v & if \ c_A < c_B < p_A^M. \end{cases}$$

4.4.3   Stackelberg Oligopoly

In the Stackelberg model firms compete by deciding on their respective *quantity*, like in the Cournot duopoly model. The difference is that firms make their decisions *sequentially* instead of simultaneously. At first, firm A (called the leader) decides about the quantity q_A, taking firm B's reaction into account in that decision. Perfect information is assumed so that firm B can observe firm A's decision. Thereafter, firm B (called the follower) reacts by choosing the quantity q_B.

The Stackelberg model is solved by backward induction. Firm A asks how firm B would react? The answer is given by firm B's best-response function, which we already know from the Cournot model. We substitute Equation 4.8b into the market demand function (Equation 4.5) and solve for the price as a function of firm A's output:

$$p(q) = \frac{a + c}{2} - \frac{b}{2} q_A.$$

Taking into account this price, firm A now maximizes profits:

$$\max_{q_A} \pi_A = q_A(p - c) = q_A \left(\frac{a + c}{2} - \frac{b}{2} q_A - c \right).$$

The FOC telling us the quantity that firm A will supply is given by $q_A^* = \frac{a-c}{2b}$. Substituting in firm B's best-response function gives us the quantity that firm B will supply in equilibrium: $q_B^* = \frac{a-c}{4b}$. The price is given by $p^* = \frac{a+3c}{4}$.

The Stackelberg duopoly also results in a situation in which the equilibrium price exceeds the competitive price. In contrast to the Bertrand and Cournot models firms are in different roles as leader and follower. The leader has the so-called first-mover-advantage and generates higher profits than the follower.

4.5   NATURAL MONOPOLY

4.5.1   The Rationale for Natural Monopolies

Real-world markets are characterized by high market concentration. Beside private-sector monopolies, in many societies utilities like electricity, gas, water, and fixed-line telephone services are government-regulated monopolies. Since monopolies are associated with deadweight loss and extra profits which would provoke market entry by competitors, the stability of monopolies and their governmental toleration require an explanation.

One reason for the stability of a monopoly market may lie in the fact that there are so-called natural monopolies. A natural monopoly is characterized by a *subadditive cost function* which indicates that it is cheaper to produce a given amount of output for a single firm than for many smaller firms. A cost function is subadditive if

$$\sum_{i=1}^{m} C(q_i) < \sum_{j=1}^{n} C(q_j) \ \forall \ m < n, with \ \sum_{i=1}^{m} q_i = \sum_{j=1}^{n} q_j = q.$$

Believing that there are natural monopolies, governments frequently grant monopoly rights to public utilities to provide essential goods or services, since given the conditions for a natural monopoly it is more efficient to have only one firm serving the market.

Subadditivity may arise due to economies of scale, for instance. Since, in this case average cost falls as output increases (strict subadditivity), the company with the largest production volume in the market could offer the output at the lowest price and displace its competitors. Hence, the market would tend toward a monopoly. To avoid the cost of parallel investments, it may be useful to grant monopoly rights to a company and regulate it.

This is the case in almost every infrastructure sector, where high fixed costs are required to establish the network that delivers a specific good (transport facilities, energy, water) to consumers, but where the marginal cost of supply is constant, so that average costs decline as output rises. If more than one firm takes up production, the average cost is going to be higher because each additional firm adds a fixed cost. For a graphical representation, compare quantities and average costs per firm, c^{TAC} in Figure 4.5. The superscripts f and s designate first- and second-best outcomes. First-best signifies the efficient solution, where price equals marginal cost. The second-best outcome is characterized by the equality of price and average costs.

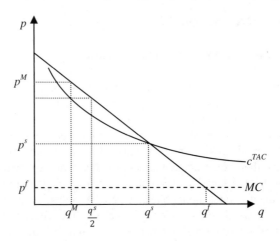

Figure 4.5   Strictly subadditive cost curve

Decreasing average costs are a sufficient condition for a natural monopoly but not a necessary one. If average costs increase again as output increases beyond a certain point (U-shaped average cost function), there can nevertheless be subadditivity, depending on the level of demand (weak subadditivity). In this case not every level of output provides the condition for a natural monopoly. Figure 4.6 depicts a U-shaped average cost function.

A natural monopoly is able to supply the total output at lowest costs. However, because of its monopoly position the price it charges can be expected to be higher than its total average cost. The actual price charged depends on how contestable the market is.

A monopoly position is sustainable, if there is no incentive for a competitor to enter the market. That is the case if the natural monopoly sets a price in a way so that any competing firm that tries to enter the market will incur a loss.

Contestable markets are characterized by free market entry meaning potential competitors (entrants) have free access to the prevailing technology and can enter the market without any penalty if the entry fails. This implies the absence of sunk costs, since the entrant can easily leave the market because the capital equipment that was acquired can be sold or used elsewhere.

In the following we examine the sustainability and efficiency of the natural monopoly in a contestable market and in a market with entry barriers.

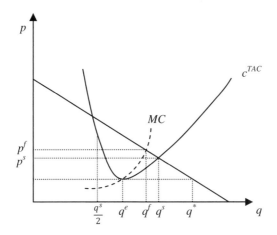

Figure 4.6   Weakly subadditive cost curve

4.5.2   Sustainability and Efficiency of the Natural Monopoly in a Contestable Market

In a contestable market a monopoly price above average cost attracts competitors (entrants) who have free access to the same technology as the established firm (incumbent). The entrants can set a price below the existing monopolist's price and take consumers away. The incumbent firm cannot deter entry if it cannot adjust its prices downwards quickly enough. Then, the entrant can engage in a hit and run strategy, entering the market when the price is high, making short-term profits and leaving it without any costs, when the incumbent lowers its price.

Strict subadditivity
In case of strict subadditivity (Figure 4.5), the threat of entry of a competitor forces the incumbent to lower the charged price to the level of its average costs to deter entrants. The charged price p^s is the second-best welfare optimal price since it is higher than the marginal cost of the corresponding

quantity. The price output combination (p^s, q^s) allows no profitable entry strategy by a competitor, thus the natural monopoly is sustainable, without, however, realizing profits. However, as average costs are higher than marginal costs at this point, the result is not technically speaking efficient.

Weak subadditivity
If the incumbent firm has a U-shaped average cost curve (Figure 4.6) and the demand level allows the subadditivity condition to hold, the threat of entry of a competitor would also lead the incumbent to charge the second-best welfare-optimal price p^s. But the resulting price output combination (p^s, q^s) is not sustainable, although the incumbent gains no profits. The firm is not protected from market entry by rival firms, since there is a profitable entry strategy for an entrant. An entrant could challenge the established monopoly by producing a level of output at minimum efficient scale (q^e) and charging a price below p^s. This may cause a price competition that has an end at price p^e. At that point, the demand q^*-q^e is not met. This outcome can be improved by regulating the market through an *entry barrier* or through a *guaranteed minimum price*.

4.5.3 Sustainability and Efficiency of the Natural Monopoly in a Market with Entry Barriers

In real-world markets there are market entry and exit barriers. Thus, the monopoly is not threatened by an entry and has no incentive to set a social-optimum price. On the other hand, subadditivity given, the cheapest way to produce any given level of output is to have one firm producing for the whole market. This raises the question of how to reach a socially optimal price and socially optimal costs simultaneously.

Strict subadditivity
Sunk costs are not relevant for the decision to produce for an incumbent since they cannot be recovered. However, they are strategic instruments to deter the entry of a competitor. If an entrant decides to challenge the established monopoly it has to take into account that the incumbent can trigger a price competition that hinders the entrant from charging a price that would allow for positive profits. Since an entrant has no sunk cost before entering the market, the sunk costs are relevant for its decision to enter the market. Considering the credible threat of the incumbent lowering the prices, a potential entrant may decide against an entry. If the incumbent is protected from market entry by rival firms, it will set the Cournot monopoly price p^M. Society incurs welfare losses. Moreover, the monopoly position is sustainable.

To prevent this loss of welfare the market should be regulated. If the government required the monopoly to set the first-best welfare optimal price p^f, the monopoly would incur losses, since $p^f < c^{TAC}$. Hence the state would have to subsidize the monopoly or allow the second-best price p^s. This price allows for maximum welfare under the constraint that the company makes no loss.

Weak subadditivity

In the case of weak subadditivity the incumbent sets the Cournot monopoly price, since it does not have to fear the market entry of a competitor. Hence the result is inefficient and the monopoly position is sustainable. But the government has the opportunity to set the first-best price regulating the market, because at p^f the monopoly makes positive profits. For a brief overview see Table 4.1.

Table 4.1   Effects of strong and weak subadditivity in contestable and non-contestable markets

	Strong Subadditivity	Weak Subadditivity
Contestable Market	- p^s (Inefficient) - Sustainable	- p^e (Inefficient) - Unsustainable - Output scaling
Market with Entry Barriers	- p^M (Inefficient) - Sustainable	- p^M (Inefficient) - Sustainable

4.6   HETEROGENEOUS OLIGOPOLY AND MONOPOLISTIC COMPETITION

In the oligopoly models presented above, we were able to gain a first overview of situations in which companies' decisions have a mutual influence on their respectively resulting profits. In a first extension, we can follow P. Sweezy (1939) asking how prices in already existing markets may change. This thought integrates the notion that markets have historically grown and that companies in such an oligopolistic setting find themselves in an equilibrium. In that case, does any company have an incentive to change its prices and if so, how would the others react? Instead of formulating assumptions that help to define one specific equilibrium that rational companies would find themselves in if they met in a market yet without any history of prior relations, we now say, if companies have over time reached one of the possible equilibria in their market, how may the situation change from that point onward, with a specific view on their price-policies.

Another basic assumption in the oligopoly models is that the companies offer a homogeneous product. We relax that assumption in Section 4.6.2 where we introduce the concept of monopolistic competition that has been introduced by E. Chamberlin (1933) and J. Robinson (1933). In that approach, a number of companies offer incomplete substitutes in a market. The intuition is that in order to avoid pure price competition, companies can try to differentiate their products and thereby gain a certain degree of pricing power (depending on the degree of substitutability between their products).

In fact, companies in real markets have a number of tools at hand to help them stabilize markets and market shares or profits and avoid price competition by using tools aiming at variables influencing customers' product choice other than price. This point will subsequently be taken, when we turn from the models of oligopolistic markets to addressing issues that emerge in real-world markets.

4.6.1   Sticky Prices in Oligopoly Markets

Sweezy (1939) addressed the question of sticky prices in markets. Instead of asking what a clearly defined equilibrium in an oligopoly market would look like (given a set of assumptions), he asked how companies might behave in an equilibrium. The point was to find reasons for observed stickiness of prices in markets, especially in markets where you might expect price competition to drive prices down if you applied a more standard model formulation in the analysis. In order to illustrate the point, he assumed that competitors react in different ways to price changes by other companies, depending on whether these would increase or lower their prices. These different reactions introduce a kink in the demand curve of companies. This means that in situations characterized by strategic interdependence, a standard demand function would not be useful.

The basic premise is that companies seek the protection of their market shares. In that case, Sweezy reasoned that it was unlikely that price increases by a company would be met by increases by their competitors. The result is a relatively elastic demand-schedule for a firm for prices above the currently charged one. Market share would be lost and total revenue would be reduced if a firm single-handedly raised the price for its product. On the other hand, he assumed that reductions of prices would be met by competitors. Therefore, the demand schedule for prices below the current one is relatively inelastic. Market shares would not change much, and total revenue would decrease as a consequence. The demand schedule a company faces and its marginal revenue are shown in Figure 4.7.

Once firms find themselves in an equilibrium in an oligopoly market, the approach can therefore help to understand why market conditions (the price asked by firms) may not change. Price competition does not make sense for the companies. Then, competition could be expected to be exercised through other, non-price instruments aiming at strengthening monopoly power and increasing customer loyalty (see below).

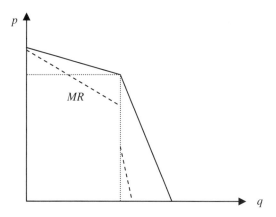

Figure 4.7   The kinked demand curve

4.6.2   Heterogenization and Monopolistic Competition

The concept of monopolistic competition was introduced by Chamberlin in 1933, and in parallel by Robinson. Observing market structures, he concluded that the available models of perfect competition and monopoly, respectively, were only incomplete approximations of real markets, where advertising and product differentiation played a significant role. Commonly observed market structures, rather, allow firms some degree of market power, without enjoying full monopoly power, though. At the outset of his concept, thus, stand firms that can behave like monopolists in their market segments. They do, however, face competition from firms offering imperfect substitutes to their products. The reasoning is that in order to avoid price competition that reduces their profits, firms could divide markets and create market segments through product differentiation. As a result, they are assumed to face downward-sloping demand curves, albeit more elastic ones than a pure monopolist would (even though the basic reasoning applied to monopoly markets as explained above remains valid here).

More specifically, two separate demand curves are introduced to illustrate a company's problem structure (Figure 4.8). One gives a demand schedule for the situation in which all its competitors keep their prices constant, this is relatively elastic (dd). The other refers to a situation in which all firms set the same price. This one is assumed to be relatively inelastic (DD). Note that the reasoning corresponds to that of the kinked demand curve that Sweezy formulated. To the left of the intersection between dd and DD curve Sweezy's kinked demand curve corresponds to the dd curve, to the right it corresponds to the DD curve.

As long as free entry is assumed, eventually a situation with many companies in the market realizing zero profit would result. This connects the idea of a monopolistic component to the competitive market. If companies realize profits, more competitors enter the market. As companies face downward sloping demand curves, the resulting price would in the end correspond to their average costs, whilst still lying above their marginal cost, though. The situation is reversed if the original set-up is characterized by losses. In that case firms leave the market until zero profits are realized.

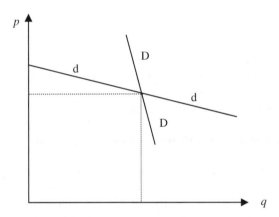

Figure 4.8   Demand schedules in monopolistic competition

If entry barriers can be erected the companies in a market may be smaller in number, and we will observe an oligopoly with heterogeneous products. We will return to this point momentarily, in Section 4.7. Even though the market structure is described as monopolistically competitive, and continuing entry would eventually drive profits down to zero unless countermeasures were taken, such heterogeneous oligopolies may in fact be closer to what Chamberlin had in mind. The importance of product differentiation that he noted, and the fact that real competition includes a number of non-price variables that allow companies to create market niches in which they can exercise market power, point in this direction.

4.7   INSTABILITY OF OLIGOPOLISTIC COMPETITION: POSSIBILITIES FOR STRATEGIC BEHAVIOR OF FIRMS

In reality, there are factors leading to oligopoly markets being unstable: Reinforced size growth through economies of scale in production technology, net effects on the user side, and the other factors mentioned above (in Section 4.2). To avoid endless price wars and related turbulence in the oligopoly, oligopolists have chosen early in history to calm their direct competition down and *reduce their direct interdependence* through dissolving an important condition of direct dilemma-prone interdependence, which at the same time is an important common condition of all oligopoly models: Product homogeneity.

Oligopolists may, of course, avoid price competition through 'meet the competition' clauses (used also as an entry deterrence), i.e., a publicly declared self-commitment and *credible threat* to meet a price-cut by another oligopolist (or potential entrant) through the same price cut on their sides. What may look like fierce price competition in fact is a device to enforce price stability as a coordination form. If a price cut can be expected to be met by price cuts by competitors, oligopolists would of course choose the high-price strategy coordination (compare to the considerations forwarded by Sweezy). But with this, we still would move in the world of homogeneous oligopolies.

Beyond the homogeneous oligopoly, product and price differentiation, through branding, advertising, or quality differences allowing market segmentation have occurred as a result of the growing action capabilities of corporations vis-à-vis their customers, users, consumers, and the market as a whole. Large oligopolistic firms divide the market and generate their own market segments, where they can behave similarly to monopolists. Consumers are induced into spending on goods and services because of the name and its image, for instance, rather than because of rational examinations of functional or instrumental quality. We may call this ceremonial belief or ceremonial institutionalized trust. The resulting set of phenomena that emerged this way in real-world markets from the second half of the 19th century onwards, was first analyzed in the early 1930s as monopolistic competition, describing a heterogeneous oligopoly. Monopolistic competition understood this way nowadays applies to virtually all important goods and services such as cars, computers, software, telecommunication and internet services, private water and energy supplies, fuel, etc. Given differentiated products, the customer/user/consumer will have to incur higher costs to collect and process information on the different brands that, in turn, are deliberately made non-transparent, incomparable or even incommensurable to customers by the monopolistic competitors.

Against this background, it becomes obvious that binding consumers/ customers/users to the oligopolist's brand name by advertising, brand management, and reputation building would be a prime strategy for an oligopolist in monopolistic competition. The more she succeeds in steepening her sales curve (the demand curve), the more the sales price *p* that she can realize will tend to be above her marginal revenue (see the Amoroso-Robinson relation above).

4.8   A FINAL CONSIDERATION ON FIRM SIZE, STRATEGIC COOPERATION, MONOPOLISTIC COMPETITION, AND REAL-WORLD MARKETS

In the end, the two perspectives of strategic interaction with some collusion/ cartelization and price cooperation and of heterogeneous oligopoly, i.e., *monopolistic competition plus strategic cooperation*, would need to be integrated into a more realistic model of real-world markets.

At any rate, though, the oligopoly – far beyond just either oligopolistic equilibrium with homogeneous goods or monopolistic competition – remains *a complex and unstable form* that probably will keep *real-world markets overly complex, unstable, and turbulent*. Finally, some core issues and their persistent tensions should be remembered (see Figure 4.9).

A broader perspective would have to consider and analyze the firm, particularly the large and global firm and monopolistic rivalry systems, not only in the economy, but its wider impacts, through the *openness of the economy*, on the power, redistribution, and exploitation processes vis-à-vis the social and ecological systems, where all three subsystems form a complete system – and the threat of *entropy*.

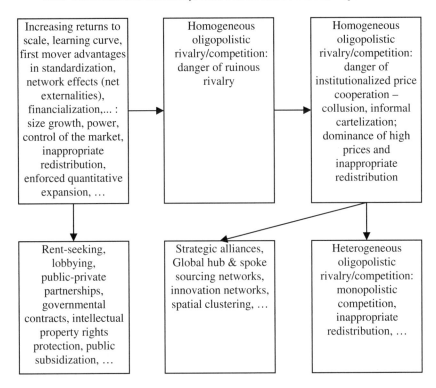

Figure 4.9   Factors and issues of real-world markets and their persistent non-optimality and disequilibrium

FURTHER READING

For a list of selected advanced textbooks, monographs, and articles on monopoly and oligopoly theory and industrial economics, see the textbook website at www.microeconomics.us.

5. Ideal Neoclassical Market and General Equilibrium

The neoclassical method and research program is to develop a 'pure theory', an abstract model, starting from some abstract axioms and taking as little as possible as givens. The objective is to construct an equilibrium model of a market economy in a *price-quantity world* and logically deduct general laws applicable therein.

However, any model is an imagery, analogy or metaphor only, relating variables to one another, mostly rather few, and not a theoretical explanation per se. Models can be set up to yield unique predetermined equilibria, in simple and 'closed' deterministic models, or they can be complex, with many variables, agents and relations, positive feedback loops, etc., no longer apt to yield unique solutions, with open boundaries and being open-ended.

Neoclassical economics typically ends up in price-quantity-spaces employing the mathematics of *maximization with restrictions*. *Economism* in that sense is the idea of a 'pure' economy, isolated from the rest of society and from the natural environment. *General Equilibrium Theory* (GET) as the study of interdependent ideal markets, is the comprehensive formulation of neoclassical economics. But the neoclassical paradigm (as any paradigm) cannot straightforwardly be tested and rejected, since 'data' are always selected, 'stylized facts', evaluated, and adapted to the world view of the measurer.

GET is often named *Walrasian economics*, after its 'inventor', Léon Marie-Esprit Walras (1834-1910). Walras considered an exchange economy where agents trade given goods not with each other but with a fictitious auctioneer. There is no direct interdependence of agents. But he was the first to emphasize the interdependence of individual partial markets in his 'Elements of Pure Economics' published in 1874, three years after the works of William Stanley Jevons and Carl Menger. Walras, Jevons, and Menger are considered to be the leaders of the *marginalist revolution* whose key elements are marginal utility (and marginal productivity in production) and scarcity.

For constructing the models, perfect competition and perfect information are assumed. This means that all agents (firms and households) get all relevant information, reflected in prices, at no costs. They take equilibrium prices as given and maximize utility (households) or profits (firms). Preferences and production technologies are exogenously given. It is implied that trade only takes place at market-clearing prices which are computed by the fictitious auctioneer. In this setting a competitive equilibrium is characterized by prices and allocations at which decisions are mutually consistent. Agents can buy and sell exactly the amount they want to at those prices. Supply equals demand. At equilibrium there is no endogenous mechanism that causes a change in prices. However, an exogenous change in preferences or technology will result in a shift of the equilibrium position, hence, a change to new equilibrium prices. An equilibrium allocation, as the 'first welfare theorem' (see below) shows, is Pareto-optimal.

Early GET models were static models of an economy, abstracted from the time-dimension. Soon, they were extended to take into account intertemporal decisions as well as risk. With the Ramsey growth model, the general equilibrium model was modified to integrate economic growth.

In our explanation of GET the starting point is an economic system consisting of households (or consumers) and firms whose behavior we describe in the next two sections. Consumers own given resources at the outset which they can consume or sell. Firms buy inputs which they transform into outputs in a production process. The economy is considered to be an exchange economy, that is, there is no money. However, we can think of one commodity (e.g., gold) as a money commodity, serving as numéraire.

Having introduced consumer and production theory (Sections 5.1 and 5.2) we briefly explain partial equilibrium analysis, the analysis of one market in isolation (Section 5.3), before we proceed to general equilibrium analysis. In a general equilibrium, the partial markets are connected and all agents' decisions are mutually consistent. The general equilibrium, its implications, and the conditions necessary for the model to offer the desired results, are considered in Section 5.4. Thereafter, we briefly review the Ramsey growth model and the 'New Keynesian' model in Section 5.5.

5.1   CONSUMER THEORY

5.1.1   Preferences

With Descartes' division of the world into an inner subjective domain (res cogitans) and an outer objective domain (res extensa), active mind and passive matter became separated. The mind was conceived as having values and being subjective; the individual was defined with reference to reason and consciousness, that is, with reference to itself. This is known as his famous

Cogito ergo sum, 'I think, therefore I am' (Discours de la Méthode, 1637). The outer world, matter, was portrayed as objective and values-less, working according to universal and unchanging rules.

The Cartesian dualism is at the root of the neoclassical conception of the individual. The subjective mind was relegated to the unscientific domain and it was assumed that individuals do not interact on a subjective level. The individual's autonomy is derived from her 'tastes' which remain unchanged. While the unscientific inner world of individuals (tastes) was treated as unobservable and unchanging, choice was observable. The focus shifted from the individual towards choice behavior and individual decision making. Moreover, with this conception the individual was completely detached from her social structure (e.g. class).

The preference-based approach to individual decision making starts from an assumed preference relation. If an individual is offered a choice between apples x and oranges y, she will choose apples if she prefers apples to oranges, formally $x \succsim y$. We assume that the individual has a rational preference relation over the set of all possible choices. Let x, y, z be mutually exclusive alternatives in the set of all possible choices X. A rational preference relation is characterized by

- completeness: for $x, y \in X$, $x \succsim y$ or $y \succsim x$ or both
- transitivity: for $x, y, z \in X$, $x \succsim y$ and $y \succsim z \rightarrow x \succsim z$
- reflexivity: $x \sim x$ for all $x \in X$.

Moreover, by assuming continuity we exclude lexicographic preferences. Let's illustrate this with a simple two-good example. An agent with lexicographic preferences will choose the bundle that offers the largest amount of the first good x_1 no matter how much of the other good is in the bundle. That is $(x_1, x_2) \succ (x_1', x_2')$ if $x_1 > x_1'$. If both bundles have exactly the same amount of the first good, $x_1 = x_1'$ then the amounts of the second good are compared and the bundle with more of the second good will be preferred. A lexicographic preference relation is rational but cannot be represented by a continuous function since it is not preserved under limits. With the sequence $\left\{ \frac{1}{m} \mid m \in \mathbb{N} \right\}$ the bundle $\left(\frac{1}{m}, 0 \right)$ will always be preferred to $(0,1)$. In the limit, however, this preference relation will be reversed, $lim_{m \to \infty} \left(\frac{1}{m}, 0 \right) = (0,0) \prec (0,1)$.

5.1.2 Utility, Maximization, and Demand

Some words on notation: We use subscript $n \in \{1, \dots, N\}$ to indicate goods, and superscript $i \in \{1, \dots, I\}$ to indicate individuals. Superscript $j \in \{1, \dots, J\}$

is used for indexing firms. Equilibrium values are denoted by an upper bar. Prices are denoted as row vectors, allocations, endowments, and demand as column vectors, hence their product (e.g. $p\omega$) gives us a scalar (for an overview of the symbols used see Table 5.1).

Table 5.1   Symbols, variables, and parameters for neoclassical GET

Symbol	Meaning
$p = (p_1, p_2, ..., p_N)$	price vector
$\mathbb{R}^N$	commodity space
$\mathbb{R}^N_+$	consumption set
$x^{i\prime} = \left(x^i_1, x^i_2, ..., x^i_N\right) \in \mathbb{R}^N_+$	commodity bundle or demand individual i
$x' = (x^1, x^2, ..., x^I) \in \mathbb{R}^{IN}_+$	allocation
$\omega^{i\prime} = \left(\omega^i_1, \omega^i_2, ..., \omega^i_N\right)$	endowment individual i
$\bar{\omega} = \sum_{i=1}^{I} \omega^i$	aggregate endowment
$w = p\omega$	wealth
λ	Lagrange multiplier
∇	gradient vector
$\bar{x}, \bar{x}^i_n, \bar{p}$	equil. allocation, equil. demand agent i good n, equil. price vector

An individual's wealth acts as a constraint on her demand since prices are assumed to be positive (goods are desirable). The consumer cannot spend more than she has. We assume that each consumer has a strictly positive (and finite) endowment of at least one good ($\omega^i_n > 0$ for all i and some n). This results in the attainable set being non-empty and, more importantly, bounded. Our rational consumer is assumed to maximize utility, taking prices as given.

Let there be a finite number of commodities n and assume that utility functions satisfy the following conditions. The utility function u is

- continuous
- strictly increasing in every argument
- at least differentiable twice on the interior of $\mathbb{R}^N_+$
- strictly concave $\dfrac{\partial u}{\partial x_n} > 0$ and $\dfrac{\partial^2 u}{\partial x_n^2} < 0$
- satisfies $lim_{x_j \to 0} \dfrac{\partial u(x)}{\partial x_n} = +\infty$.

The utility function maps all possible choices of commodity bundles into the real numbers, mathematically $u: \mathbb{R}_+^N \to \mathbb{R}$. Commodity bundles that are preferred give a higher utility. The first part of the assumption follows from continuity of preferences and is made primarily for mathematical convenience. The second part means that goods are good, i.e. by consuming more of any good the consumer gets higher utility. Differentiability is assumed for mathematical convenience. Concavity is derived from the assumption of diminishing marginal utility, that is, the additional amount of utility gained from consuming one extra unit decreases with the amount of the good the individual already consumes. Marginal utility is positive but decreasing. The last condition of this assumption ensures that quantities and prices will be strictly positive in equilibrium. The budget set of consumer i containing all possible bundles that the consumer could buy, given her endowments, is

$$B^i = \{x^i \in \mathbb{R}_+^N : px^i \leq p\omega^i\}.$$

Box 5.1   *The Lagrange Multiplier Method*

The utility function $u(x)$ itself has no maximum, utility increases as more of the goods is consumed. The utility maximization problem is a constrained optimization problem, that is, utility is maximized subject to the constraint that consumers cannot spend more than their available wealth. One way to transform an unconstrained maximization problem into a constrained maximization problem and to solve it is the method of Lagrange multipliers.

For the sake of illustration assume a consumer in a world with only two goods, x_1 and x_2, and wealth ω. We can write the utility maximization problem as a constrained maximization problem. The constraint $p_1x_1+p_2x_2=\omega$ is rewritten so that we have zero on the right-hand side, $p_1x_1+p_2x_2-\omega=0$. Then, the left-hand side of the rewritten budget constraint is multiplied by the Lagrange multiplier λ and the whole term is subtracted from the utility function:

$$\max_{x_1,x_2,\lambda} \Lambda = u(x,y) - \lambda(p_1x_1 + p_2x_2 - \omega)$$

The term λ is called Lagrange multiplier and ensures that the budget constraint is satisfied. The first-order conditions for a maximum are obtained by taking the first partial derivatives of the Lagrange function Λ with respect to x_1, x_2 and λ and setting them equal to zero. Since we assume that the utility function is concave the first-order conditions are necessary and sufficient conditions.

$$\frac{\partial \Lambda}{\partial x_1} = \frac{\partial u}{\partial x_1} - \lambda p_1 = 0$$

$$\frac{\partial \Lambda}{\partial x_2} = \frac{\partial u}{\partial x_2} - \lambda p_2 = 0$$

$$\frac{\partial \Lambda}{\partial \lambda} = p_1 x_1 + p_2 x_2 - \omega = 0.$$

Now we have a system of three equations which we solve for x_1, x_2 and λ. The specific form of the solution depends on the specific form of the utility function. As can be seen from the last of the three equations, the budget constraint is satisfied. The consumer spends her wealth completely.

By dividing the first and the second equation we obtain an interesting result:

$$\frac{\partial u/\partial x_1}{\partial u/\partial x_2} = \frac{\lambda p_1}{\lambda p_2} = \frac{p_1}{p_2}.$$

At the optimum, the ratio of prices equals the ratio of marginal utilities (= marginal rate of substitution). For our consumer this means that, at the optimum, the utility from the last monetary unit spent on each good must be the same.

The solution to the consumer's utility maximization problem (UMP) is a bundle of commodities as a function of prices and wealth $x^i = x^i(p, w)$. This is called a Walrasian or Marshallian demand function[1]. For positive prices and wealth let $v\,(p,\,w)$ denote the indirect utility function, giving the value of u at $\bar{x}(p)$ (the value of the solved utility maximization problem). Since the utility function is strictly increasing (assumption 1) we know that the budget constraint will hold with equality. The consumer spends her wealth completely:

$$v(p, w) = \max_x u(x) \text{ subject to } px = w. \tag{5.1}$$

Using the Lagrange method (see Box 5.1) we maximize

$$\Lambda = u(x) - \lambda(px - w) \tag{5.2}$$

and get the following first-order conditions:

$$\frac{\partial u}{\partial x_n} = \lambda p x_n \forall n \in N \tag{5.3}$$

$$px = w. \tag{5.4}$$

Assuming that all consumers have positive endowments and thus $w > 0$ we know that in equilibrium they will consume a positive quantity of each good, hence $x_n > 0$ for $n \in \{1,2,...,N\}$. From Equation 5.3 we know that in this equilibrium for consumers marginal utilities (weighted by prices) are equalized, formally

$$\frac{\partial u/\partial x_{n1}}{p_{n1}} = \frac{\partial u/\partial x_{n2}}{p_{n2}} \iff \frac{p_{n1}}{p_{n2}} = \frac{\partial u/\partial x_{n1}}{\partial u/\partial x_{n2}} \tag{5.5}$$

where $n_1, n_2 \in \{1,2,...,N\}$. Call this the equilibrium condition for consumers[2]. Equation 5.4 tells us that the budget constraint will be binding, that is, consumers spend their wealth completely. The FOCs of the UMP give us $N+1$ equations and $N+1$ variables (x_1, x_2, ..., x_N and λ), a system that is solvable in principle. Using a simple example we illustrate how we can use the FOCs of the utility maximization problem to derive the demand functions. Assume a world with just two goods, x_1 and x_2. (For simplicity we omit the superscript i indexing individuals.) The utility function is given by

$$u(x_1, x_2) = \alpha ln x_1 + (1 - \alpha) ln x_2.$$

We set up the Lagrange function and derive the FOCs:

$$\max_{x_1, x_2, \lambda} \alpha ln x_1 + (1 - \alpha) ln x_2 - \lambda(p_1 x_1 + p_2 x_2 - w) \tag{5.6}$$

$$\frac{\alpha}{x_1} = \lambda p_1 \tag{5.7}$$

$$\frac{1-\alpha}{x_2} = \lambda p_2 \tag{5.8}$$

$$p_1 x_1 + p_2 x_2 = w. \tag{5.9}$$

We combine Equations 5.7 and 5.8 to get

$$p_1 x_1 = \frac{\alpha}{1 - \alpha} p_2 x_2$$

and rearrange Equation 5.9 into

$$p_1 x_1 = w - p_2 x_2.$$

From the last two equations we get

$$\frac{\alpha}{1 - \alpha} p_2 x_2 = w - p_2 x_2.$$

This equation can be solved for x_2 as a function of prices and wealth:

$$\overline{x_2}(p_1, p_2, w) = (1 - \alpha)\frac{w}{p_2}. \tag{5.10}$$

Substituting Equation 5.10 in Equation 5.9 and solving for the demand of x_1 we get

$$\overline{x_1}(p_1, p_2, w) = \alpha\frac{w}{p_1}. \tag{5.11}$$

The last two equations are the individual's Walrasian or Marshallian demand functions, telling us how much of each good the individual will demand as a function of prices and wealth. Note that the demand for each good increases in wealth and decreases in the price of the good. If wealth increases the consumer buys at least as much of each good as before. And if the price of a good increases she will buy less of this particular good. The consumer's utility at the optimum is given by the indirect utility function:

$$v(p, w) = u(\overline{x_1}, \overline{x_2}) = \alpha ln\left[\alpha\frac{w}{p_1}\right] + (1 - \alpha)ln\left[(1 - \alpha)\frac{w}{p_2}\right].$$

5.2 PRODUCTION THEORY

5.2.1 The Production Function

We describe firms' production possibilities by a production function F stating the relation between inputs and outputs. For simplicity assume that there is one output, y, which is produced with two inputs, capital K and labor L.

A technology that is often used is the Cobb–Douglas technology, which is defined for $\alpha \in (0,1)$ and two inputs (K,L) by the following production function:

$$y = F(K, L) = AK^\alpha L^{1-\alpha}. \tag{5.12}$$

In this context it is also useful to define the marginal product which is the change in total output that occurs in response to a one-unit increase in a variable input, keeping all other inputs fixed (the slope of the surface in Figure 5.1). Mathematically this is the partial differential of the production function with respect to the variable input.

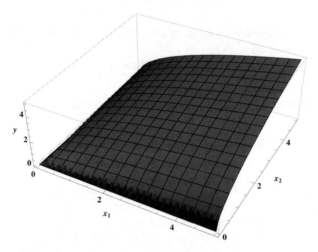

Figure 5.1   The Cobb–Douglas Production Function (α=0.5)

Assume that the production function is differentiable. Then, the marginal rate of technical substitution (MRTS) tells us at which rate one input can be exchanged for another input without altering the quantity of output. To derive the equation for the MRTS we start with the total differential of the production function (5.12) and set it equal to zero. This is the equation for an isoquant, a contour line through the set of points at which the same quantity of output is produced. We stick to the Cobb–Douglas production function for the derivation, with $A = 1$:

$$dy = \alpha \left(\frac{L}{K}\right)^{1-\alpha} dK + (1 - \alpha) \left(\frac{K}{L}\right)^{\alpha} dL = 0.$$

If we solve it for the MRTS it is obvious that the MRTS equals the ratio of the marginal products which is nothing else than the absolute value of the slope of the isoquant:

$$MRTS_{KL} = \left|-\frac{dL}{dK}\right| = \frac{\alpha}{1-\alpha}\frac{L}{K}. \tag{5.13}$$

Figure 5.2 shows isoquants for different levels of output. The shaded areas in the figure are input sets, that is, combinations of inputs that produce at least some specified amount of output. Formally, isoquant $S(y)$ and input requirement set $I(y)$ are defined as follows:

$$S(y) = \{(L, K): F(K, L) = y\} \tag{5.14}$$

$$I(y) = \{(L, K): F(K, L) \geq y\}. \tag{5.15}$$

The isoquant is the boundary of the input requirement set. Here we assume free disposal, that is, by increasing one input we can produce at least as much output. Moreover, we assume that the law of diminishing returns holds. The law states that if all but one input is fixed, the increase in output from an increase in the variable input eventually declines. For the production function this implies:

$$\frac{\partial F}{\partial K} > 0 \text{ and } \frac{\partial^2 F}{\partial K^2} < 0$$

$$\frac{\partial F}{\partial L} > 0 \text{ and } \frac{\partial^2 F}{\partial L^2} < 0.$$

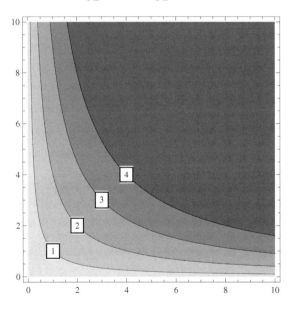

Figure 5.2   Isoquants and input sets for a Cobb–Douglas Production Function ($\alpha=0.5$)

5.2.2   Cost Minimization and Cost Functions

Let there be a firm with Cobb–Douglas production technology with $\alpha = 0.5$. Input costs are given by the cost of capital r and the wage w. The firm wants to produce output $y = \bar{y}$ taking prices as given. Which amount of capital and labor will the firm choose? To answer this problem we set up the Lagrangian of the firm's cost-minimization problem:

$$\min_{K,L} rK + wL \text{ subject to } F(K,L) \geq \bar{y}$$

$$\Lambda(K,L,\lambda) = rK + wL - \lambda(F(K,L) - \bar{y}). \tag{5.16}$$

Note that we replaced the inequality from the constraint by an equality in the Lagrange-function since the firm will not use more of any input than necessary, i.e. production will take place on the isoquant. To figure out which point on the isoquant is cost minimizing we take first-order conditions (FOC) and set them zero:

$$r = \lambda\frac{\partial F}{\partial K} \text{ and } w = \lambda\frac{\partial F}{\partial L}$$

$$F(K,L) = \bar{y}.$$

The last FOC states that production will be on an isoquant, i.e. no inputs will be wasted. Combining the first two FOCs we get the firm's optimality condition for the relative amounts of inputs used:

$$\frac{r}{w} = \frac{\partial F/\partial K}{\partial F/\partial L} = MRTS_{KL}. \tag{5.17}$$

At the optimum, the relative price of inputs has to equal the marginal rate of technical substitution.

We now derive the firm's cost function, giving us the minimum cost for producing output $\bar{y}$. For simplicity we use the Cobb–Douglas production function with $\alpha=0.5$ (see Figure 5.3):

$$C(r,w;\bar{y}) = \min_{L,K} wL + rK \text{ subject to } \bar{y} = K^{0.5}L^{0.5}. \tag{5.18}$$

Solving the constraint for K yields $K = \bar{y}^2/L$. By substitution we rewrite the cost function as

$$C(r, w; \bar{y}) = \min_{L} wL + r\frac{\bar{y}^2}{L}.$$

Taking the FOC and setting zero yields $w = r\bar{y}^2/L^2$. We rearrange the terms to get the conditional factor demand for labor:

$$L(w, r, \bar{y}) = \left(\frac{r}{w}\right)^{0.5} \bar{y}. \tag{5.19}$$

In the same way we can derive the conditional factor demand for capital:

$$K(w, r, \bar{y}) = \left(\frac{w}{r}\right)^{0.5} \bar{y}. \tag{5.20}$$

We can now write the cost function as

$$C(r, w; \bar{y}) = wL(w, r, \bar{y}) + rK(w, r, \bar{y}) = 2w^{0.5}r^{0.5}\bar{y}. \tag{5.21}$$

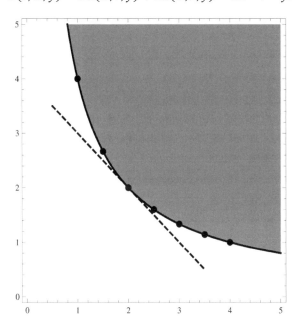

Figure 5.3   Input requirement set (grey), isoquant (boundary) and relative prices (dotted line) for a Cobb–Douglas Production Function

5.2.3 Profit Maximization

Using the cost function we now turn to the firm's profit maximization problem. A firm's profits are defined as revenue minus cost:

$$\pi(y, L, K; w, r, p_0) = p_0 y - (wL + rK). \tag{5.22}$$

Since profit maximization implies cost minimization we can substitute the cost function for *(wL+rK)*. The firm's task is now to choose the level of output *y* that maximizes profits, taking input prices (*w* and *r*) as given. The price of the output p_0 is also taken as given.

$$\max_{y \geq 0} \pi = p_0 y - C(r, w, y). \tag{5.23}$$

The solution depends on p_0 and the specific form of the cost function. Assume that the firm can sell its complete output at price p_0. The Cobb–Douglas production function exhibits constant returns to scale (see Box 5.2) since

$$F(cK, cL) = A(cK)^{0.5}(cL)^{0.5} = cAK^{0.5}L^{0.5} = cF(K, L).$$

This means that the cost function is linear and average costs $(AC = \frac{C(r,w,y)}{y})$ as well as marginal costs $(MC = \frac{\partial C(r,w,y)}{\partial y})$ are constant[3].

Box 5.2 Returns to Scale

The form of the cost function depends on whether the technology exhibits increasing, decreasing, or constant returns to scale. Will the technology work the same way if the level of production is changed? Constant returns to scale prevail, i.e., by doubling all inputs we get twice as much output; formally *F(cx)= cF(x)* for all *c* ≥ 0. If we multiply all inputs by two but get more than twice the output our production function exhibits increasing returns to scale, *F(cx)> cF(x)* for *c > 1*. Vice-versa, decreasing returns to scale are defined by *F(cx)< cF(x)* for *c > 1*. Increasing returns to scale might prevail if a technology becomes feasible only if a certain minimum level of output is produced. On the other hand, limited availability of scarce resources (natural resources or managerial talent) might be limiting firm size in which case decreasing returns to scale are more likely. Also, it is possible that a technology exhibits increasing returns at low levels of production and decreasing returns at high levels.

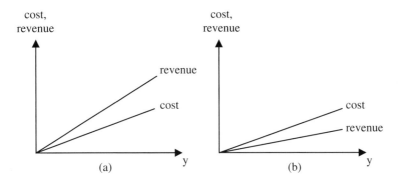

Figure 5.4   Revenue and cost for constant returns to scale

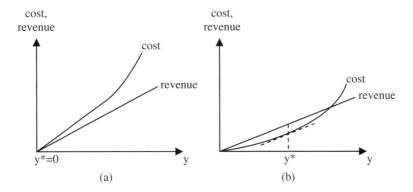

Figure 5.5   Revenue and cost for decreasing returns to scale

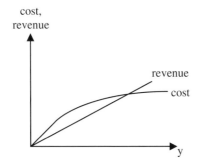

Figure 5.6   Revenue and cost for increasing returns to scale

If the price p_0 is below average costs, the firm will do best if it produces zero output (Figure 5.4 (b)). And if $p_0 > AC$ the firm maximizes profits by producing as much as possible since every additional unit of output increases profits. In this case the maximum of the profit function is not well-defined (Figure 5.4 (a)). Profit can be visualized as the distance between the revenue-function (yp_0) and cost-curve ($C(r, w, y)$), as can be seen in Figure 5.4.

With decreasing returns to scale the cost function is convex in y, that is, the more output is produced the higher the average costs. If the cost of producing one unit of output is larger than p_0 it is optimal to produce nothing (Figure 5.5 (a)). Otherwise, it is optimal to increase production up to the point where marginal costs (the costs of increasing production by one unit) are equal to p_0. In Figure 5.5 (b) this is the case where the slope of the cost-curve, which gives us marginal costs, is equal to the slope of the revenue-function[4].

In the case of increasing returns to scale there exists no optimum. The cost function is concave and average as well as marginal costs decrease. At some point marginal costs are below p_0 (and still decreasing), so the firm can increase its profit by expanding production (Figure 5.6).

Note that the above discussion of a firm's profit maximization problem relies on two assumptions. First, all output can be sold at the price p_0. Second, all inputs are available in unlimited supply at constant prices. In general, these assumptions will not hold.

5.3   PARTIAL EQUILIBRIUM

We consider a single market in isolation from all other markets and assume that in this ideal market the demand of one consumer (representative consumer) and the supply of one firm (representative firm) come together. We assume that the consumer and the firm take prices as given, that is, there is no strategic interaction and they behave as if they were in a perfectly competitive market.

Figure 5.7 shows a downward-sloping demand function as it is assumed in neoclassical economics (though it is not necessarily linear). We have seen demand functions before in Equations 5.10 and 5.11. The demand function specifies the quantity the consumer wishes to purchase at various prices. Individual demand functions are assumed to be downward sloping. At all points on the demand curve the consumer is at her optimum.

In a similar way we can depict the firm's supply schedule connecting all price-quantity pairs which are consistent with the firm's optimum (Figure 5.8). The higher the price of a good, the more a firm is willing to produce and offer, hence, the supply function is upward sloping. In fact, in the perfect competition market, the supply curve is the marginal cost curve. As some inputs to production are assumed to be available only in limited supply, we have a convex cost function and decreasing returns to scale (as in Figure 5.5). Increasing production is only profitable if the good can be sold at a higher price.

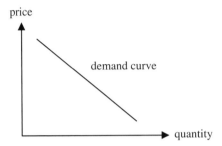

Figure 5.7   A stylized demand function

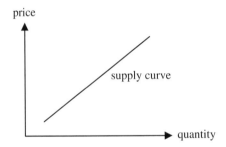

Figure 5.8   A stylized supply function

Figure 5.9 now brings the demand and supply functions together. The equilibrium price and quantity is given by the intersection of the curves and depicts the price-quantity combination at which the consumer and the firm are both satisfied. If the price is above the equilibrium price there will be excess supply. The firm wants to sell more than it can, hence the firm will cut the price and we move closer to the equilibrium. At a price lower than the equilibrium price the consumer wants to buy more than is available. There is excess demand, resulting in upward pressure on the price. At the market equilibrium excess supply and excess demand are both equal to zero. The resulting allocation is Pareto-optimal.

Note that in the analysis of supply and demand we assumed decreasing returns to scale. For the short-run in which some inputs, such as factory buildings, are available in limited supply this is a reasonable assumption. This is why the upward-sloping supply curve is also known as a short-run supply curve. In the long-run, however, all inputs can be increased (it takes some time to set up a new factory but in principle this is possible). Then the production technology can exhibit constant or increasing returns to scale. In the case of constant returns the long-run supply curve is horizontal, in the case of increasing returns it is downward sloping.

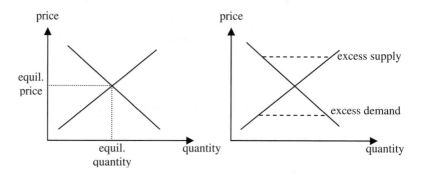

Figure 5.9   Supply and demand combined in interaction: Equilibrium price and quantity, excess demand and supply

5.4   GENERAL EQUILIBRIUM

5.4.1   Welfare Theorems and Walras' Law

Instead of just looking at one market in isolation, as we did in the preceding section, we look at the complete set of markets now. From the discussion of consumer and firm behavior above, in particular Equations 5.5 and 5.17, we know that in equilibrium marginal rates of substitution and marginal rates of technical substitution are equalized:

$$MRS_{12} = \frac{\partial u/\partial x_1}{\partial u/\partial x_2} = \frac{p_{x1}}{p_{x2}} = \frac{\partial F/\partial x_1}{\partial F/\partial x_2} = MRTS_{12}. \qquad (5.24)$$

General equilibrium analysis allows us to consider all markets simultaneously, instead of just looking at one market in isolation. A general equilibrium is a concurrent equilibrium in all markets, hence the cross effects among markets are taken into account. The combination of equilibrium prices and allocations $(\bar{p}, \bar{x})$ is also known as Arrow-Debreu equilibrium. Wealth is endogenously determined by the equilibrium price system and the endowments. For the sake of simplicity we assume that there is no production; we look at an exchange economy. From our discussion of consumer theory we know that the condition given by Equation 5.5 has to hold for all consumers, hence we have NI equations. Also, we assume that all markets are in equilibrium, that is, excess demand z (demand minus supply) is equal to zero:

$$z_n(p) = \sum_{i=1}^{I} \bar{x}_n^i(p) - \sum_{i=1}^{I} \omega_n^i = 0 \ \forall \ n \in \{1, \dots, N\}. \qquad (5.25)$$

A corollary of Equation 5.25 is Walras' Law, stating that if $N - 1$ markets are in equilibrium, the N-th market must also be in equilibrium (see Box 5.3).

Box 5.3   Walras' Law

If $N - 1$ markets are in equilibrium, the N-th market must be also in equilibrium. This follows from simple accounting. If we sum up all individual budget constraints we see that total expenditure has to equal total receipts, i.e.,

$$\bar{p} \sum_{i=1}^{I} \hat{x}^i(p) = \bar{p} \sum_{i=1}^{I} \omega^i.$$

For excess demand functions Walras' Law implies that they sum up to zero:

$$\sum_{n=1}^{N} z_n(p) = 0.$$

For the analysis of general equilibrium this result proves useful since it implies that if all markets but one are in equilibrium, the last market also has to be in equilibrium:

$$z_n(\bar{p}) = 0 \ \forall \ n \in \{1, \dots, N-1\} \Longrightarrow z_N(\bar{p}) = 0. \qquad (5.25)$$

From Equation 5.25 we get another N equations, so in total there are $N + IN$ equations and $N + IN + 1$ unknowns (N prices, IN unknowns for the allocations, and λ). Since (excess) demand functions are homogeneous of degree zero in prices we can normalize prices by choosing one good as numéraire and setting its price equal to one. Homogeneity follows from the fact that the budget set does not change if we count in Euros or cents. Now we have a system of $N + IN$ equations with $N + IN$ unknowns, and this is as far as Walras got. He just counted the number of equations and the number of unknowns and concluded that an equilibrium existed. However, this need not be true. We will discuss the conditions for existence below, together with the questions of uniqueness and stability. For now we just assume that there exists an equilibrium with positive prices and state some properties of this equilibrium (Debreu, 1959; Arrow and Hahn, 1971; Starr, 1997):

- *Theorem 1* (First Welfare Theorem): A competitive equilibrium allocation is an efficient allocation.
- *Theorem 2* (Second Welfare Theorem): Every efficient allocation can be transformed into a competitive equilibrium allocation by appropriate transfers.

The first welfare theorem just states that the equilibrium allocation is efficient in the sense of Pareto: Nobody can be made better off without making someone else worse off. It provides a major argument for market liberals.

The first welfare theorem does not mean that the competitive equilibrium allocation is the social optimum, a claim that would require the comparison of individual utilities. Strictly speaking, there are infinitely many Pareto efficient allocations. One of them can be achieved by letting individuals trade at market clearing prices. At the resulting general equilibrium no individual can increase her utility by trading at the prevailing prices.

In slightly more technical jargon an allocation $x = (x^1, x^2, \ldots, x^I)$ is Pareto-optimal if there is no other allocation $\hat{x} = (\hat{x}^1, \hat{x}^2, \ldots, \hat{x}^I)$ such that $u(\hat{x}^i) \geq u(x^i) \forall i$ and $u(\hat{x}^i) > u(x^i)$ for at least one i. In addition it has to hold that both allocations are feasible, i.e. the economy cannot consume more than the available endowments, $\sum_{i=1}^{I} x^i \leq \sum_{i=1}^{I} \omega^i$ and $\sum_{i=1}^{I} \hat{x}^i \leq \sum_{i=1}^{I} \omega^i$.

The first welfare theorem now states that the competitive equilibrium, defined by equilibrium prices $\bar{p}$ and allocations $\bar{x}$ that solve the individuals' optimization problems, is Pareto-optimal. What follows is a short sketch of the proof. Suppose that allocation $\hat{x}$ dominates allocation $\bar{x}$ in the sense that $\hat{x}^i = \bar{x}^i$ and $u(\hat{x}^i) = u(\bar{x}^i)$ for $i = 1, 2, \ldots I - 1$, and $u(\hat{x}^I) > u(\bar{x}^I)$. The hat-allocation yields the same utility for all agents except agent I whose utility is higher under the hat-allocation. Since $\bar{x}^i$ is the solution to agent i's utility maximization problem subject to the budget constraint any allocation that yields higher utility cannot be within the agent's budget set, $\bar{p}\hat{x}^I > \bar{p}\omega^I$. For all agents except agent I it holds that $\bar{p}\hat{x}^i = \bar{p}\omega^i$. Summing up the budget constraints for all users we get

$$\bar{p}(\hat{x}^1 + \hat{x}^2 + \cdots + \hat{x}^I) > \bar{p}(\omega^1 + \omega^2 + \cdots + \omega^I)$$

$$\bar{p} \sum_{i=1}^{I} \hat{x}^i > \bar{p} \sum_{i=1}^{I} \omega^i \Leftrightarrow \sum_{i=1}^{I} \hat{x}^i > \sum_{i=1}^{I} \omega^i.$$

Put in words, the last equation states that total consumption is higher than aggregate endowment. This contradicts the feasibility of the alternative allocation $\hat{x}$.

The second welfare theorem states that every efficient allocation is attainable. A way to achieve this is by reallocation of initial endowments. Wealth is transferred and then the market mechanism does its work, so the economy will arrive at the general equilibrium which is efficient. This reveals that the resulting equilibrium allocation is dependent on the initial endowments.

Box 5.4   A 3-Agents, 2-Goods General Equilibrium

This is a simple illustration of an equilibrium in an exchange economy. Agents take prices as given so there is no direct strategic interdependence. No production takes place but three consumers $i = (A,B,C)$ exchange two different goods. Their utility functions are given by

$$u^i(x_1, x_2) = x_1^{a_i} x_2^{1-a_i}$$

with $a_A = 0.4$, $a_B = 0.5$, and $a_C = 0.6$ and endowments $\omega_A = (10,10)$, $\omega_B = (20,5)$, and $\omega_C = (5,10)$. Computing and summing up the individual Walrasian demand functions and equating with aggregate supply we get the following two equations which have to hold in an equilibrium:

$$17 + 12.5\frac{p_2}{p_1} = 35$$

$$12.5 + 18\frac{p_1}{p_2} = 25.$$

Normalizing the price of the first good $p_1^* = 1$ we compute the equilibrium price of the second good as $p_2^* = 1.44$. At these prices both markets clear simultaneously. Equilibrium allocations are $x^{A*} = (9.76, 10.17)$, $x^{B*} = (13.6, 9.44)$, and $x^{C*} = (11.64, 5.39)$ and utility levels are $u^{A*} = 10.004$, $u^{B*} = 11.3307$, and $u^{C*} = 8.55475$. In comparison, the initial utility levels were $u^A = 10.0$, $u^B = 10.0$, and $u^C = 6.5975$. Hence, exchange resulted in a Pareto improvement for all agents. Moreover, from the first welfare theorem we know that the resulting allocation is efficient in the sense of Pareto.

5.4.2   Existence, Uniqueness, and Stability, and the Sonnenschein–Mantel–Debreu Conditions

The two welfare theorems discussed above give us some attractive properties of the equilibrium allocations. But with respect to existence, uniqueness and stability of equilibria they tell us nothing. In what follows we will discuss these three points. Walras counted equations and unknowns and argued that a general equilibrium existed. Formal proofs of the existence of a general equilibrium in competitive markets were developed by Kenneth Arrow and Gerard Debreu as well as Takashi Negishi. The question of uniqueness was analyzed by Hugo Sonnenschein. Finally, we briefly explain the very restrictive conditions that have resulted from these investigations as necessary for allowing for a unique and stable equilibrium, generally known as the Sonnenschein-Mantel-Debreu conditions.

Existence
What conditions must be satisfied for an equilibrium to exist? Just counting equations and unknowns is not sufficient. To guarantee existence we need convexity of preferences (a concave utility function) and a convex production set. The latter implies that we have either constant or decreasing returns to scale, but not increasing returns to scale. Also, it is assumed that each household has strictly positive endowments. Using these assumptions a general proof of existence was formulated by Arrow and Debreu. A few years later a different and more compact proof was developed by Negishi. Both proofs rely on the mathematics of set theory, in particular the fixed point theorems developed by Brouwer and Negishi. As these methods are quite sophisticated we will not discuss them here. For this, the interested reader is referred to Starr (1997, Chapter 2) and Mas-Colell et al. (1995, pp. 92-94).

Uniqueness
Knowing the conditions for the existence of an equilibrium we now turn to the question of uniqueness. Is there a single equilibrium or will there be more than one? As it turns out, there are two stringent conditions under which the existing equilibrium will be unique. In the trivial case the initial allocation is already Pareto efficient. No trade will take place and the initial allocation determines the (globally) unique equilibrium.

In the second case, global uniqueness is arrived at by assuming gross substitutability for the demand functions. This means that the demand for each good increases in the price of other goods, $\frac{\partial x_n^i(p)}{\partial p_j} > 0$ for all $j \neq i$ and all goods $n = 1, ..., N$ and individuals $i = 1, ..., I$. This requirement translates into a strictly decreasing excess demand function $z_n(p)$ which crosses the x-axis only once. The two conditions for global uniqueness will seldom be fulfilled, so it is likely that there are multiple equilibria. We do not know which equilibrium will be selected. However, if we assume that the economy is at an equilibrium we know that it will stay there if this equilibrium is locally unique and stable. Local uniqueness is likely (if we exclude perfect substitutes and perfect complements).

Stability

Connected to the question of the uniqueness of an equilibrium is the question of its stability. If the equilibrium is unique it is also globally stable. After small deviations the economy will move back to its equilibrium. However, if there are multiple equilibria, some will be locally stable while others will be unstable. Local stability depends on the process which specifies how prices change. If there is more than one locally stable equilibrium, the outcome reached depends on the starting point.

Sonnenschein–Mantel–Debreu

The conditions that have to be fulfilled for arriving at a unique and stable equilibrium are called Sonnenschein–Mantel–Debreu (SMD) conditions. The intention of those mathematical economists deriving these implications was to show that individual demand curves could be aggregated with the resulting market demand curve maintaining their basic characteristics; that society could be understood as the sum of its parts. In the end they had shown that this was not the case.

The problem results as an agent's income is determined by prices and quantities of her endowments, so that, when relative prices change, so does income. For aggregate demand curves this cannot be ignored, as now a substitution effect and a wealth effect combine in their influence on demand changes. They may be mutually reinforcing or countering one another. The substitution effect refers to relatively cheaper goods being consumed more. The wealth effect is due to changes in the value of the endowments of agents. Wealthier agents consume more, possibly countering effects in markets were demand is negatively affected by substitution effects. Additionally, more than one price vector may exist that clears markets.

A negatively sloped market demand curve can only be constructed from individual demand curves if these individuals have identical preferences and spend their income on the same goods in the same proportion independently of their income level (basically meaning a world of clones who all consume the same good). In all other cases the market demand curve can take any form at all. The market demand curve will be continuous, homogeneous of degree zero, and it will satisfy Walras' Law, but market demand is not necessarily monotonically decreasing. In consequence, the SMD conditions mean that equilibrium may be neither unique nor stable unless the very restrictive conditions mentioned are met.

5.5   FURTHER DEVELOPMENTS

5.5.1   The Ramsey Growth Model

The Ramsey Growth Model is the neoclassical growth model. It is often labeled the Ramsey–Cass–Koopmans model as the basic ideas were developed in Ramsey (1928), Cass (1965), and Koopmans (1965). In its simplest version there is one representative household and one representative firm. Household and firm are assumed to live forever. They take prices as given and maximize utility and profits respectively. There is only one produced good which can either be consumed or invested. Also, we assume that the household has no preference for leisure and supplies one unit of labor each period. In this framework the only trade-off is the intertemporal trade-off between consumption today and consumption in the future. The solution to the model is an optimal growth path which maximizes social welfare, i.e. the sum of all periods' utility, with β as the discount factor:

$$\max_{\{c(t)\}_{t=0}^{\infty}} \sum_{t=0}^{\infty} \beta^t u[c(t)]. \qquad (5.27)$$

Usually, this problem of intertemporal optimal allocation is stated and solved as a social planner's problem, i.e. the problem faced by a hypothetical social planner trying to maximize social welfare. It can be shown that a Pareto-optimal allocation that solves the social planner's problem and the allocation arrived at by exchange via free markets are equivalent.

In each time period we have three goods, labor l_t, capital k_t, and the final output y_t which can either be consumed c_t or invested i_t. Technology is characterized by the production function $y_t = F(k_t, l_t)$ and we assume that capital depreciates at a rate δ so that next period's capital is given by Equation 5.28, subject to a non-negativity constraint $k_{t+1} \geq 0$:

$$k_{t+1} = (1 - \delta)k_t + i_t. \qquad (5.28)$$

The economy is assumed to start with initial capital $k_0 = \bar{k}_0$. The representative household is endowed with one unit of productive time each period and will supply all of it since it does not care about leisure (labor is no argument in the utility function (5.27)), hence $l_t = 1 \ \forall t$. For simplicity it is assumed that there is no uncertainty but perfect foresight:

$$f(k_t) \equiv F(k, 1) + (1 - \delta)k_t. \tag{5.29}$$

The net output $f(k_t)$ can be used for consumption c_t or as capital in next period's production k_{t+1}. We can rewrite consumption as the difference between net output and next period's capital stock, $c_t = f(k_t) - k_{t+1}$, substitute in Equation 5.27 and rewrite the optimization problem as follows:

$$v(k_0) = \max_{\{k(t+1)\}_{t=0}^{\infty}} \sum_{t=0}^{\infty} \beta^t u[f(k_t) - k_{t+1}] \tag{5.30}$$

$$0 \le k_{t+1} \le f(k_t)$$

$$k_0 = \bar{k}_0 > 0 \text{ given.}$$

To derive the mathematical solution would be tedious, hence we will briefly sketch how one would arrive at the solution. First, we would derive the Euler equation, which is a second-order difference equation. Then we use two boundary conditions, namely the initial value for k_0 and a transversality condition (stating that the value of the capital stock converges to zero as time goes to infinity) to solve the Euler equation. The solution is a function which gives us the optimal value for k_{t+1} as a function of k_t, and from the optimal value for k_{t+1} we can derive the corresponding values for c_t. The complete solution to the social planner problem is an allocation $\{c_t, k_t, l_t\}$. If our economy applies this function each period it is on the optimal growth path.

A hypothetical social planner wanting to maximize welfare should follow this rule, but in reality there is no such social planner. Within the model, however, this can be solved. Negishi (1960) shows that the solution to the social planner's problem is a Pareto-optimal allocation. More precisely, the solution to the social planner's problem yields the set of all Pareto-optimal allocations. From this set we can select the allocation that is consistent with the firms' and households' first-order-conditions to get the competitive equilibrium allocation, since from the first welfare theorem we know that the competitive equilibrium allocation is Pareto-optimal. In most cases the optimization problem is nonlinear and there are no analytic solutions, so numerical methods have to be used.

5.5.2 New Classicals and New Keynesians

We saw above that in equilibrium supply and demand determine equilibrium prices which in turn determine output, and thus employment and possibly growth rates. Such a system is stable and follows a smooth and optimal growth path. In reality, however, there are fluctuations in the form of short-run variations in aggregate output and employment. Some economists claim that the fluctuations exhibit no regular pattern but are the consequences of random shocks of various types and sizes. The simplest way New Classical economists model fluctuations is to add shocks to the Ramsey growth model (such a model is fully developed and discussed in Romer (2005, pp. 180-202)). As a consequence, real shocks, i.e. shocks to preferences or technology, which come from outside the model, are propagated through the model and result in fluctuations at the aggregate level. The New Classical Macroeconomics, most prevalent in the work of Robert Lucas and Edward Prescott, was a reaction to Keynesian macroeconomics arguing that involuntary unemployment can arise if wages are too high. The New Classicals claim that a free price system balances supply and demand in each market, including the labor market, hence there is no place for involuntary unemployment, if we abstract from market imperfections. Fluctuations are explained as responses to real shocks (shocks to real as opposed to nominal variables). Demand shocks result, for example, from unanticipated changes in fiscal policy. In a supply shock unanticipated changes in technology cause productivity to change. Since households and firms are assumed to be rational optimizers fluctuations at the macro level are the aggregate effects from households' and firms' efficient responses to shocks. The question now is how to explain persistence. Economies usually show periods of boom and recession which are too long to be just fluctuations. New Classicals in the Real-Business-Cycle (RBC) school claim that shocks are propagated slowly through the whole economy[5]. Also, it is argued that technology shocks do not come in isolation but in waves. Thus, RBC macroeconomists try to explain fluctuations within a Walrasian model of a competitive economy without the need to assume imperfections, missing markets, or externalities.

According to RBC theory there is no rationale for mitigating fluctuations since they are the consequences of rational adjustments to shocks. Further, there is no place for monetary policy since monetary policy only affects nominal variables, not real variables. Monetary policy has only nominal effects since an increase in the money supply will change the absolute but not the relative price level. Real variables, like preferences and technology, remain unaffected. New Keynesian economics is a response to the New Classicals[6]. Their main disagreement is about how fast prices and wages adjust. New Keynesians have different arguments to explain why adjustment might take time. First, adjusting prices is costly (firms need to print new price lists, distribute them to customers). Second, not all firms adjust prices at the same time, resulting in staggered price adjustment so that overall prices adjust slowly[7]. Third, there can be efficiency wages (Romer, 2005, Chapter 9.2). Firms pay a wage above the market wage since this increases productivity; a high wage is presumed to increase workers' effort. As a consequence of prices adjusting slowly (sticky prices) households and firms are faced with wrong price signals, leading to misallocations and temporary fluctuations in the real economy. Here there is a role for monetary policy which can act in order to mitigate fluctuations. Monetary policy has short-run effects as, for example, an increase in money supply stimulates demand and economic activity. In the long-run, however, monetary policy has no effects since prices fully adjust. There are three fundamental assumptions of the New Keynesian model: Intertemporal optimization, imperfect competition, and rigidities. The last two components are absent from RBC models, which is the main difference between the two models. But at a fundamental level, New Keynesian and RBC models use the same methods. Both see the economy as a dynamic stochastic general equilibrium system that deviates from the optimal growth path in the short-run as a result of exogenous shocks. Both models are entirely Walrasian, i.e. they are built up from microeconomic foundations.

5.6   CRITICAL EVALUATION

In this chapter we gave a brief introduction to the basic neoclassical model without going into the technical issues. We saw this model is applied to many different settings ranging from simple static exchange economies (Box 5.4) to dynamic monetary growth models (New Keynesian model). Within all models agents maximize utility or profit, taking prices as given, which is justified by the assumption that in a perfectly competitive economy individuals are myopic and cannot influence prices. Starting from individual agents and markets, general equilibrium analysis uses a 'bottom-up' approach by which it is shown that the equilibrium allocation resulting from the decentralized decisions of a large number of individuals is Pareto efficient (First Welfare Theorem). Thus, they provide a rationale for free-markets and against state-intervention. But there is also critique. The assumptions used to ensure existence, uniqueness, and stability of an equilibrium are very restrictive. Preferences are assumed to be fixed and convex, agents are assumed to behave in an instrumentally rational manner, and technology is convex. Externalities and economies of scale, as well as transaction costs, are assumed away. By focusing on perfect competition, oligopolies, monopolies, and strategic interaction are not captured within the model. General equilibrium models generally assume complete markets, but in reality markets are incomplete. Modifying the general equilibrium model in order to make it more realistic (e.g. by introducing economies of scale or market incompleteness) would mean that equilibrium may no longer exist nor be efficient. For a more detailed critique of some selected aspects of neoclassical models, see Chapter 6.

NOTES

1. Since the utility function is concave and we optimize over a compact set B, by the Weierstrass theorem we know that a solution exists. By assuming that u is strictly concave we get a single-valued solution, that is, we get a demand function instead of a demand correspondence. Marshallian demand functions are homogeneous of degree 0 in (p,w) and they satisfy Walras' Law. A proof can be found in Mas-Colell et. al. (1995, p.52).
2. This fact was first demonstrated by Hermann Heinrich Gossen in 1854. Gossen's Laws: (1) decreasing marginal utility, $\partial u/\partial x_n > 0$ and $\partial^2 u/\partial x_n^2 < 0$; (2) utility is maximized if marginal utilities are equalized, $\frac{\partial u/\partial x_n}{p_n} = \frac{\partial u/\partial x_{n'}}{p_{n'}}$; (3) a commodity has value if there is subjective scarcity, i.e. demand exceeds supply.
3. Mathematically, average costs are the slope of the line going from the origin to a point on the cost-curve. Marginal costs are the slope of the cost curve. In the case of constant returns to scale marginal costs are equal to average costs.
4. To the right of this point profits would decrease since the costs of producing one unit more are larger than the revenue from selling the additional unit.
5. For a quick review of RBC models see Romer (2005, Chapter 4).
6. Two exhaustive references for New Keynesian economics are Walsh (2003) and Woodford (2003).
7. Sticky prices can be explained by reference to institutional rigidities and bargaining power; here the New Keynesians depart from the assumption of perfectly competitive markets. However, such rigidities can, in principle, be derived from microfoundations.

FURTHER READING

For a list of selected intermediate and advanced textbooks, and some more articles, see the textbook website at www.microeconomics.us.

6. Critique of the Neoclassical 'Perfect Market' Economy and Alternative Price Theories

6.1 INTRODUCTION

The basic model formulation of neoclassical economics has been criticized from a variety of perspectives since its inception. These include focuses on the lack of direct interdependence and the static framework applied, which does not allow us to understand the changing nature of capitalist economies (Veblen, 1898; Schumpeter, 1911); internal inconsistencies in the development of the model (overviews and detailed explanations can be found in Keen, 2009, 2011); flawed foundations of and analogies in the models derived from the application of tools used in 19th century mechanical physics (Mirowski, 1989; Smith and Foley, 2008); but also for instance the assumption of increasing marginal costs that are necessary to arrive at the stable and efficient equilibrium, which are empirically unfounded (Lee, 2004; Blinder et al., 1998; for a very early exposition of this observation, Sraffa, 1926), and related assumptions regarding the price setting by firms. We take up these last points in this chapter.

In the last section of the present chapter, we will also introduce the classical theory of prices, which is based on a very different understanding of value, equilibrium, and competition. The classical theory of prices, as we will see, provides one possible alternative to neoclassical theory. We will discuss the main differences between both. Lastly, we will also offer an outlook on Post Keynesian and Institutional price theory.

6.2 THE MIROWSKI CRITIQUE

In his book 'More Heat Than Light' (1989) Mirowski launched a profound critique on neoclassical general equilibrium theory. At the heart of his critique is the metaphor of energy as a mathematical field, and a discussion on how this metaphor including its mathematical formalism was adopted in economics. In short, Mirowski claims that the metaphor is inappropriate because neoclassical economics has imitated classical physics but neglected one of the fundamental principles of physics, the conservation of energy, which according to Mirowski has no meaningful equivalent in economics.

Mirowski describes the marginalist revolution in great detail and shows how the metaphor of utility as a field is imported from physics to economics. According to him the field metaphor is inappropriate because by explicitly taking into account the conservation of energy, several inconsistencies arise in the neoclassical core model. Neoclassical economists did not see the inappropriateness because the use of the field concept in physics was not fully grasped at the time. Consequently, the field metaphor was developed further in economics although upon closer inspection it becomes clear that the field metaphor has only weak explanatory power and leads to several inconsistencies. In addition to that, the field metaphor is not the all-encompassing concept which was dominant in 19th century physics any longer but has been supplanted by newer developments in quantum mechanics and thermodynamics.

In this section we explain the analogy between classical physics and neoclassical economics. We explicitly discuss the analogy between energy and value, before we review Mirowski's critique based on the theory's ontological significance and epistemological interpretation.

6.2.1   Classical Mechanics

According to classical mechanics we can predict the trajectory of any particle if the particle's position, its mass, and the forces (impulses) acting upon it are known. The philosophical worldview associated with classical mechanics points to a deterministic world in which the behavior of any particle can, in principle, be described accurately. An equilibrium position of the particle is then a point at which the particle comes to rest.

A crucial assumption in classical physics is the conservation of energy, one of the fundamental principles of classical mechanics. It states that in any closed physical system, a system that does not exchange energy with its environment, total energy is conserved over time. More precisely, energy is quantitatively indestructible but can undergo qualitative transformations, for example if work is transformed into heat (Mirowski, 1989, p. 37). The conservation of energy is a specific form of a conservation principle, meaning that a 'particular aspect of a phenomenon remains invariant or unaltered while the greater phenomenon undergoes certain specific transformations' (Mirowski, 1989, p. 13). The particular aspect which is conserved in classical physics is the amount of energy in a closed system. But what exactly is energy?

6.2.2   From Substance to Field

Early theories described energy as a substance, being embedded in and exchanged between bodies. With the discovery of Leibnitz's calculus of variations the motion of bodies could be described mathematically. An equilibrium corresponds to a stationary value for the function. Later, Hamiltonians were used to describe mechanical systems and mechanical problems were solved for their equilibrium values by integrating the Hamiltonian. The gradient of the Hamiltonian describes a vector field within which each point is associated with a specific amount of energy which depends on the coordinates but is independent of time.

Box 6.1   Vector Fields
A vector field is a mathematical concept, which is used to describe the strength and forces in a subset of the Euclidian space. Maybe the best-known example is a magnetic field. If a magnet is placed in the middle of a table the magnetic field is not immediately visible. But if shavings of iron are scattered around the table, the shavings will adjust to the forces of the field so that the magnetic field becomes visible. Since the vector field defines direction and strength of its forces, it can be used to represent movements within a space.

While energy was described before as a substance residing in a body (with the possibility of being transferred to another body), now energy was described as a mathematical field, i.e. a relation between different potentials (see Box 6.1). A potential can be understood as a point in the field characterized by the amount of energy required to bring a particle to this point. The interpretation of energy as a field and the associated mathematical formalism was widely accepted in physics, but on an ontological and epistemological level it was not clear how energy should be perceived. According to Mirowski, '[e]nergy, it seems, has finally become a purely instrumental and mathematical entity, transformed along its history from a substance to an entity to a relation to, finally, a gestalt' (Mirowski, 1989, p. 93).

   Formally, classical mechanics works with equations of motion which may be written as a Lagrangian. This method is analogous to Lagrangian optimization in microeconomics (Box 5.1) though the approach is used for a different purpose and also applied differently in classical mechanics. The Lagrangian $\mathcal{L}$ is defined as the difference between kinetic engergy T and potential energy V, hence

$$\mathcal{L} = T - V.$$

T, the kinetic energy, generally is defined as

$$T = \frac{m\dot{q}^2}{2}$$

in mechanics (m denoting the mass of the body in question, $\dot{q}$ the velocity). As m is constant in closed systems in classical mechanics, kinetic energy is a function of position q and velocity $\dot{q} = \frac{\partial q}{\partial t}$ (t being the time), hence $T = T(q, \dot{q})$. q and $\dot{q}$ are vectors containing the position q_i (or respectively velocity) in each space dimension i; derivatives are component-wise. Potential energy V is a function of position only $V = V(q)$. Consequently, the Lagrangian reads

$$\mathcal{L}(q, \dot{q}) = T(q, \dot{q}) - V(q)$$

and the Lagrange-Euler equations, derived by differentiating

$$\frac{d}{dt}\left(\frac{\partial \mathcal{L}(q, \dot{q})}{\partial \dot{q}}\right) - \frac{\partial \mathcal{L}(q, \dot{q})}{\partial q} = \frac{d}{dt}\left(\frac{\partial T(q, \dot{q})}{\partial \dot{q}}\right) - \frac{\partial T(q, \dot{q})}{\partial q} + \frac{\partial V(q)}{\partial q}.$$

The Euler-Lagrange equations may be used to derive the path of motion of a mechanical system, specifically with Hamilton's principle of the least action by minimizing physical action (the integral of this Lagrangian over time).

Define $p_i = \frac{\partial \mathcal{L}}{\partial \dot{q}_i}$ as the generalized momenta of the system. The Hamiltonian $\mathcal{H}$ discussed above is defined as

$$\mathcal{H} = \sum_i \dot{q}_i p_i - \mathcal{L}(q, \dot{q}).$$

Since $\dot{q}_i p_i = \dot{q}_i \frac{\partial \mathcal{L}(q,\dot{q})}{\partial \dot{q}_i} = \dot{q}_i \frac{\partial T(q,\dot{q})}{\partial \dot{q}_i}$ and by definition $\frac{\partial T(q,\dot{q})}{\partial \dot{q}_i} = m\dot{q}$

$$\sum_i \dot{q}_i \frac{\partial T(q, \dot{q})}{\partial \dot{q}_i} = 2T$$

and consequently the Hamiltonian equals the sum of kinetic and potential energy, which must be conserved in closed systems:

$$\mathcal{H} = 2T - \mathcal{L}(q, \dot{q}) = 2T - T + V = T + V.$$

A more detailed discussion may be found in any mechanical physics textbook; for a good and extensive explanation see for instance Calkin (1996).

6.2.3 The Fall of Classical Physics

With the development of modern physics, especially quantum physics, at the beginning of the 20th century several ideas of classical mechanics have been undermined. Modern physics emphasizes the wave-particle duality, according to which all matter exhibits both particle and wave properties. With the wave-particle duality modern physics moved away from the deterministic worldview which was associated with classical physics. According to quantum physics, the dynamics of particles at the atomic or subatomic level cannot be described deterministically because the particle's mass, position, and the forces acting upon it cannot be measured simultaneously with certainty (Heisenberg's uncertainty principle). Moreover, the discovery of Planck's constant revealed that a particle's energy level cannot take all values from a continuum but only certain discrete values, rendering the application of the calculus of variations impossible. Lastly, Henri Poincaré's discoveries in nonlinear dynamics revealed that there are many systems which are not integrable. Integrability, however, was a crucial condition for solving the Hamiltonian function of a dynamic system. The analogies taken from classical physics are by themselves not suitable for an open system, such as a socio-economy. Additionally, much of economic theory did not move beyond them, even as developments in natural sciences pointed away from such concepts to become more refined in their approaches to natural phenomena.

6.2.4 The Mistaken Energy-Value Analogy

In tracing the theory of economic value, Mirowski points to the similarity between physical energy and economic value. In classical physics, energy was considered as a substance residing in a body. In classical economics, utility was conceived as a substance residing in a commodity. As the interpretation of energy changed from a substance to a field, a similar development occurred in economics. While the classical economists held a substance theory of value (e.g. in Marx labor is the substance which produces value) starting with the marginalist revolution value was being interpreted as the result of opposing forces of buyers and sellers. The strength of the forces is independent of any substance but is derived from buyers' and sellers' utility functions. In transferring the model from classical mechanics to a simple exchange economy the following analogies arise. The three-dimensional Euclidian space corresponds to the n-dimensional commodity space, individuals' endowments correspond to the particles' initial positions, and the forces are derived from individuals' preferences. Knowing individuals' endowments and preferences, an equilibrium position, i.e. an allocation of commodities in which no further mutually beneficial trades are possible, can be computed.

In economics, the use of the Lagrangian method is commonplace but the Hamiltonian, though straightforwardly constructed from the Lagrangian is usually avoided. The analogies are:

- $\mathcal{L}$=T-V: utility
- q: commodity quantities (in physics position in space)
- p: commodity prices (in physics generalized momenta)
- $\dot{q}$: the exchanged volume in commodities (in physics velocity)
- $p\dot{q}$: expenditure (in physics twice kinetic energy)
- $\mathcal{H}$ and its conservation: the conservation of expenditure – utility which has no useful interpretation in economics (in physics energy and its conservation).

6.2.5   The Epistemic Break between Classical and Neoclassical Economics

Mirowski refers to the change from value as a substance to value as a field as the epistemic break between classical and neoclassical economics. Reasons for the epistemic break are (1) physics envy, i.e. the imitation of physics because physics was considered the most developed and a 'serious' science, (2) the promise of the unification of all sciences, and (3) a shift in academic standards towards sophisticated mathematical modeling, precision and internal consistency. The 'Achilles heel' in this epistemic break, however, is, as Mirowski argues, the conservation principle, which was ignored by neoclassical economics. In order to apply the mathematical apparatus from classical physics to economics one has to take the conservation principle into account. But if this is done, several anomalies arise, leading to Mirowski's claim that the neoclassical theory of value is a bad description of reality, has no ontological significance, and no epistemological interpretation.

Let us pause for a moment to see how Mirowski arrives at this claim. The neoclassical theory of value as a mathematical field is derived from agents maximizing their utility subject to a budget constraint. If the mathematical analogy from classical physics is transferred and the conservation principle is taken into account such a model gives rise to the following results:

1. The model illustrates the interdependencies of markets and the resulting equilibrium prices are such that all markets clear simultaneously (see Chapter 5.4). Trade is only allowed at equilibrium prices. Unfortunately, equilibrium prices are not necessarily unique.

2. Another weakness of the neoclassical theory of value concerns the system's behavior out-of-equilibrium. For simplicity let us assume that it is possible to compute unique equilibrium prices for a set of interdependent markets. The question of how markets actually arrive at equilibrium prices cannot be answered, making the model highly stylized and abstract compared to how markets are described by the classical theory of prices. In the neoclassical world there is perfect competition and the law of one price holds as a consequence. This is radically different from the classical theory, in which natural prices act as center of gravity and market prices fluctuate around them. According to the classical theory, goods are traded at different market prices but competition forces prices towards natural prices (see Section 6.4). Such a mechanism, explaining how prices converge towards equilibrium prices, is absent in neoclassical theory. This is closely related to the question of stability, which is concerned with the behavior of the system at positions close to equilibrium. If small deviations from the equilibrium position will be corrected and the system converges back to its equilibrium position, the system is said to be stable. The problem of stability has a fundamentally different structure than the problems of existence and uniqueness because stability is concerned with the adjustment of the system over time, as has been further elaborated by Wellhöner (2002). The neoclassical theory of value, however, remains silent about what happens at positions outside equilibrium and hence cannot answer the question of stability.

3. A consequence of modeling value as a field is that the order of consumption does not matter, meaning that an agent is indifferent about eating soup first and desert second, and eating desert first and soup second. This follows from the fact that the vector field is independent of time.

4. Close adherence to the conservation principle yields the result that the sum of utility and expenditure is constant. According to Mirowski this is the 'Achilles heel' of neoclassical economics because it implies that on an ontological level money and utility are the same thing (Mirowski, 1989, p. 231). If utility and expenditure were not the same thing, adding them up would be impossible and the neoclassical theory of value would break down.

In Mirowski's critique, the fundamental difference between classical and neoclassical theory of value was mentioned several times. Also, the classical theory of prices represents an alternative which has been adopted by different strands of heterodox economics. Hence, a more detailed discussion of the classical theory of prices will be useful in order to get a deeper understanding between these two competing theories of value. Before we turn to this in Section 6.4, however, we will briefly explain another line of criticism that is concerned with internal inconsistencies of the neoclassical core model and results that can be found for firms' behavior in markets and resulting market structures and outcomes.

6.3   INTERNAL INCONSISTENCIES AND A MORE REALISTIC MARKET OUTCOME

6.3.1   Atomistic Markets and the Impossibility of a Horizontal Demand Curve

Whereas Mirowski focuses his critique on the construction proper of the neoclassical core model, other authors have focused on questions regarding the appropriateness of several of the core assumptions used within the model, a point that we will take up below (and have in part already explained above, in Section 5.4.2 dealing with the Sonnenschein-Mantel-Debreu conditions). Yet others have addressed inconsistencies that arise within this model if we take the assumptions as given and follow their implications. An overview of these points is given by Keen (2011). In this section, we take up a couple of the matters that he presents.

One fundamental assumption of the neoclassical core model, regarding the supply-side, is that companies do not influence each other, that there is no direct interdependence between them. That means there is no functional relation between the decisions of one company and those of others. Additionally, no single company's decisions have an influence on the overall market result, their impact is assumed to be so marginal that it can be ignored in the analysis of the overall market. Therefore, companies act as price-takers who adjust their output so that their marginal costs equal the market price. This assumption is reflected in individual firms facing demand schedules that are horizontal. The overall demand schedule in the market, on the other hand, is assumed to be negatively sloped, as a reflection of presumed 'normal' demand patterns (a price-increase reduces demand).

If companies make their decisions independently of one another, that means the decision to increase output q_i that one firm i may take does not lead to reactions by any other producer k in the market, so that $\frac{dq_k}{dq_i} = 0$. As a consequence, overall output changes in the market, dQ, and changes in output by one individual firm are the same, $\frac{dQ}{dq_i} = 1$.

Now, we have the negatively sloped demand function, or the corresponding inverse demand function $p = p(Q)$. The slope of this market demand function is $\frac{dp}{dQ}$. We can multiply this by 1 and use the above relation to arrive at:

$$\frac{dp}{dQ} = \frac{dp}{dQ} \frac{dQ}{dq_i} = \frac{dp}{dq_i}.$$

We could also apply the chain rule to derive:

$$\frac{dp}{dq_i} = \frac{dp}{dQ} \frac{dQ}{dq_i} = \frac{dp}{dQ}.$$

In any case, we arrive at the result that given the assumptions regarding companies in perfectly competitive markets, the slope of the market demand schedule and the demand schedule that an individual company faces are equal. This introduces a direct contradiction between two of the core assumptions on which the supposed market outcome in a perfectly competitive market rests. If the slope of the market demand curve is negative, $\frac{dp}{dQ} < 0$, and the atomistic structure is maintained, the individual demand curve cannot be horizontal.

Keen (2011) explains this in more detail and develops some additional implications, including a negative profit for companies that results from decisions ignoring the above relation. The condition $\frac{dQ}{dq_i} = 1$ was originally pointed out by eminent neoclassical economist George J. Stigler (1957, fn. 31).

This aspect is complementing the already explained Sonnenschein-Mantel-Debreu conditions that set out the very restrictive conditions under which an aggregate demand function could be constructed from individual demand schedules (Section 5.4.2).

6.3.2   Market Outcomes in a more Realistic Simulation

Using simulation as a tool for investigating market outcomes, Keen finds that the monopoly prediction of a market outcome and simulation results coincide. For a market with many firms, however, there are substantial differences between the prediction in the 'perfect market'-model and simulation outcome. The demand curve for both sets of simulations was the same, and so was, in fact, the overall outcome – the competitive market result (with 10,000 firms in the simulation) and the monopoly result showed basically the same total supply, and hence the same market price.

In the simulations, behavior of firms in competitive markets included a provision for changing their individual supplies. The rule was that if a change in individual output resulted in a reduction of individual profits, that change was reversed (so that if an increase in output reduced profits, in the following period output was reduced). Individual firms showed a variety of different output levels, the aggregate result was that of the monopoly market, though. The different output levels may be taken to point to another aspect of real-world markets, namely the tendency towards larger and smaller companies being present in a market, tending towards oligopolization or even monopolization (see Chapter 4).

That means if we take the assumptions seriously and for the sake of a thought experiment ignore the possible critique formulated on a different level of analysis, as set out in the preceding section, we still arrive at rather unflattering results (and in fact, if monopolies enjoy cost advantages in production, you might even say that the whole neoclassical apparatus offers arguments for monopoly markets, instead of against them). As a by-product of the points presented by Keen, we can also clearly see that the efficient reference point of the perfect market is fictitious even within the neoclassical core model. Even given its assumptions there will be no socially optimal outcome (understood as maximizing the sum of consumer and producer rents) in the interplay of agents. The foundation for arguments employed to argue for a reduction of government presence in the economic sphere is thereby void. Note, however, that this does not mean that government was necessarily needed and would always improve the outcome achievable; quite to the contrary. What we do find are reasons for more careful arguments and analyses of specific situations before formulating policy proposals. The 'black or white'-solutions implied by the simplistic model structures discussed above cannot hope to lead to policies and actions that would systematically improve real-world economic results.

6.4   THE CLASSICAL THEORY OF PRICES AND THE SRAFFIAN CRITIQUE OF THE NEOCLASSICAL THEORY OF VALUE

6.4.1   Foundations of the Classical Theory of Prices

In neoclassical theory prices are determined by marginal productivities of inputs. Prior to the marginalist revolution (see Chapter 5), which marked the starting point for neoclassical economics there was no notion of marginal utility, marginal costs and marginal productivity. Then how are prices determined without any notion of marginal utility, marginal costs and marginal productivity? According to the classical economists, Smith, Ricardo, and Marx, prices are determined by the costs of production. The costs of production depend on technology and distribution.

Classical economists differentiated prices into market prices and natural prices. Market prices are the prices at which goods and services are exchanged. Natural prices are a theoretical construct. Natural prices cannot be observed directly but can be computed based on costs of production. It is assumed that competition will equalize the wage rate and the profit rate. If wage and profit rates are not equalized natural prices and market prices will differ. Competition, however, will give rise to a process in which capitalists move from sectors with low profit rates to sectors with high profit rates, and workers will move from sectors with low wages to sector with high wages, thus there is a tendency towards uniform rates of profit and wages. Due to this tendency market prices will fluctuate around natural prices which act as a center of gravity. Natural prices are conceived as long-run prices determined by technology and distribution. To simplify the analysis we assume that labor is homogeneous. Furthermore, we assume:

1. Constant returns to scale: If we double the amount of all inputs we will receive exactly double all outputs. (Actually, Sraffa does not assume constant returns to scale, but most of his followers did. If no assumptions are made regarding returns to scale we cannot make any meaningful statement about what happens when the quantity of outputs produced changes. Hence in the following we assume constant returns to scale.)
2. Fixed proportions technology: There is only one technology, i.e. one combination of inputs that produces the output. Input factors are used in fixed proportions and there is no substitution of inputs.
3. Circulating capital: All inputs are completely used up in the production process.
4. No joint production: Each production process will produce exactly one output.

In the following sections we will delineate Sraffa's critique of neoclassical economics, show a one-commodity model to illustrate the concept of feasibility and the inverse relation between profits and wages. Then we will introduce a general model with n commodities to illustrate how prices depend on distribution. As mentioned above, the concept of natural prices goes back to the classical economists, especially Ricardo (1817). It was formulated mathematically by John von Neumann (1946) and Piero Sraffa (1960) and an in-depth treatment can be found in Kurz and Salvadori (1997).

6.4.2   Sraffian Critique of Neoclassical Theory of Value

Sraffa's critique of the neoclassical theory of value is based on the problem which arises when defining an aggregate measure of capital. He claimed that neoclassical models, which rely on an aggregate measure of capital K, are logically flawed because an aggregate measure of capital cannot exist independently of prices. To define an aggregate measure of capital is impossible because in order to aggregate diverse capital goods (e.g., tractors and computers) into one single quantity of capital requires prices (e.g. the price of tractors and the price of computers). However, prices cannot be taken as given since the neoclassical theory is intended to determine prices endogenously.

Sraffa's alternative is to use time-dated commodities, i.e., the quantities of commodities and labor which are used as inputs, and the quantities of commodities which are produced. Following Sraffa, we use the term 'relations of production' to refer to the processes of production of all commodities by means of commodities and labor per period of time. Since we can (in principle) measure the amounts of inputs and outputs, this implies that Sraffa's theory is based on observables. Of course, this only holds for the actual relations of production since we cannot observe the amounts of inputs and outputs that would be obtained in a hypothetical situation when the scale of production is changed. Using the assumption of constant returns to scale, however, allows us to make inferences about the amount of inputs and outputs that would be observed in any hypothetical situation.

Sraffa shows that, given the relations of production, prices depend on distribution. He goes on and argues that distribution and prices cannot be determined simultaneously and concludes that distribution has to be determined prior to the determination of prices. For a given distribution Sraffa is then able to determine natural prices (using the assumption of a uniform wage rate and a uniform rate of profit). In contrast to the neoclassical theory of value, Sraffa is able to determine prices without any reference to demand. This implies that his theory of prices is immune to the weaknesses that arise from the Sonnenschein–Mantel–Debreu conditions in

Section 5.4.2 above. The next two sections show Sraffa's idea in an analytical way and thus depict an alternative theory of value, which does not require marginal analysis and an aggregate measure of capital.

6.4.3   A Classical One-Commodity Model after Sraffa

In the world of the classical economists, production is conceived as a circular flow. At the beginning of the production period we have a given number of inputs, say x bushels of corn. In the production process the inputs are transformed into outputs, say y bushels of corn. Production is viable if the surplus or net-output y-x is positive, i.e. the system is able to reproduce itself or to expand. If all of the surplus is consumed then there are exactly x bushels of corn at the beginning of the next period, so the system just reproduces itself. If only part of the surplus is consumed and the rest is invested, our economy starts the next period with more than x bushels of corn and the system grows.

Assume that there is only one commodity, say corn. For the production of one unit of corn we need a units of input (seed corn) and l units of labor. Let p denote the price of corn, w the wage rate (the price of one unit of labor) and r the profit rate. Assuming that wages are paid at the end of the production period, costs of production are given by

$$P = (1+r)ap + wl. \tag{6.1}$$

Since we assume that production is feasible we assume $a < 1$, meaning that less than one unit of seed corn is needed to produce one unit of corn. We can normalize the price of our single commodity corn by setting $p = 1$ and rewrite Equation 6.1 to see that the net output $(1 - a)$ is distributed between profits and wages:

$$(1 - a) = ra + wl. \tag{6.2}$$

Another way to see this would be to solve Equation 6.1 for the wage as a function of the profit rate:

$$w(r) = \frac{1-(1+r)a}{l}. \tag{6.3}$$

We see that there is an inverse relation between the wage rate and the profit rate, illustrating the class struggle that is inherent in capitalist production. Setting the wage equal to zero we can solve for the maximum rate of profit R. Vice-versa, we can set the profit rate equal to zero and solve for the maximum wage rate W. Now we know that the wage rate will be in the interval $[0, W]$ and the profit rate will be in the interval $[0, R]$. Equation 6.3 is an equation with two unknowns, w and r. By setting the wage (the profit rate) we can solve for the profit rate (the wage) and hence arrive at a solution. In order to close the system we have to fix one of the parameters. We will come back to this issue below.

6.4.4   A Classical N-Commodity Model after Sraffa

Let us now move to an n-commodity world. Assume that there is only one technique for the production of each of the n commodities. This way we do not have to deal with the choice of techniques. Let $p = (p_1, p_2, \ldots, p_n)$ denote the n-dimensional vector of prices, and let $l = (l_1, l_2, \ldots, l_n)$ denote the n-dimensional vector of labor inputs. Labor is assumed to be homogeneous and profit and wage rates are defined as above. The coefficient a_{ij} denotes the amount of input of commodity j that is needed to produce one unit of commodity i. Cost of production for commodity i is then given by

$$p_i = (1 + r) \times [a_{i1}p_1 + a_{i2}p_2 + \cdots + a_{in}p_n] + wl_i.$$

Collecting all coefficients in a matrix

$$A = \begin{pmatrix} a_{11} & a_{12} & \cdots & a_{1n} \\ a_{21} & a_{22} & \cdots & a_{2n} \\ \cdots & \cdots & \cdots & \cdots \\ a_{n1} & a_{n2} & \cdots & a_{nn} \end{pmatrix}$$

allows us to write the prices for all n commodities as

$$p = (1 + r)Ap + wl. \tag{6.4}$$

This economy is viable if the largest real eigenvalue of the matrix A is smaller or equal to one (eigenvalues are explained in Box 9.1). To see how this result is derived the interested reader is referred to Kurz and Salvadori (1997, pp. 96-97).

Equation 6.4 is a system of n linear equations. The values for A and l are given by technology. The unknowns of the system are the n prices, the wage rate and the profit rate. Fixing one price as a numéraire (for example by setting $p_1 = 1$) we are left with n equations and $n + 1$ unknowns. The system is underdetermined; in order to solve it we need to fix one additional parameter. There are various possibilities to solve this: First, we could argue that the wage is determined by class struggle. Second, we could argue that there is a socially determined subsistence wage. And third, we could argue that the profit rate is determined in the financial sector. No matter which way we go, as soon as we fix the wage rate or the profit rate we can compute all remaining prices. These prices are natural prices which depend on technology (the matrix A and the vector l) and on distribution. If the distribution changes relative prices are affected. If, for example, the wage rate moves up, prices of labor-intensive commodities increase and prices of capital-intensive commodities fall.

The classical theory of prices is an alternative to the neoclassial theory of prices. Characteristic for the classical theory of prices is the absence of any notion of marginal productivity and the emphasis on distribution, as illustrated by the inverse relation between wages and profits.

6.5   AN OUTLOOK ON POST KEYNESIAN AND INSTITUTIONAL PRICE THEORY: SETTING AND ADMINISTERING PRICES

More generally, price theory in the setting of Post Keynesian economics and institutional economics, particularly the economics of American (or Original) Institutionalism, provide a further, and more far-reaching alternative to the neoclassical modeling of prices. As Lee (2004), amongst others, points out, *Post Keynesian* as a term for grouping theoretical approaches is not easily defined. In fact there are a number of broader or narrower definitions of what constitutes Post Keynesian economic theory. This may partly be the case because a number of theoretical approaches that are not counted as Post Keynesian in the narrow sense are in fact complementary to these narrow formulations. Therefore, even though more diverse, a broader field can be formulated as well, that would then include a number of different, but complementary perspectives, on, for instance, questions of long-term investment and growth dynamics, distribution, the role of the institutional framework in those dynamics, and, especially interesting for us here, prices, approached from a basis that is firmly rooted in real-world economics.

In the final section of this chapter, therefore, we offer a brief explanation of Post Keynesian price theory's principal conceptions, for which we follow Shapiro and Sawyer (2003). Amongst other issues, Post Keynesian approaches to companies' price setting allow overcoming another conceptual problem in neoclassical theory, namely the fact that costs cannot be fully determined (but would have to be for strict profit-maximization to be possible) and that prices therefore have to be set in a manner that always includes an arbitrary and rule-based element.

At the center stands *pricing power* of the firms. Prices are not cost- or demand-determined but set according to strategic considerations by firms.

These prices are operationalized as *markup prices* (in detail, Lee, 2004). The markup is added onto the average variable costs (AVC) in a period. Depending on your needs in a model, you can capture the markup as a percentage m of AVC or as a fixed amount M added to ACV:

$$p = (1 + m)AVC$$

or

$$p = AVC + M.$$

Usually, prices are set to cover additional costs and allow for the realization of profits. However, in practice, there is no fixed relation between average cost and markup. Changes in average costs may, for instance, lead to a reduction in the markup, if the overall competitive or demand structures are not permissive of (extensive) price increases for a certain product. Vice versa an increase is conceivable as well. Hence, the markup depends on the conditions a company faces in its market segment and its *discretion* with regard to price-setting (note that distributional issues are involved here as well). The *objectives* pursued by a company come into play as well, and different ones may be conflicting here. For instance, aiming at an increase in market share may lead to the acceptance of reduced profits at times. Costs matter in those decisions, but so do, for instance, targeted sales, or the difference between targeted and realized sales, and actions taken by competitors (see also Chapter 4 for discussions of related aspects).

A problem that is very specifically pointed to is connected to the impossibility of the full determination of *real unit costs*. Their final value depends on a number of aspects that can only be known after a few periods; in fact, can definitely be known only once production has stopped. Examples on such influences are the cost of acquiring equipment, whose contribution to unit cost can only be determined once the machine's use is discontinued and the number of units produced with it known; but also marketing expenditure that influences future sales where the impact on unit costs depends on the number of units sold after they were undertaken, etc. Running costs may also include research expenditure for new products, which have to be covered by revenues from the existing product line.

The covering of costs in a period and realization of a desired profit can of course be attempted based on experience and expectation, but the resulting price to be set will always be somewhat arbitrary under true uncertainty and only local knowledge; and a 'profit rate' will likewise be, as true costs cannot properly be determined. Strict profit maximization is hence logically impossible, and not only because of issues of true uncertainty and strategic interdependence, and therefore true strategic uncertainty. True costs and demand (which may depend on a number of factors unknown to or outside the company's scope) would have to be known, but are not and cannot be. Experience and expectations, and rules of thumb for price setting, in turn, are formulated within the institutional (cultural) framework that companies operate in, and the rules they have come to learn and adopt over time that are related to their own learned firm culture and the culture prevailing in their environment, their industry, sector, region and peer group.

Still, obviously, general requirements are known that have to be fulfilled by companies and guaranteed by the prices they set and can be integrated into economic theory. These provide the foundation for the alternative understanding of the setting of prices introduced here. As said, the operationalization of these concepts is undertaken by means of the markup.

Another aspect to be mentioned here is *administered prices* introduced by the institutionalist economist Gardiner C. Means in the 1930s (Means, 1939; compare Lee, 2004). As Nell (1998) points out, mechanisms for reacting to changes in market demand patterns have undergone significant changes between the period before World War I and the period following World War II. Technical conditions in production up until the beginning of the twentieth century were such that changing demand conditions directly led to changes in prices as production structures were set up for producing a specific amount of a product and changes in that amount were difficult to implement. Prices in this regime fluctuated pro-cyclically to adjust demand to supply (and if nominal wages are assumed to be more slowly adjusted, real wages moved countercyclically, providing some endogenous counterbalance). In the following decades, through a process that had consolidated itself by the middle of the twentieth century, production structures underwent significant alterations with the result that changes in demand have since then usually been addressed by adjusting the use of production factors, which in the short term is predominantly labor. Prices are kept constant, or slowly increasing, and fluctuations in demand lead to pro-cyclical fluctuations in employment.

The mentioned administered prices can be seen as a complementary aspect of these broader changes. Companies enter into repeated interactions and contractual relations. Prices are thereby set for a period of time. These are called administered prices; they can be maintained if companies have some degree of market power. The rationale for the company can be understood from a *long-term* perspective, allowing *strategic considerations* regarding growth and market share to become important factors in their considerations and price policies. Prices that can fluctuate in the short term, on the other hand, are called market prices.

The parallel existence of these two types of prices can result in *endogenous macroeconomic cycles*, as demand developments are mutually reinforcing. A reduction in aggregate demand would lead to a reduction in prices in the market sector, and a reduction in employment in the administered sector. Unemployed workers and stable administered prices would further reduce effective macroeconomic demand and thus economic activity. Increasing aggregate demand would be necessary to counter downward adjustments in economies with a mixed price structure, such as the ones that have been emerging since the beginning of the twentieth century. On the other hand, administered prices may also introduce an inflationary dynamic. If companies enjoy market power, they can increase prices even under stable conditions, possibly resulting in dynamics at the end of which stands a generally increasing price level in an economy (possibly leading to *stagflation* as effective demand may subsequently be reduced as well).

FURTHER READING

For a list of selected textbooks, monographs, and articles on classical and Post Keynesian economic theory, see the textbook website at www.microeconomics.us.

7. Methods for Analyzing Complex Processes: An Introduction to Computer Simulation

7.1 INTRODUCTION

Simulation is a method to acquire data about the behavior of highly complex systems. It may reveal information about the system, that could not be revealed by deterministic computation. Nevertheless, the system under investigation has to be well-specified in order to compute its future behavior. The fundamental difference from exhaustive deterministic analysis of the whole system is that simulation does not attempt to investigate any possible state, let alone the possible relations between the states of the system. Rather, for a finite set of valid states, the behavior is traced to establish a general idea of the resulting trends. The initial state can be modified slightly to derive knowledge about the consequences of particular modifications, particular influences or particular patterns in the system's state.

While manual simulation (with pen and paper) is basically possible, it is convenient to employ computers, as only large computation power enables both, to deal with highly complex systems and to derive sufficient data for sufficiently many different settings to investigate a system of greater complexity. This is also why simulation as a scientific method was not developed before the advent of computers.

This chapter will give an overview of basic techniques, common problems, and the resulting advantages and disadvantages of computer simulation. It will further provide an example of the use of computer simulation in a microeconomic context and thereby offer an introduction to the discussion of models of direct interdependence in Chapter 8.

It is to be noted that simulation is not an exact method in a formal-analytical sense, as there is always the possibility that the results of the simulation do not or only partly match the true behavior of the system under investigation. Therefore, simulation should only be employed if other scientific techniques are not available. Moreover, the weaknesses of this method have always to be taken into account focusing especially on the typical errors arising from these weaknesses (as discussed in Section 7.3).

However, if a system is indeed highly complex, simulation may be very useful. This is especially the case, if

- a system's solution or dynamics is not computable exactly in a formal-analytical way;
- a system is basically computable but would take an unacceptably long computation time;
- a system does not show regular convergent behavior. That is, if the trajectories diverge, not only the system's future variable values, but its future behavior, depend on the initial values, and, if present, stochastic shocks.

7.2　METHOD

While it is possible to compute targeted approximations for not exactly computable values, the usual application of computer simulation is to study the general behavior, or aspects of that behavior, of systems. Simulation provides a powerful tool to investigate not only results but also development paths. The following procedure will typically be employed:

1. *Identify the system under investigation.* At this stage, it has to be determined what will be included in the system and what will not. The scope of the system has to be chosen such that the complexity is kept as small as possible, however without neglecting important influences in order to be able to derive meaningful results that resemble the real-world model of the system.
2. *Formalize the system under investigation.* A mathematical model has to be developed; the components of the system have to be transformed into variables and equations.
3. *Determine, whether simulation is a viable and effective method* to investigate the system.
4. *Formalize the mathematical model as a computer program.* Note that this is the most important stage; the behavior of the model is shaped by the program. While the mathematical formalization is a great simplification of the real world, the program formalization differs again fundamentally from the mathematical model. There are considerable limitations to numerical computation that will be discussed in detail below, which is why this stage is the main source of errors. Specifically, it is defined how data is to be shaped and how it is to be transformed. That may include *constants*, which are unchangeable, *parameters*, set at the beginning of the particular simulation run, and *variables*, that may be changed through

the process of the simulation. Of course, the program specifies also when and how a variable shall be changed.

5. *Define the input value or value range for each parameter,* that is, determine which part of the system is to be investigated and how deeply it is to be studied. Firstly, several evenly or randomly distributed points of the state space may be chosen to monitor the general behavior. Secondly, to eliminate volatility (if stochastic variables are included) the simulation may be run several times for the same input values. Thirdly, to study the sensitivity of the results, a particular state and several points of its 'close neighborhood' (in terms of variable values) may be investigated. These may of course be set for each variable independently.

6. *Run the simulation.*

7. *Analyze the results.* This includes determining whether the model is indeed a representation of what was to be investigated (validation), and if the results are reliable (verification); see below.

A simulation model is said to be valid if it resembles the problem it was designed to simulate. (In other words, it is valid if its formulation is correct.) It is called reliable if the data it produces resemble the behavior of the real-world structure it simulates. A valid simulation model may or may not be reliable, e.g. if the produced data is theoretically possible, but the structural behavior of the real world is not matched or is not identically reproduced in different simulation runs.

No simulation model can be completely valid and perfectly reliable. An unreliable or invalid model may produce data, that is not related to the real-world behavior at all (arbitrary / random data generated by the model). Models may further produce data that is correlated to the real-world behavior, but shows other systematic influences that do not resemble the real-world – these models are said to be biased. A systematic bias represents an invalidity in the formulation of the model.

7.3   PARTICULAR ISSUES IN COMPUTER SIMULATION

7.3.1   Entities

A model of a system is by definition a simplification of the real system which it however only approximates. This is not a particular issue of computer simulation, but is an extraordinarily important one. The model usually has to be *finite* which for the real-world system is not necessarily the case. Thus, the model will consist of a finite number of well-defined (often homogeneous) entities with well-defined behavior, representing substantially more complex structures in the real world.

7.3.2   Numbers

Computers cannot deal with irrational numbers and will perform better for rational ones the easier they are *representable* (as fractions of integers). Therefore, numbers in the model will be approximated by easier representable numbers, if necessary. This happens at the expense of exactness but there are benefits in terms of storage space and computation time. This has considerable consequences, as rounding errors may sum up over time. But there are even more problems: Computers employ specific number types, able to store a defined range af numbers each. If a value that is to be stored does not fall into the range of the type the corresponding variable is defined as, there are three possible behaviors of the program that may result from this: The variable type might be changed, the program might fail or (worst of all) the variable might 'overflow'. (An 'overflow' of a variable is the transgression of the maximum value it can hold. All bits of the variable are 1 at this point; further 'increment' by 1 will change all bits to 0 such that the variable takes its lowest possible value and the program will return wrong results.)

7.3.3   Time

Time has to be *discrete* in computer simulation. To work with continuous time, the computer would have to be either infinitely fast, or able at least to deal with irrational numbers (for a variable representing continuous time). Continuous time systems can be approximated, but will actually always be time-discrete. Of course, not every simulation needs time as a feature, but dynamic systems are usually the most complex ones, for which computer simulation is required. The simulation's frequency will be different from the computer's frequency, as there are usually several to many necessary arithmetic operations per time step – therefore the simulation will need its own clock, its own internal time variable.

7.3.4   Randomness

A special problem is how to generate stochastic influences, that is, random numbers and stochastic distributions. This is an unsolvable problem, as computers work deterministically and computably and are therefore not able to generate true randomness but only pseudo-random numbers.

As mentioned above, some numbers are more easily representable than others, all distributions will therefore be discrete, and all values are of finite complexity. Hence for each level of complexity, there is only a finite number of representable values. Partly because of this, partly as the complexity of the computer itself is finite, each sequence of random numbers generated by computer is repetitive from a certain point on – called the *period* of the random number generator.

Pseudo-random number generators usually work with the *modulo* (denoted by % – the remainder of a division) *operation,* but may be extended using other operations or constantly changing globally available variables, such as the computer's system clock. The most common basic pseudorandom number generator, also employed in the programming language C++'s rand()- and srand()-functions is the linear congruential generator

$$X_{n+1} = (aX_n + c) \% m \qquad (7.1)$$

where X_n is the sequence of the random numbers, a, c and m are integers, a and m positive, c at least non-negative.

7.3.5 Simplicity

The more complex a simulation model is, the more difficult is the interpretation of the obtained results. With a vast number of parameters, it becomes more challenging to identify the crucial influence for a certain observed behavior; a more complicated program makes it more difficult to find and correct errors and complex interrelations of variables may lead to genuinely chaotic behavior of the system itself. It is therefore a crucial principle to keep simulation models (as well as formal models) as simple as possible. However, it is also important to retain descriptiveness in order not to diverge too far from the system to be simulated. This second principle conflicts with the former one (simplicity) to some degree.

7.4 ADVANTAGES AND DISADVANTAGES OF SIMULATION

As was already mentioned above, consideration should be given to whether simulation is the appropriate method for the problem in question. The ease and convenience of computer simulation is counterweighted by several considerable disadvantages. The advantages include:

- Simulation as a scientific technique enables approximation of some otherwise incomputable results.

- Highly complex systems become, if modeled appropriately, predictable within the technical limits such as reasonable computation time.
- Sufficiently modeled systems (i.e., given the model is valid) allow quite flexible investigations; it is possible to study each element of the system, each modification in this element and it is possible to change the scale of the variables (e.g., to contract or expand space and time).
- A great variety of possible states and dynamics may be studied, therefore it is much easier to identify complex mechanisms and constraints of the system.
- Preliminary testing prior to more in-depth analysis is possible, which may save time and other resources.

The particular disadvantages on the other hand are:

- Simulation results in general are to some degree unreliable, and may not be treated as certain data.
- The results might be difficult to understand and to interpret, which is another source of error.
- The capacity of computation in general is limited and (given the capacity) also restricted to certain types of values and operations. This may influence the quality of the result. There is, for example, no guarantee that a discrete-time model will behave in the same way as a real-world system with continuous time.
- Unawareness of these limitations or the functioning of specific tools may lead to further errors.
- The chosen scale of variables and parameters may bias the results.

7.5   MICROECONOMICS AND COMPUTER SIMULATION

7.5.1   Computer Simulation in Microeconomics

Simulation as a method is particularly useful when dealing with systems that are inherently complex. This is especially the case for economics and other social sciences where even the basic elements – humans – are complex and indeed incomputable systems. This forces general analytical models such as the neoclassical equilibrium theory as discussed in Chapter 5 to make a number of greatly simplifying assumptions – among others the homogeneity of agents to which we get back to the following section. Computer simulation does however allow the analysis of more complex settings though some degree of simplification is required to keep the simulation models simple enough for a conclusive interpretation of the results. Most importantly, simulation as a method in economics helps to bridge the gap between microeconomic and macroeconomic models.

Most simulation models in microeconomics follow a common pattern: They contrast a micro-level of similar but not usually homogeneous agents with the aggregate level of the simulation, in turn representing the system or sector level. In turn, there are *macro and micro variables* respectively describing the system or one agent. *Macro and micro states* describe the entire variable set of the system or the agent at one point in time and *macro and micro parameters* refer to the basic values or properties of the system or an individual agent beyond that entity's 'control'. The simulation program usually cycles through the agents letting them behave as if they were making independent decisions and taking the appropriate actions. According to specified (homogeneous or heterogeneous) decision rules, the agents manipulate their micro variables while their control over macro-variables and their own micro-parameters is minimal. Those change as a result of all actions of all agents but have significant effects on the individual agent's decisions. This modeling approach is called *agent-based modeling*, the distinctive property being that such programs behave as if micro-level agents were acting independently. As with all simulations, agent-based modeling uses discrete (or quasi-continuous) time (the time steps being called iterations). Note that agents follow defined rules, thus implying a concept of bounded rationality. The accuracy of such a model in the real world is limited; for details on this question, see Chapters 1 and 2 above.

7.5.2 Homogeneous vs. Heterogeneous Agents

The assumption of homogeneity among agents (representative agent) was of course most radically developed in neoclassical microeconomics. It reduces, like the assumption of independence of these actors, the complexity of the system to such an extent, that it becomes computable by deterministic means.

Let N agents be represented by the state vectors $a_{1,t}, \ldots, a_{N,t}$ at time t. Furthermore, P shall denote a vector of global variables or parameters, which might represent environmental conditions, or in standard neoclassical microeconomics, most importantly, prices. The system is then described by equations (f denotes a function that is for this setting homogeneous for all agents)

$$a_{n,t+1} = f\left(a_{n,t}, P\right) \qquad n = 1, \ldots, N. \tag{7.2}$$

However, as argued repeatedly in this book, both assumptions are not entirely realistic: Real-world actors are neither homogeneous in their incentives nor in their properties though microeconomic modeling may start with relatively homogeneous settings in order to keep complexity moderate. But first and foremost, the agents are interdependent and interacting. By this, the system becomes highly complex. First, the assumption of homogeneity is abandoned:

$$a_{n,t+1} = f_n(a_{n,t}, P) \qquad n = 1, \dots, N. \tag{7.3}$$

While Equation 7.3 is doubtlessly more complex, it is presumably still computable and predictable as a whole, as will be shown. This, however, changes if the assumption of independence is dropped:

$$a_{n,t+1} = f\left(d_1 * a_{1,t}, d_2 * a_{2,t}, \dots, d_N * a_{N,t}, P\right) \qquad n = 1, \dots, N \tag{7.4}$$

where $d_n = 0,1$ are N dummy variables, indicating if the state of agent a_n depends on the previous state of the agent a_m or not. Note that this implies a network structure between the agents where positive dummy variables ($d_n = 1$) are indicating edges (links). Also note that this formulation includes the above stated standard neoclassical setting: For the neoclassical system, for any agent n all dummy variables, except d_n are zero.

7.5.3 Simulating Games on Networks: The Example of a Prisoners' Dilemma

Consider a system of 100 interactive agents playing repeated Prisoners' Dilemma games in pairs, three repetitions with each opponent in each iteration. They are either cooperative players, employing the tit-for-tat (*TFT*) strategy (see Chapter 3), or non-cooperative, defecting always (*All-D*). Initially, there are 30 cooperative and 70 non-cooperative agents. The numerical payoff structure of Figure 7.1 is chosen as in a similar but more extensive simulation study by Axelrod (1984/2006).

		Player B	
		Strategy 1	Strategy 2
Player A	Strategy 1	3 3	5 0
	Strategy 2	0 5	1 1

Figure 7.1   Prisoners' Dilemma with the incentive structure as in Axelrod (1984/2006)

Those whose aggregated payoff exceeds the mean of the payoffs of their interacting partners, will 'reproduce' their habit. One among their less lucky interacting partners adopts their strategy (unless all of their interacting partners are either already playing the same strategy or have already adopted another strategy in the same iteration).

7.5.4   Direct Interdependence and Computability

The strategies and the switching behavior can equivalently be described as the functions f_n. If, however, all agents have the same interaction partners, that is, if each agent interacts with each other agent (*total connectivity*), the system can be deterministically computed with the current strategy shares as global variable P

$$a_{TFT,\ t+1} = f_{TFT,\ t}(P)$$
$$a_{All-D,\ t+1} = f_{All-D,\ t}(P).$$

Specifically, the payoff each defector gets, is

$$3(n_{All-D} - 1) + (5 + 2)\, n_{TFT} = 417,$$

(n_{All-D} and n_{TFT} denoting the number of All-D and of TFT players respectively) while the *TFT*-players get

$$3 * 3 * (n_{All-D} - 1) + 2\, n_{TFT} = 401.$$

(a)   (b)

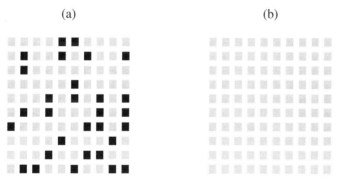

Notes: TFT Players (Dark) and Defectors (Light) in a Network Game (Repeated Prisoners' Dilemma) on a Complete Network (Total Connectivity): (a) Initial state (30% TFT Players), (b) after 1 iteration (0% TFT).

Figure 7.2   Network Game on a complete network

(a)   (b)   (c)

(d)   (e)   (f)

(g)   (h)   (i)

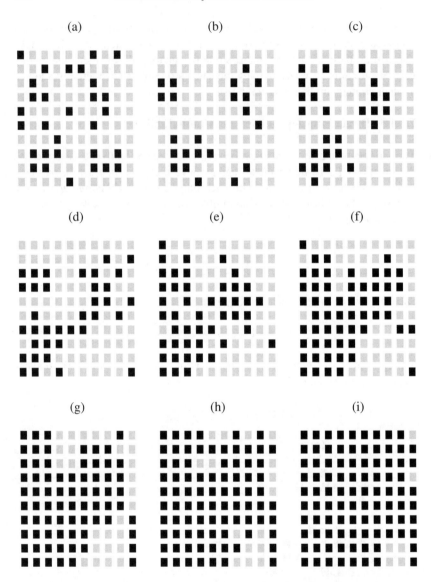

Notes: TFT Players (Dark) and Defectors (Light) in a Network Game (Repeated Prisoners' Dilemma) on a Lattice Network with Moore Neighborhood: (a) Initial State (30% TFT Players), (b) After 1 Iteration (22% TFT), (c) After 2 Iterations (26% TFT), (d) after 3 Iterations (36% TFT), (e) After 4 Iterations (46% TFT), (f) After 5 Iterations (57% TFT), (g) After 6 Iterations (73% TFT), (h) after 7 Iterations (84% TFT), (i) After 8 Iterations (94% TFT).

Figure 7.3   Network Game on a lattice network

As the average is $(417 * 70 + 401 * 30)/100 = 412.2$, the *All-D* players finish all above this average, hence the system will switch all 30 TFT players to defective behavior in the very first iteration.

If there is no total connectivity, this is not that obvious any more. Let the actors be arranged on a two-dimensional 10x10 lattice, where the upper end is attached to the lower end and equally the left to the right end and the interacting partners are their direct horizontal, vertical and diagonal neighbors (*Moore neighborhood*).

The simulation of both a system with total connectivity in Figure 7.2 and a system with Moore neighborhood in Figure 7.3 show that while the above prediction of the total connectivity system is correct, its behavior is hence trivial and predictable, the Moore neighborhood system shows complex and maybe chaotic patterns.

7.6 OUTLOOK

This chapter has given an overview of methodology and common issues and errors of simulation. An example illustrated how to use the particular advantages of simulation: Simulation was applied to acquire a prediction of the behavior of a system that would have been both difficult and resource-intensive to solve analytically. A set of independently acting agents, described by a number of equations of the same order as the set itself is difficult to solve, but easy to compute for particular sample values. Thus, even for very complex systems a prediction of the dynamics can be obtained fast. However, the reliability of that prediction has to be studied by careful analysis of the volatility and the sensitivity of the results and possible different predictions for other values. (For reasons of simplicity, this analysis has been omitted in this chapter).

Chapter 8 will discuss several instructive models of modern micro-economics with the majority of it either relying on computer simulation or providing techniques for simulation modeling. Simulation is used to explain special segregation patterns as a general structure in complex populations, to model potentially impeding technological lock-ins as well as the phenomenon of the emergence of cooperation – the latter model similar to the simple example discussed above in Section 7.5.

FURTHER READING

For an annotated list of textbooks and general introductions to computer simulation, see the textbook website at www.microeconomics.us.

8. Recent Core Models of Complexity Microeconomics

8.1 INTRODUCTION

Having discussed both the game theory framework for interactive models of an evolutionary-institutional economy and the neoclassical general equilibrium perspective in the early chapters of this textbook as well as simulation as a method to analyze complex systems in Chapter 7, one question remains: How can a powerful evolutionary-institutional theory be derived without falling back onto the same heroic assumptions neoclassic theory forces its followers to make?

It is not too difficult to model single interactive situations and even complex societal phenomena using game theory. An integrated powerful general theory, however, is still lacking in spite of promising approaches by both evolutionary game theorists as discussed in Chapter 2 and complexity economists as discussed in Chapter 9. The present chapter shall serve to offer a few particularly inspiring building blocks, non-neoclassical models that are both striking in their simplicity and powerful in the scope of their explanatory potential.

We are going to explain the models of institutional emergence by A. Schotter, R. Axelrod, and K. Lindgren, and models of the emergence of social segregation by T.C. Schelling and successive authors. Further, this chapter will discuss the path dependence in positive feedback processes such as arguably the technological standardization (following P.A. David and W.B. Arthur), S.A. Kauffman's technology landscapes, a model of technological progress under uncertainty and D.J. Watts and S.H. Strogatz's approach to the modeling of social networks (small-world networks). The final section will discuss the more qualitative theory of institutional change by P.D. Bush.

8.2 A. SCHOTTER (1981), R. AXELROD (1984/2006), AND K. LINDGREN (1997) ON THE EMERGENCE OF INSTITUTIONS

8.2.1 Schotter

Andrew Schotter proposed a theory of institutional emergence that centers on the development of *mutually consistent expectations* of agents regarding their respective behaviors (in Schotter, 1981; especially Chapter 3, with Simeon M. Berman). He stressed the function of institutions as 'informational devices ... that help (the agents) place subjective probability estimates over each other's actions' (p. 109). More secure expectations enhance individuals' decision-making capacity because they make it easier to choose one's own behavior in situations characterized by uncertainty and interdependence (see Chapter 1 in this textbook). Focusing on this aspect in his model, the emergence of specific institutions depends on the *observed behavior* of agents. However, the agents' behavioral choices also include a stochastic element, and so the eventual institution is not determined from the outset; rather, from one initial situation we may see the development of different institutional settings.

For his analysis Schotter chose a set-up in which agents would meet repeatedly in strategic interactions, as can be described by game-theoretic tools. The agents thus can create a relationship and learn what behavior to expect from one another. They choose their own behavior according to their expectations about the others. Once all agents' expectations are correct, no more adaptations of expectations are needed and the individual behavioral choices no longer change. The expectations regarding the others' behavior are shaped by the common observations of behavior, as an action today influences expectations about behavior tomorrow and so on. To describe the emergence of institutions, Schotter employs a Markovian diffusion process to model the adjustment of the expectations of the agents (that means a process in which the state of a system in the subsequent period depends only on its state in the current period, or, more technically, where the conditional probability distribution of the future depends only on the current state) the absorbing points of which (where the probability distributions no longer change) are interpreted as corresponding to stable social institutions embodying the 'behavioral modes' of the agents.

As institutions are devices to help the players move more securely in strategic interactions with others, they need to contain some reference to the other players' behaviors (even if that is, 'continue doing what you did no matter what anybody else has been doing'). Realizing that this is an important part of the institutional content, we can understand why Schotter based his model on supergame strategies – only in the repetition (the memory of the agent) do we find the basis for references to the others' behaviors.

To illustrate the model, we limit ourselves to four strategies to describe the behavioral modes of the agents. These strategies can be very basic ones (play a^1 as long as the other one plays a^1, play a^1 as long as the other one plays a^2, etc., where a^j is a pure strategy in the constituent game). In fact, rather simple formulations of strategies/behaviors are seen as sensible choices insofar as for institutions to be established it seems reasonable to assume that they do not consist of overly complicated behavioral rules. In the case of a 2x2 normal-form game, the strategy set S_i including the supergame strategies σ_i for a player i is given by

$$S_i = \left(\sigma_i \begin{bmatrix} a_i^1 \\ a_j^1 \end{bmatrix}, \sigma_i \begin{bmatrix} a_i^1 \\ a_j^2 \end{bmatrix}, \sigma_i \begin{bmatrix} a_i^2 \\ a_j^1 \end{bmatrix}, \sigma_i \begin{bmatrix} a_i^2 \\ a_j^2 \end{bmatrix} \right). \tag{8.1}$$

As said, in the example, these are the four behavioral modes the players choose from.

In the next step, Schotter defined a *convention* as including the compatible strategies of two players. The two strategies in such a convention are called a *pair* b^k. Thus, if the convention $\sigma = \left(\sigma_i \begin{bmatrix} a_i^1 \\ a_j^1 \end{bmatrix}, \sigma_j \begin{bmatrix} a_j^1 \\ a_i^1 \end{bmatrix} \right)$ is observed we call the pair $b^1 = \left(a_i^1, a_j^1 \right)$. The purpose of the model is to account for the process through which agents arrive at such conventions – mutually compatible behavioral decisions.

Now, instead of assuming that the agents formulate expectations regarding the others' behavior based on the payoff matrix alone, Schotter chose a different approach. The agents start by assigning a uniform probability vector to the pure strategies in the game which Schotter calls a *norm p*, giving them a uniform norm $p_i^u = \left(\frac{1}{4}, \frac{1}{4}, \frac{1}{4}, \frac{1}{4} \right)$ as the starting point ($1/n$ for each of the n strategies). Based on this probability distribution each agent calculates her own optimal mixed strategy $s_i = (s_i^1, s_i^2, s_i^3, s_i^4)$ for the first interaction with another player. These mixed strategies assign the probabilities that govern the choice of a pure strategy in an interaction so that based on the mixed strategies we can calculate the probability for each pair b^k to occur.

As an example for a probability of a supergame strategy take $s_1(\sigma_1[a_1^1/ a_2^2])$. This instructs player 1 to play strategy 1 as long as player 2 plays strategy 2 and attaches a weight s to it in the optimal mixed strategy calculated. The probability that a player chooses a supergame strategy starting with his strategy 1 is given by $\sum_{j=1}^2 s_1(\sigma_1[a_1^1/a_2^j])$ and analogous for his second strategy and the strategy options of player 2. That means the probability q of observing a strategy pair b^k that for example consists of both players choosing strategy 1 is given by

$$(a_1^1, a_2^1) = \left[\sum_{j=1}^2 s^1 \left(\sigma^1 [a_1^1 / a_2^j] \right) \cdot \sum_{i=1}^2 s^2 \left(\sigma^2 [a_2^1 / a_1^i] \right) \right]. \qquad (8.2)$$

At any moment there may thus be a positive probability for any strategy pair to be chosen.

For the process of institutional emergence, we now define a rule according to which the agents update the norm p for the calculation of their optimal mixed strategy before each interaction. For this update, we let the agents assume that the strategies they observed in their previous interaction represent a pair b^k. Such a pair is then translated into the corresponding supergame strategy. In the updated norm, the probability assigned to this convention is increased (the probabilities for the others are reduced accordingly). Specifically, in the example given here, the agents increase the probability for one convention by an amount ε and decrease the probabilities for the other three conventions by $\varepsilon/3$. Then, the best mixed strategy against this updated norm is calculated.

The solution procedure, the iterated adjustment of the probability vectors, lets players adjust expectations until the same equilibrium probability n-tuple is continuously prescribed. In the eventual equilibrium one strategy is chosen with probability one (as values less than one in one interaction would lead to an altered probability vector in the following interaction). At that point the agents arrive at a stable rule or institution for their, mutually consistent, behavior. The process is historical insofar as the changes in probabilities in the current norm depend on the observed strategy choice(s) of the opponent(s) in the preceding round. The stochastic element results from the fact that optimal strategies are mixed strategies during the process of emergence. That is, a pure strategy chosen in one encounter may be any of the (in the example four) pure ones included in the strategy set, as long as each one is included in the optimal set with a positive probability.

If you choose a Prisoners' Dilemma as the constituent game of the supergame there are two attractors. The institution may thus prescribe mutual cooperation or defection as the behavioral mode of the agents. A combination of cooperation/defection in a population is effectively not possible, as that would mean a mixed population in which every players' expectations are always fulfilled, meaning that every player is always matched with a player of the other type, something that is not going to happen in groups larger than two.

In his model, although based on game theory, Schotter did not employ any of the usual solution concepts for finding equilibria in games. Instead, he formulated a rule for the continuous adaptation of expectations regarding the other agents' behavior. As a result, there are a number of attractors in the system (as many as pure strategies in the constituent game, in fact). Additionally, because in Schotter's model the process of institutional emergence includes a stochastic element, it is not determined at the beginning, which of the behavioral modes eventually results.

8.2.2   Axelrod

Robert Axelrod (1984/2006) has also investigated the possibility of the emergence of institutions on the basis of iterated Prisoners' Dilemma games. However, while in Schotter's approach the process leading to the behavioral prescription (i.e., institution) is historical as well as stochastic, Axelrod, in turn, based his approach solely on the *payoffs* different strategies would achieve against each other in a supergame to see which one would prove advantageous for the players. For this, he held two tournaments in which a number of strategies were entered (a smaller one with 14 entries first and subsequently a second, larger one where 62 strategies were entered). All strategies played against all others, and then their respective average payoffs were calculated to see which one fared best. As this was not a theoretical approach to model the process of institutional emergence, but rather a lab experiment to see the returns strategies would generate against each other in supergames, the strategies considered are more complex than the four that have served as the basis for Schotter (where it was unnecessary to include more, or more complicated strategies, to make the point).

In the first tournament interactions were fixed at 200 rounds to at least limit if not completely avoid endgame effects from dominating the results; in the second tournament this set-up was altered slightly, as interactions continued with a given probability, p=0.99654. This leads to an expected 200 interactions in each round, but eliminates endgame effects. The payoff matrix was the same both times awarding 3 points to each agent for mutual cooperation, 1 point to each agent for mutual defection, and 5 points to a defecting agent exploiting cooperative behavior, with the cooperating agent receiving 0 points in that case.

After all strategies played against each other (including playing against a 'twin' strategy and a random strategy that was cooperating and defecting with a 50% probability respectively), the average results of their interactions were calculated. At the end, strategies were ranked according to the average points scored. The winning strategy was the same both times, the simplest of all strategies entered, Tit-for-Tat (TFT).

Given this result, Axelrod tested the strategy specifically over a number of additionally constructed tournaments with a variety of distributions of strategies, to see whether TFT was a robust strategy, or depended significantly on specific environments for its success. For the construction of these altered tournaments, Axelrod used the fact that in the second tournament, a group of five out of the 62 strategies had actually proven sufficient to predict the overall results in the tournament with very high accuracy. He then let all strategies play against these five, increasing the number of rounds played with one of the five in turn, thus increasing their weight in the calculation of the overall returns achieved by all strategies in the respective altered tournaments. In all those additional trials, TFT proved remarkably successful as well.

Based on these tournaments, Axelrod also constructed repeated tournaments in which updating rules for strategy choices were included – these were meant to reflect the fact that highly unsuccessful strategies would in all likelihood not be chosen again whereas the more successful ones should be chosen more frequently. The shares of strategies in subsequent tournaments were assumed to correspond to their relative payoffs (if strategy A's average payoff is twice as large as B's, A's share will be twice as high). Again TFT proved quite successful, representing the plurality of the population (with 1/6 of the population).

The results of the tournaments show, underlining the argument of Schotter to focus on simple strategies, that strategies in games involving complex decision problems (particularly social dilemma games), and hence the institutions reflected in them, should not be too complicated so that agents can understand them easily and are able to adapt their behavior without excessive effort. Additionally, Axelrod, based on the large dataset from the results of the tournaments, was able to formulate more detailed requirements for successful strategies in PD-based supergames. They should be *friendly* (nice), thus avoiding unnecessary conflict as long as the opponent cooperates, embody a *sanctioning mechanism* should the opponent cease to cooperate, in order to punish defections immediately (retaliation), but also show a capacity to *forgive* in case a deviating opponent returns to cooperative behavior (forgiving).

As the results further show, *cooperation* can emerge in a 'world of egoists without central authority'. The central aspect upon which its eventual emergence depends is the *likelihood of repeated interactions*, the probability that agents will meet again in the future. In the case that the probability of future interactions is sufficiently high, cooperation based on reciprocity can be established between individual agents; and, once established, in this set-up a cooperative strategy is actually able to defend itself against an invasion by less cooperative strategies.

In fact, in the tournaments, 'nice' strategies, those that did not have an option of defecting first, did significantly better than those that were not nice (with the first half of the ranking in the final tableau being taken by 'nice' strategies and the bottom half by the 'not-nice' ones). Among the nice strategies, those that were forgiving (like TFT that punishes only once and then possibly reverts to cooperation) did better than the less forgiving ones (in fact, as Axelrod points out, an even more forgiving strategy than TFT, namely Tit-for-Two-Tats, would have won had it been entered into the first tournament). However, the punishment of an unprovoked defection was also a necessary characteristic of a successful strategy. Finally, those that attempted more complicated patterns did not do nearly as well as the simpler ones even if the underlying rationale of the more complicated strategies seemed compelling at first sight.

8.2.3   Lindgren

In a next step, Kristian Lindgren (1997) further extended Axelrod's analysis by allowing for a number of variations in the games. He introduced the possibility that agents make *mistakes*, and for *learning* and *mutation* possibilities. When mistakes are allowed (meaning that with a certain probability a player may execute an action he had not intended – say, to choose 'defect' instead of 'cooperate') the advantageous strategies turn out to be some variant of TFT (nice, forgiving, retaliatory) but with an additional provision that lets them recover a cooperative relationship in case of accidental mistakes in the execution of a strategy by one of the players in an interaction.

However, if simulations run long enough, given the option for mutations (where Lindgren uses a provision that leads to an increased memory length of strategies) that is included, strategies may emerge that are capable of exploiting the error correction mechanism of a previously successful strategy. The *arbitrary endpoint* of simulations (as in Axelrod, for instance) only allows making statements regarding a *temporary advantage* of one specific strategy; for instance, in some runs, Lindgren finds strategies dominating a population for 10,000 generations (repetitions of the underlying game) only to then be replaced by another one dominating for 15,000 generations. Given such long dominance in combination with subsequent changes, there is no possibility of determining a possible stable equilibrium that may or may not emerge eventually. Nevertheless, the (temporarily) dominant strategies are generally *variants of TFT*, somewhat more elaborate for sure, but, as mentioned above already, respecting the same principal concepts with the differences lying in the details of length of retaliation period and the error correction mechanism (where strategies may eventually be distinguished by their ability to react to mistakes that are made in the process of correcting prior mistakes).

Finally, specifically including neighborhood structures in the analysis, in simple iterated PD games, where All-D would become dominant in a so-called mean-field set-up (especially in large groups where all interact with all), a lattice structure (where interactions are limited to the direct neighborhood, meaning smaller groups; see also Section 8.3 in this Chapter) usually leads to cooperation (TFT) being able to at least stay present in the population – either as the strategies change in waves of ascent and retreat, or due to the establishment of stable islands of cooperation in parts of the lattice.

8.3   T.C. SCHELLING (1978) AND R. AXELROD (1984/2006) ON SEGREGATION

Many common instances of segregation are caused by gender, such as toilets, showers, changing rooms, sports matches, or even schools sometimes. However, from a broader perspective the phenomenon of segregation often has more to do with personal individual choices. Different kinds of agents with weak preferences regarding their more frequent interaction partners may cause a strong degree of segregation as a collective result. And furthermore, neighborhood structures likewise lead to distinct patterns of interaction – the process of developing different topologies on which interactions takes place has been the focus of some of the seminal works of Thomas Schelling (1971, 1978) and Robert Axelrod (1984/2006).

8.3.1   A Spatial Proximity Model

In a first approximation to the segregation phenomenon, Schelling (1971, 1978) applies two models, one is a linear and the other is a two-dimensional neighborhood, in which agents with different preferences are divided into two groups where everyone can recognize its belonging. Agents' preferences simply consist of a minimum requirement regarding the number of their own group's members in their neighborhood. If anyone is dissatisfied with her neighborhood composition, she can move and find a satisfying place. For these moves, different rules are formulated to compare the resulting neighborhood structures.

Under the *linear distribution* condition there are 40 agents, 20 stars and 20 zeros, randomly distributed on a line (see Figure 8.1). All are concerned with their neighbors and want at least half of them to be like themselves. The neighborhoods extends to four neighbors in each direction (fewer to one side, obviously, for those on either end). Figure 8.1 shows a possible initial random distribution. In the case depicted there, 13 individual agents (marked with dots) can be found whose neighborhood does not meet their demands.

$$0 \dotplus 000 \dotplus \dot{+}0 + \dot{0}0 \dotplus +\dot{0}\dot{0} + + + \dot{0} + +\dot{0} + +\dot{0}0 + +00 + +0\dot{0} + \dotplus000 \dotplus$$

Figure 8.1   The initial distribution of agents

Now, anyone dissatisfied with her neighborhood can move in order for her preferences to be met. Starting from the left, the dissatisfied group members move to the nearest spot that meets their demands regarding the neighborhood composition. In Figure 8.1 that means, the first to move is the first star, on the second from the left, followed by the second star, on the sixth from the left, and so on.

After a few more rounds, while agents seek new positions in order to find satisfying neighborhoods we eventually arrive at a situation where no agent wants to change her position any longer. As depicted in Figure 8.2, the stable endpoint that we arrive at following the rules as set out above shows a segregated pattern with three clusters.

$$000000 +0000000000 \ 0000$$

Figure 8.2   Segregation in a linear distribution

Summarizing the above model, we can identify the determining elements for arriving at the final result as follows: The neighborhood size, the required percentage of one's own type in the immediate neighborhood, the share of different types of agents in the total population, the rules governing movement, and the original configuration. These mechanisms and conditions do, however, only shape the specific endpoint reached; the general pattern of a development towards segregation holds more broadly.

Another possible formulation for analyzing segregation dynamics is not to choose a linear pattern, but an *area distribution* in a two-dimensional space instead. Divide a space up into squares (imagine a chess board) and let some of those squares be occupied by agents, with one agent per square. Some squares stay empty to allow agents to move if necessary. Neighborhoods are defined as a set of squares (e.g. 3x3, 5x5) in which the agent under consideration occupies the center position. No fewer than 60% of an agent's neighbors are to be of the same type as she is. For those whose current position does not meet that specification, the moving rule used in the succession shown in Figure 8.3 is specified as follows: An agent has to move to the nearest vacant square meeting her demands regarding the composition of her neighborhood, crossing horizontally or vertically through other squares.

Figure 8.3 (a) shows a possible initial random *area distribution*. There are 2000 agents (two kinds of color of agents, 50 to 50), of the occupying agents, initially 66.6% are discontent and move as the above assumption requires 60% of the neighborhood to be of the same type for the agent to be satisfied. A first round of movement will leave new agents behind unsatisfied, and moving will continue until eventually all agents have settled in neighborhoods that leave them content. Figure 8.3 (b) shows the final stable segregation state after a number of rounds via simulation. For details, see Wilensky (1997, 1999).

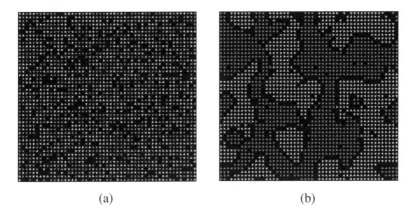

(a)   (b)

Figure 8.3: Segregation model in an area distribution

8.3.2   A Bounded-Neighborhood Model

Another variation of a segregation model is the bounded-neighborhood model. Each agent in this case is concerned with the ratio of agents in her neighborhood. We have two types of agents, blue and white. The more tolerant an agent is, the higher the share of members of the other group she is willing to accept in her neighborhood. Again, when the limits are crossed, agents leave and move to a neighborhood that satisfies their preference setting.

The different ratios that agents are willing to tolerate allow us to draw a *distribution of 'tolerance'*. An example of a linear distribution schedule is shown in Figure 8.4 (a). For the whites, the vertical axis presents the *upper tolerance limits* measured by the ratio of blues to whites. The horizontal axis is the amount of whites, 100 in total. If the median white can live with an equal number of blues in her neighborhood, the ratio is 1:1. In the example, the most tolerant white is willing to accept a ratio of blue to white of 2:1, and the least tolerant white only tolerates all white groups.

Suppose now that the tolerance of blues is identical to that of whites. The total number of blues is 50, half that of the whites. We can translate the straight-line tolerance schedules for the single groups into a parabola, respectively, translating the shares agents are willing to accept into absolute numbers (with blues on the vertical and whites on the horizontal). The resulting parabolas divide the quadrant into four areas. The figure allows us to graphically depict the direction that the changes of compositions of neighborhood populations take starting from all possible initial combinations, as indicated by the arrows. Already a first glace shows that there are strong forces pulling towards equilibria in which fully segregated neighborhoods will have resulted. For almost every agent that means that, due to the heterogeneity of preferences regarding the neighborhood population ratio, they live in a much more segregated environment than they would have been willing to live in.

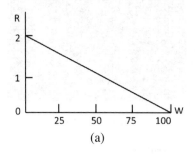
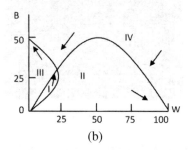

(a)   (b)

Source: T.C. Schelling, 1971, p. 169.

Figure 8.4   Distribution of tolerance

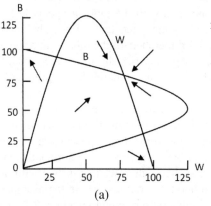
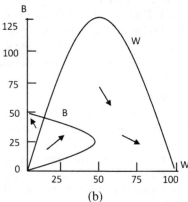

(a)   (b)

Source: T.C. Schelling, 1971, p. 173.

Figure 8.5   Alternative instances of tolerance distribution

The direction of the population movement given a composition of a neighborhood is marked by the arrows in each area. In the overlapping area, area I, the numbers of whites and blues will both be increasing until the schedules cross. That point would mark an equilibrium composition for the neighborhood, however, an unstable one, for any change pushing the composition into areas II or III would lead to substantial changes. In area II, whites would be entering, while the blues are departing. The process would continue until the lower right is reached, leaving an all-white neighborhood. Within area III, the opposite dynamic would be playing out, leaving an all-blue neighborhood. Finally, in area IV, outside both curves, the motion depends on the initial ratio between blues and whites. From area IV, the dynamics of segregation lead to two stable equilibria, of which one is formed of all whites and no blues, the other vice versa.

The detailed results are attributable to the specific *tolerance schedule* and the *size of population*; if we change them, a different outcome can be arrived at. Figure 8.5 (a) shows the situation of two colors with the same tolerance schedule and equal numbers (of 100 agents each). The median white (or blue) agent can tolerate a ratio of 2.5 blues to whites (vice versa). In this case, a linear tolerance schedule runs as a straight line with a vertical intercept at 5.0, which is the upper limit. As the graph shows, there are two stable equilibrium states at 100 blues or 100 whites respectively in a neighborhood, and a stable equilibrium at a mixture of 80 blues and 80 whites.

Leaving the tolerance schedule unchanged while reducing the number of blue agents produces the situation depicted in Figure 8.5 (b). Due to a change in the size of population, one curve now lies within the other one, and the stable mixed equilibrium disappears, leaving only the two equilibria of complete segregation. From this situation we can further alter conditions in order to be able to produce a stable mixed neighborhood again.

8.3.3   A Territoriality Model

Axelrod (1984/2006) dedicated some space to an analysis of the stability of strategies in territorial social systems as compared to his baseline case of social systems in which everyone can meet everyone else. In social systems of (weak or strong) total connectivity, a TFT strategy can be stable, meaning that it cannot be invaded by an All-D agent; this, Axelrod calls 'collectively stable' strategies. An interesting question that follows is whether conditions change when agents are confined to interacting with their neighbors only; in other words, are collectively stable strategies territorially stable as well.

In general, we see that a collectively stable strategy is territorially stable as well. To see why, imagine a structure in which every agent interacts with four neighbors (north, east, south, west). If one of these neighbors does better on average than the others, the direct neighbors subsequently copy his strategy. The strategies under consideration are All-D and TFT. If TFT is collectively stable that means that TFT against TFT does better than All-D against TFT in a PD supergame. In a neighborhood structure in which one agent plays All-D, the All-D player may do better than the TFT players with which he interacts. But it also follows from this that the average result achieved will be below the result of a TFT player playing against TFT players only. If only one All-D agent invades then no other agent has a reason to copy the All-D strategy, because there will always be direct neighbors playing TFT who are more successful. If a strategy is collectively stable, it will thus always be territorially stable as well. For an illustration of a very similar model, see Figure 7.3 in Chapter 7.

8.4   W.B. ARTHUR ET AL. (1982), W.B. ARTHUR (1989), AND P.A. DAVID (1985) ON INCREASING RE-TURNS, POSITIVE FEEDBACK IN TECHNOLOGY CHOICE PROCESSES, AND LOCK-IN

8.4.1   Standardization and Technology Choice in Economic Systems

Economic systems require a certain level of coordination in order to function properly. The types of coordination range from unified measures to standardized intermediate products to common technologies and to universally agreed communication systems. Contrary to the assumptions needed for neoclassical microeconomic optimization, this leads to increasing returns to the number of users of such standards (network externalities). As a consequence, there is no optimal share of users that should use a standard but the largest benefits are realized if the standard is used by the entire economy. This in turn brings about new problems such as the realization of technological progress: Given the entire economy uses the currently best possible option and a new and better technology is developed, there is no feasible way to switch to this technology which of course has no user base and therefore does not generate network externalities. Hence, technological progress is hampered in a standardized economy (lock-in); further, in the case of several competing standards there is not necessarily a way to predict which one of the standards would be the socially best option to establish.

David was among the first scholars to study this phenomenon in detail using the case of the QWERTY keyboard as an example. At the time, keyboard layouts were still mainly physical devices (i.e. mostly mechanical typewriters) that could not be changed. Almost everyone in the English speaking world and certainly the major corporations adhered to the QWERTY standard that continues to dominate the default layout of today's computer keyboards. Yet David discovered evidence that the alternative but rarely used DVORAK keyboard layout would have significantly increased the average typing speed in turn generating noticeable efficiency gains (though the credibility of this evidence was later contested, see Liebowitz and Margolis, 1990). Network externalities and the (not surprising) failure to achieve a coordinated switching to the better standard with a significant share of the population prevented the economic system from leaving the lock-in, the inefficiency trap it was caught in. With various collaborators, David (David and Bunn, 1988; David and Steinmueller, 1994) continued to analyze similar historical cases in other industries, including the dominance of alternating current over direct current in today's electricity grids and the success of the VHS video tape standard over several allegedly better alternatives.

8.4.2   A Formal Model of Technology Choice and Lock-In

The formal approach to model such cumulative feedback processes, however, is by Arthur et. al (1982). Arthur and David were mutually aware of each other's work and worked together to some degree. Arthur later applied the purely theoretical work of 1982 to more illustrative examples of network effects in economic systems (Arthur, 1989); other game theory models (for instance Katz and Shapiro, 1985) follow similar lines.

The core of the formal approach is the feedback loop inherent in these standardization processes that allows for path dependent development of the technological or organizational system, i.e. a state variable (the usage share x of a standard) as a function of itself:

$$x = f(x). \tag{8.3}$$

This, however, is to be the consequence of individual technology choice. Let A and B be two competing technologies generating utilities u which are composed of an intrinsic utility r and a network $v(n)$ the latter one being a strictly increasing function of the number of users n. In turn

$$u_A = r_A + v(n_A). \tag{8.4}$$

Further, let δ be the difference in the intrinsic utility $\delta = r_A - r_B$ and $v(n)$ be a linear function. The decision problem consequently comes down to

$$u_A - u_B = \delta + v(n_A - n_B) \tag{8.5}$$

which is either positive or negative; the agent adopts standard *A* or *B* accordingly. Adoptions occur sequentially; the agents choose one after another. They are perfectly informed about the state of the system. Consequently the direction of the path dependent development is determined by the values and distribution of δ for the agents and by the sequence in which the agents get to choose a technology. In a theoretical homogeneous case, i.e. δ is identical for all agents, the process – given as the probability that an agent chooses technology *A* – comes down to

$$p(A) = \begin{cases} 1 & if\ u_A - u_B > 0 \\ 0 & if\ u_A - u_B < 0. \end{cases} \qquad (8.6)$$

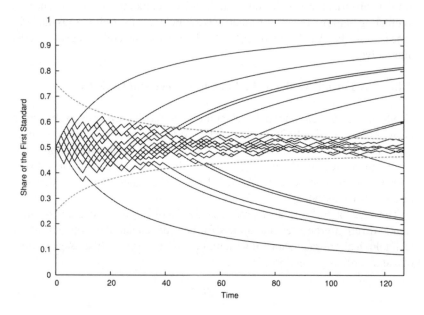

Figure 8.6   Simulation of a technology choice process with two homogeneous groups, network utility in absolute user numbers

As all agents are identical and $v(n)$ is strictly increasing, all agents would follow the decision of the first adopter reducing the process to a one period process. The more interesting case of two distinct homogeneous groups (1 and 2) exhibits absorbing barriers at which the behavior of the system changes abruptly: Once the network effect $v(n)$ for one technology favored by one group has grown large enough to surpass the intrinsic preference of the other group for the other technology, everyone will make the same choice. Before the absorbing barrier is reached, the process follows the distribution of agents among the two groups (assuming a uniform 0.5:0.5 distribution for the further considerations here):

$$p(A) = \begin{cases} 1 & if\ u_{A,1} - u_{B,1} > 0,\ if\ u_{A,2} - u_{B,2} > 0 \\ 0.5 & if\ u_{A,1} - u_{B,1} > 0,\ u_{A,2} - u_{B,2} < 0 \\ & or\ u_{A,1} - u_{B,1} < 0,\ u_{A,2} - u_{B,2} > 0 \\ 0 & if\ u_{A,1} - u_{B,1} < 0,\ if\ u_{A,2} - u_{B,2} < 0. \end{cases} \qquad (8.7)$$

We simulate the process (20 runs) to illustrate the behavior of the system; the simulation result is given in Figures 8.6 and 8.7. The dynamic properties of this process depend on the scale of δ with respect to the slope of the linear net utility function $v(n)$, shifting the absorbing barriers outward or inward (see Figure 8.6). Note that the absorbing barriers are constant if the net utility is a function not of the absolute user numbers n but of the usage shares $x_A = \frac{n_A}{n_A + n_B}$ (see Figure 8.7).

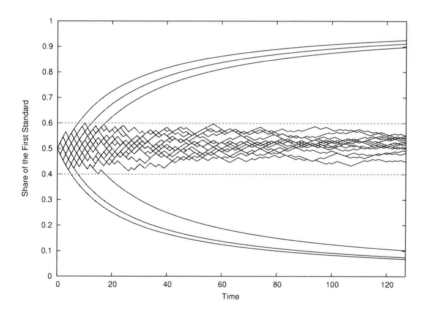

Figure 8.7   Simulation of a technology choice process with two homogeneous groups, network utility in usage shares

Considering truly heterogeneous agents, the probability function $p(A)$ becomes a continuous function:

$$p(A) = f(n_A - n_B) \tag{8.8}$$

or, using usage shares instead of absolute numbers,

$$p(A) = f\left(\frac{n_A}{n_A + n_B}\right) = f(x_A) \tag{8.9}$$

which, in effect, is the positive feedback function 8.6. The system is thus given by a stochastic recurrence equation that shares the same dynamic properties and equilibria (fixed points) with its corresponding non-stochastic form (that is, the function $f(x)$ is not treated as a probability distribution but rather a deterministic function)

$$x_{A,t+1} = f(x_{A,t}) \tag{8.10}$$

the fixed points of which are the points for which the function crosses the 45°-line, i.e.

$$f(x_{A,t}) = x_{A,t}. \tag{8.11}$$

For a graphical illustration using a typical (s-shaped) network externality function as an example, see Figure 8.8. Specifically the fixed points are stable (attractors) if the crossing occurs from below the 45°-line, i.e.

$$\frac{\partial f(x_A)}{\partial x_A} < 1 \tag{8.12}$$

and unstable otherwise. Arthur et al. (1982) showed that if the set of stable fixed points of such a positive feedback function is non-empty (i.e. there is at least one attractor), the process converges to one of the attractors with certainty.

Arthur emphasized that positive feedback processes, in other theory traditions also known as circular cumulative causation, are a central feature in economic systems especially when considering technological progress. While such processes are difficult to account for using methods of neoclassical theory, it is relatively straightforward when applying dynamic systems as discussed in more detail in Chapter 9.

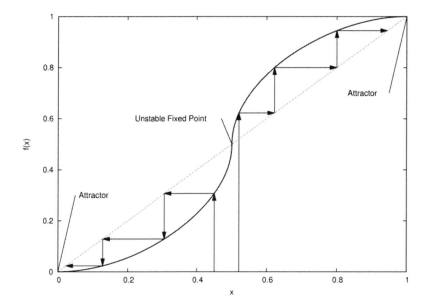

Figure 8.8 S-shaped Arthurian technology choice function

8.5 S.A. KAUFFMAN (1993) ON SEARCH ON LANDSCAPES

Evolutionary processes describe the change in the traits of an organism through successive generations. Change comes about by recombination or mutation. In evolutionary-institutional economics a technology was always understood as a combination of different tools. Innovation can then be conceived as the recombination of existing tools (Ayres, 1944, Chapter VI).

A landscape visualizes all different combinations of traits the organism can have. Associated with each point on the landscape there is a fitness level, which can be thought of as the height of the landscape at that particular point. If the landscape is simple and has only one peak, like a mountain in the middle of the desert, then this peak can easily be found. But if the landscape is very rugged having multiple peaks, like the Alps, finding the highest peak is more diffcult. Figure 8.9 illustrates the difference between simple and complex landscapes. Although we can easily find the highest peak on the complex landscape (lower graph) if we look from above, finding the highest peak can be very dificult for agents who do not have this bird's-eye-view but are situated on the landscape.

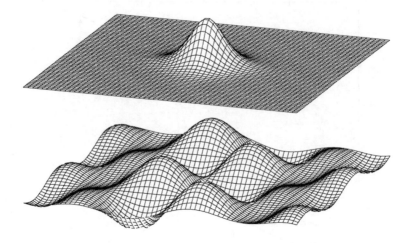

Figure 8.9   A simple landscape (upper graph) and a complex landscape (lower graph)

8.5.1   Illustrative Example

In order to model the search for better technologies in a complex environment we choose an NK landscape. *N* and *K* are two parameters. As we will see below, *N* is related to the size of the landscape and *K* is related to its complexity. By choosing an NK landscape we follow Kauffman (1993) and Kauffman et al. (2000). This section will present an illustrative example and the next section will give a more formal representation of NK landscapes.

As an example assume that a homogeneous good is being produced by the combination of *N* different tasks. Let us assume that we produce coffee by combining three tasks, (i) picking the beans, (ii) roasting the beans, and (iii) grinding the beans. Further we may assume that each task can be done in one of two ways. Picking the beans can be done manually or automatically, the roasting can be done for either 10 or 20 minutes, and grinding can be coarse or fine. We codify the two alternatives for each task by 0 and 1. A technology for producing coffee can then be codified as a unique combination of the 0 or 1 states of each task. In total we have $2^3 = 8$ technologies for producing coffee, (000); (001); (010); (100); (011); (110); (101); (111). The quality (fitness) of our finished product coffee depends on which tasks are used. But, and this is the crux of NK landscapes, the contribution of one task might depend on the state of other tasks. Fine grinding might improve the quality tremendously but only if the beans were roasted for 20 minutes. If the beans were only roasted for 10 minutes fine grinding might not improve the quality at all.

8.5.2 NK Landscapes

In an NK landscape N corresponds to the number of tasks and K corresponds to the number of other tasks on which the contribution to overall fitness depends on. For $K = 0$ each task's contribution to overall fitness depends only on the state of the task. For $K > 0$ each task's contribution to overall fitness depends on the state of the task as well as the state of the K other tasks. By changing the parameter K we are able to vary the complexity of the landscape and the corresponding search problem, as the number of local optima increases with K.

More generally, an NK landscape is a metaphor for modeling an environment of varying complexity characterized by two parameters N and K. Each point on the environment is specified by N coordinates. Associated with each point on the landscape is a fitness level. In search models one or more agents navigate through the landscape with the goal of finding higher peaks, where local peaks correspond to local optima and the highest point on the landscape corresponds to a global optimum. In our example from above the environment is a technology consisting of $N = 3$ different tasks and the quality of coffee corresponds to fitness.

Keeping as an example the landscape as a technological environment in which agents search for a better technology, the technology landscape is defined as the set of all possible technologies and the associated fitness levels. A step uphill on the landscape is then a metaphor for finding a better technology.

We call the N-dimensional vector $v = (v_1, \dots, v_N)$ a technology. A technology assigns a state to each of its elements (tasks) where each element can occupy one of S states. The variable v_j thus indicates the state of task j. For simplicity we assume that $S = 2$ and

$$V_{j \in \{1,\dots,N\}} \in \{0,1\} \tag{8.13}$$

which allows us to represent each technology as a binary string (a vector of 0 and 1) of length N. The space of all possible technologies is then given by $V = \{0,1\}^N$ and the size of the technology space is given by 2^N. We can represent the technology space as an undirected graph. A specific technology $v \in V$ is represented as a vertex and is connected to its $d = 1$ neighbors. A d-neighbor is a technology that differs exactly by d tasks, that is, d tasks have to be changed to turn one technology into another. Using the Hamming distance (to be explained below) as a metric allows us to measure the distance between technologies where distance refers to similarity not spatial distance. Formally the set of neighbors of technology $v \in V$ is

$$N_d(v^{i'}) = \{v^i \in \{V - v^i\} : \Delta(v^i, v^{i'}) = d\}. \tag{8.14}$$

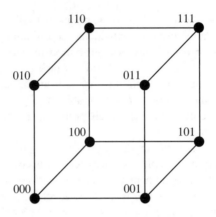

Figure 8.10 A 3-bit binary cube

For $N = 3$ the technology space is an undirected graph which can be visualized as a 3-bit binary cube (Figure 8.10). The $d = 1$ neighbors of technology (000) are the technologies (010), (100) and (001). The Hamming distance is just the number of bits that have to be changed, so for example the Hamming distance between (100) and (111) is 2 since the last two bits have to be changed. From the cube we see that there are $2^N = 2^3 = 8$ different technologies, each represented by a vertex of the cube. By increasing N, the technology space grows rapidly. If we take, for example, $N = 15$ there are 32,768 possible technologies in total. Firms do not know these technologies and searching the complete space of technologies would be too costly and time-consuming. Thus, firms try one technology after another, as we will see later.

8.5.3 Fitness Levels

Next we link the positions on the landscape to fitness levels. With each possible technology $v \in V$ a specific level of efficiency or fitness $e(v) \in [0,1]$ is associated. A fitness function e transforms the state space into a fitness landscape. In our case this is a mapping

$$e: v \in V \rightarrow \mathbb{R}^+ \tag{8.15}$$

which associates a specific level of efficiency to each technology. The levels of efficiency are drawn from the set of positive real numbers.

The contribution to efficiency by task j depends on the state of the task v_j, as well as on the state of K other tasks $v_{j1}, ..., v_{jk}$. For the simplest case, $K = 0$, there are no connections (intranalities, epistatic relations) between individual tasks, i.e. no intranalities (Kauffman et. al, 2000, p.145; by intranality we mean a task has an externality, i.e., the performances of two tasks affect each other. For the technology, however, this effect is not external. Some authors, for example Frenken and Nuvolari (2004), use the term epistatic relation instead of intranality). The value of each bit v_j is independent of every other bit for a particular state. For $K = 0$ we have the simplest possible landscape with only one maximum. If we increase K the complexity of the landscape increases and with it the number of local optima increases. This means that search becomes more complicated.

To every bit we assign a value $e_j(v_j)$ which is drawn from a 0-1 uniform distribution. We generate a value for $e_j(0)$ and for $e_j(1)$ for $j = 1; ...; N$; so we generate $2N$ values in total. Then, overall efficiency is given by

$$e(v) = \frac{1}{N}\Sigma_{j=1}^{N} e_j(v_j) \qquad (8.16)$$

Table 8.1   Fitness levels associated with technologies and fitness contributions of each task for N = 3 and K = 2

V	e_1	e_2	e_3	$e(v)$
(0,0,0)	0.6	0.3	0.5	0.47
(0,0,1)	0.1	0.5	0.9	0.5
(0,1,0)	0.4	0.8	0.1	0.43
(0,1,1)	0.3	0.5	0.8	0.53
(1,0,0)	0.9	0.9	0.7	0.83
(1,0,1)	0.7	0.2	0.3	0.4
(1,1,0)	0.6	0.7	0.6	0.63
(1,1,1)	0.7	0.9	0.5	0.7

Source: Adapted from Kauffman, 1995, p. 172.

If we move to the more interesting cases we have $0 < K \leq N - 1$. The efficiency of process j depends not only on v_j but also on K other values $v_{j1}; ...; v_{jK}$; i.e. $e_j = e_j(v_j; v_{j1}; ...; v_{jK})$. Overall efficiency e for state v is then given by

$$e(v) = \frac{1}{N}\sum_{j=1}^{N} e_j(v_j, v_{j1}, \dots, v_{jK}).$$ (8.17)

The number of random values we have to generate is $2K + 1N$. Table 8.1 illustrates this for $N = 3$ and $K = 2$.

8.5.4   Search

Search can be modeled in a number of ways. In general, search algorithms are used. The algorithm is a set of rules. Following the rules the agent navigates through the landscape. One particularly simple search algorithm is the adaptive walk or hill-climbing (Kauffman, 1995). Agents, which are firms in our example, start at their initial position and change one randomly chosen task. For $N = 3$ and initial position $v(t) = (1; 0; 1)$ the new position on the technology landscape could be $v(t + 1) = (0; 0; 1)$. That is, the firm tries one technology out of the set of neighboring technologies with distance one:

$$v(t + 1) \in N_1(v(t)).$$ (8.18)

If fitness at the new position is higher, that is, if the new technology is better, the firm moves to the new position. Otherwise it stays at the old position. Regardless of the efficiency of the new position firms have to pay the cost of search. A problem with this search algorithm is that it gets stuck at local optima since only $d = 1$ neighbors are considered. To overcome this problem more sophisticated algorithms have to be devised. The example of a firm's search for a better technology is only one particular example illustrating the characteristics of NK landscapes. In principle it is possible to model a wide range of phenomena as landscapes and let agents search on it. The NK model illustrates that if technologies are complex (N and K are large) the best technology cannot be easily found. Here it is assumed that agents do not have perfect information about the technology, i.e. they do not know the landscape in advance. Boundedly rational agents might easily get stuck at suboptimal outcomes since there are no simple rules for finding the global optimum. Instead of trying to find the global optimum, which implies searching the whole landscape, agents could change their approach and try to arrive at a local optimum without searching too long. Taking this perspective, which obviously becomes relevant for boundedly rational agents engaging in costly search in complex environments, the next step would be to find efficient search algorithms.

8.6   D.J. WATTS AND S.H. STROGATZ (1998) ON SMALL-WORLD NETWORKS

'The world is small' is a common saying for many people to describe a somewhat surprising phenomenon: We may meet a complete stranger and are surprised to find we share a mutual friend, or, more generally, everybody in the world can be reached on average with only six steps of relationships. This is commonly referred to as the *small-world phenomenon*, the name already suggests its intriguing characteristic within social networks, which has been explored in many scientific experiments by Milgram and others (see, Milgram, 1967; Mitchell, 1969; Korte and Milgram, 1970). After a number of explorations, for instance, by Pool and Kochen (1978), Skvoretz (1985) and Kochen (1989), who theoretically investigated small-world phenomenon, Watts and Strogatz (1998) provided the first model of the small-world phenomenon, appearing widespread in the social and natural sciences. In this section, we explain what the small-world phenomenon is, and how it has been formalized by Watts and Strogatz (1998).

8.6.1   The Small-World Phenomenon

In an experimental study in the 1960s in the United States, Milgram (1967) asked more than three hundred people in Kansas and Nebraska to send letters to targets in Boston (i.e. people randomly chosen in Boston). Each sender was only given the name of target – no address. If the targets were complete strangers to them, they could have intuitively sent the letter to whichever of their friends may possibly know the target. This procedure was repeated several times. Finally, each process of transfer generated a chain from the sender to the recipient. Statistically, Milgram found that sixty persons out of three hundred finished the tasks, of which the average number of links in the chain was six. The same results were also found in experiments by researchers such as Mitchell (1969) and Korte and Milgram (1970). From a series of experimental results, it may be concluded that the small-world phenomenon exists, namely that we are connected by a series of short links, or, in other words, we can connect any persons in the world over several acquaintances, even those vastly separated.

Of course, research specific to the small-world phenomenon had a considerable history after Milgram's (1967) experiment, but none of these works before Watts and Strogatz's (1998) succeeded to provide a comprehensive model. In reality, many phenomena, such as the spread of diseases, rumors, and fashion, are based on contacts between individuals. More importantly still, if many other large, sparse networks such as biological networks, neural networks, etc. have this deep feature – that an element can connect with any other in a network over several elements – new discoveries would be made. Therefore, it is necessary for an effective model to be built to improve the understanding of related areas.

8.6.2   Formalization of the Small-World Phenomenon

Before going further, it is best to understand the following definitions to simplify explanations.

Definition 1: Characteristic path length (L), for a given graph, is defined as the average number of edges that must be traversed in the shortest path between any two pairs of vertices in the graph (Watts, 1999a).

Often the small-world phenomenon is described as 'everybody in the world can be reached by only six steps'. Roughly, 'six steps' here would be characteristic path lengths. Concretely, L would be the average chain length from any sender to the recipient (in the edge set), which appeared in Milgram's (1967) experiment, or, in other words, the *shortest path length* between m and j. Namely, that it is the median of the means of the shortest path lengths connecting each vertex $m \in G$ (graph) to all other vertices and, specifically, we first calculate $d\,(m,j)\,\forall\,j\in G$ and find mean d_m for each m, then L is defined as the median of $\{d_m\}$ (Watts, 1999a).

Definition 2: Clustering coefficient (C) is a measure of the local graph structure (Watts, 1999a). Concretely, C measures the degree to which vertices in a graph tend to cluster together.

That is, assuming vertex v having m_v as immediate neighbors, then the immediate neighbors of m_v form a subgraph where $m_v\,\dfrac{m_v-1}{2}$ edges exist if every neighbor is connected. If the number of actual connections in the neighborhood (subgraph) is k, C_v is $\dfrac{2k}{m_v(m_v-1)}$, then C is this fraction over all vertices in the graph.

To form a model of the small-world phenomenon, Watts and Strogatz (1998) proceeded in the following way.

Firstly, recognizing that while the real world is a rather large, sparse and decentralized structure this is impractical for creating a simple model. In order to reduce complexity, a minimal and simplified structure is required for the graph; no vertex should be special. For instance, in star networks, there is a central node, chain networks have endpoints. A topological ring structure (see Figure 8.11) however, fulfills this requirement. Starting from such a regular geometric shape allows us, as will be discussed below, also to control and quantify the reduction of such regularity, and thereby the transition to a random network as well as the corresponding clustering and path length properties.

Secondly, Milgram's (1967) experiment showed that we are connected by a series of short links in the world. Hence alongside the ring structure, there should also be some short links connecting different parts of the ring. Starting with a regular ring network, Watts and Strogatz (1998) use a probability p to rewire nodes randomly. If $p = 0$, the ring network is unchanged, for $p = 1$ all vertices are changed randomly, resulting in a random graph. Then let $0 < p < 1$ represent the real world case. Watts [1999b, Chapter 4] gives the following algorithm to simulate the features above: Each vertex i in the ring connects, in a clockwise sense $(i, i + 1)$, to its nearest neighbour. It ensures formation of an ordered world first.

A random deviate $r\ (0 < r < 1)$ is generated (it will be created by computer). If $r > p$, connections $(i, i + 1)$ are unchanged. If $r < p$, $(i, i + 1)$ is deleted and rewired to a vertex which is chosen at random from the ring. Thus, if $p = 0$, r is always greater than p, resulting in an ordered graph, and when $p = 1$, r is always smaller than p, creating a random graph. When $0 < p < 1$, r is smaller than p in some cases and greater than p sometimes so that the formation of connections lies somewhere between randomness and order.

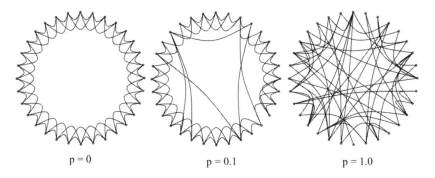

p = 0   p = 0.1   p = 1.0

Figure 8.11   Regular ring network (p=0.0), Watts–Strogatz small-world network (p=0.1), and random graph (p=1.0)

Finally, three graphs in Figure 8.11 are created by simulating the algorithm above (for how to simulate, see Chapter 7). Watts and Strogatz (1998) found the graph was highly clustered when $0 < p < 1$ (clustering coefficient), yet the characteristic path lengths were small, and called it a 'small-world' network, in reference to the small-world phenomenon. In fact, this model not only simulates the real world by combining a topological ring and formation of social connections, but also simulates 'small' by small characteristic path lengths. It therefore is an approximation of the small-world phenomenon.

8.6.3   Properties of Small-World Networks

Small-world networks are an important contribution to the modeling of economic reality not only because they seem to resemble real-world structures better than other types of networks but also as a consequence of their distinct properties. The network structure shapes the communication of agents, the spreading of epidemics, and, most importantly for our context of interactive economies, the diffusion of ideas, fashion, and innovations, of attitudes and strategies. Small-world graphs combine relatively high clustering with relatively short path lengths. Clustering gives rise to a number of distinct closely connected subgraphs that provide a protected environment for the development and evolution of new ideas and strategies; yet the distances in the graph are short enough to allow a rapid spread through the network once the time is right.

Consider as an example the population playing Prisoners' Dilemma supergames in networks as discussed in the final section of Chapter 7. In a two-dimensional environment, only the two limit cases ($p = 1$, total connectivity and $p = 0$, regular grid network) were considered; Watts and Strogatz (1998) did a more extensive analysis in their (one-dimensional) random graph context. Using a computer simulation, they found that when p was increased from 0 to 1 the fraction of cooperation was decreased. This result suggests that small-world networks can support cooperation (although random networks cannot). Furthermore, from this result, we can also see that, in reality, choices of people are often constrained by the networks they belong to.

8.7   P.D. BUSH (1987) ON THE INSTITUTIONALIST THEORY OF INSTITUTIONAL CHANGE

In Chapters 1 and 3, institutions were presented as solutions of complex social dilemma problems and an introduction to Veblenian conceptions of institutionalist theory was given. This approach, starting with Veblen, furthered by Ayres and Foster, and during the 1980s advanced by Bush (1983, 1987) to constitute a comprehensive theory of institutional change, has come to be known as the Veblen-Ayres-Foster-Bush paradigm. In contrast to the formal models for the emergence of institutions discussed in the first sections of the current chapter, the present section deals with the dynamics of existing institutions between their instrumental and ceremonial potentials following Bush's more qualitative approach in the Veblenian evolutionary-institutionalist tradition.

8.7.1   The Institutionalist Definition of Institutions

Bush (1987) first defines an institution as '*a set of socially prescribed patterns of correlated behavior*' (p. 1076). The term 'socially prescribed' in this definition stresses the fact that institutions mostly appear as received preexisting normative phenomena to individual agents, having emerged earlier and being received in a process of 'reconstitutive downward causation'. They may be objectively either still instrumental, i.e., problem-solving, or already fully abstract and detached from the original problem, thus ceremonial, i.e., mostly preserving power and status differentials, with regard to the agents. In the latter case, the original instrumental context of their emergence usually has faded away.

This is often not just a 'social behavioral rule (plus endogenous sanction)' as conveyed by social conditioning and enculturation, but above that, an explicit feeling of individuals of a 'must' or 'must not' of behavior, similar to semi-conscious habituation, as explained in Chapters 1 and 3.

Further, as the definition quoted above states, institutions require *correlated* behavior. In our instrumental derivation of institutional emergence, behaviors are correlated first between two agents who learn to correlate their behaviors in recurrent interaction to solve a problem at hand, particularly correlated (or reciprocal or mutual) cooperation learned in a Prisoners' Dilemma supergame. 'Correlation' may also be any coordination in a broader sense, including both institutionalized cooperation and some repeated mutual defection, carried out as a rule. Such 'correlated' behavior, therefore, can be not only correlated cooperation in an instrumental sense, but also defection in a ceremonial sense, as we will explain below. Repeated (mutual or one-sided) defection, in fact, may in this way have become established as a certain individualist, hyper-rational, ceremonial 'culture'. And while in a Prisoners' Dilemma supergame defection typically will be mutual among hyper-rational agents, under some particular assumptions, there may also be power and status exertion by one agent and corresponding acceptance by the other one. This would be a continuous, institutionalized exploitation.

Furthermore, any such behavior is correlated not only among agents, but also over time, since it emerged as a recurrent, repetitive, just rule-based behavior. In fact, a rule would be no rule (a 'strategy' in game-theoretic terms) if this behavior were not somehow correlated with itself over time. Thus, a set of correlated behaviors may refer to a set of *coordinated agents* carrying the institution and/or a set of repetitions of coordinated behaviors, i.e., a set of *coordinated interactions over time*.

Finally, according to the institutionalist conception, different institutions can be correlated among each other to form larger *institutional sets* and whole institutional arrangements or cultures. However, they cannot actively correlate themselves but will be correlated by agents through the values that motivate agents' behaviors and thus warrant individual institutions or sets of – then, and by this – correlated institutions.

8.7.2   Values Correlating Patterns of Behavior

The central aspect of determining the character of institutions (predominantly instrumental or ceremonial) and correlating different institutions (and determining the character of those together) in the institutionalist approach, which has not explicitly been accounted for in the game-theoretic treatment so far, is *values*. As Bush puts it, '*Values function as the "correlators" of behavior within and among patterns of behavior*' (Bush, 1987, p. 1077). That is '*two behaviors [..] [are] correlated by a value*' (ibid.). In a game-theoretic perspective, for instance, cooperative behavior in a Prisoners' Dilemma – and also, basically, coordinated behavior in a coordination game, particularly if coordinated on a superior Nash equilibrium in a stag-hunt game – are correlated among agents and over time through the 'instrumental value' (or valuation or motivation) of problem-solving, which seems quite obvious. Defection, aimed at unilateral exploitation and the often resulting mutual defection, on the other hand, is justifiable – also in game-theory – through the value of Veblenian 'invidious distinction', i.e., the striving for superior power and status, in a word, ceremonial value. This dual characterization of institutions by instrumental or ceremonial warrant is called the '*institutional dichotomy*', as originally introduced by Veblen.

Those motivations (values, valuations) may simultaneously determine the characters of, and thus correlate, different institutions coexisting in different arenas. The basic scheme of this institutionalist argument is

$$B - V - B,$$

with V for the correlating values and B for the patterns of behavior or institutions. V correlates behaviors B, again either *interpersonal* and/or *intertemporal* or *inter-institutional*.

The characters of and relationship between the Bs are fundamentally determined by the type of V. Therefore, first, all kinds of constellations, including conflicting ones, between instrumental and ceremonial Vs and their determined institutions have to be expected, and, second, *institutional change* must entail (or require, presuppose, or just go along with), basically, a change of the value correlating the behaviors.

8.7.3   The Asymmetry in the Institutional Dichotomy, Ceremonial Dominance, and Ceremonial Encapsulation

Again, behavior warranted by ceremonial values is based on invidious distinction and differential status and power. The logic of ceremonial warrant is, as Veblen has already put it, one of 'sufficient reason', which means that ceremonial values refer to tradition, received authority, and suitable myths, and are beyond critical scrutiny and scientific inquiry. The *operative criterion* for such behavior thus is 'ceremonial adequacy', i.e., just conformity with the myths of differential power and status, without any proof of real efficacy – conformity is just sufficient.

Instrumental values, on the other hand, are bound to some specified problem solving, and thus their logic is that of 'efficient cause' rather than just 'sufficient reason'. The operative criterion by which instrumentally warranted behavior is judged, therefore, is that of 'instrumental efficiency' (rather than 'ceremonial adequacy'), i.e., efficacy. Typically, with new 'technological' knowledge (in the broadest sense), instrumental behavior would have to be scrutinized and properly adapted.

Several qualifications are to be made here:

- First, there are two *pure forms* of behavior that can be expressed in the values-behaviors scheme:

$$B_c\text{-}V_c\text{-}B_c \quad \text{and} \quad B_i\text{-}V_i\text{-}B_i,$$

  where c and i stand for ceremonial and instrumental, respectively.
- Second, it is most important in the institutionalist approach to institutional change that most behavior is *dialectical* in the sense of having *both ceremonial and instrumental* characteristics or potentials. These are patterns of behavior to be symbolized by B_{ci} (or equivalently, B_{ic}), which are ambivalent and open, and in their final significance depend on the type of values that warrants them. Thus, there can be added the following forms:

$$B_{ci}\text{-}V_c\text{-}B_{ci} \quad \text{and} \quad B_{ci}\text{-}V_i\text{-}B_{ci}$$

and, of course, also

$$B_c\text{-}V_c\text{-}B_{ci} \quad \text{and} \quad B_i\text{-}V_i\text{-}B_{ci}.$$

Both ceremonial and instrumental values can warrant and correlate either 'dialectical' patterns of behavior or a 'pure' form of their own kind with a 'dialectical' or ambivalent form.

- Third, there is a *fundamental asymmetry* between instrumental and ceremonial modes of valuation, as already apparent from the two different logics and operational criteria given above: The instrumental logic and operational criterion of efficient cause and instrumental efficiency are inapplicable to purely ceremonial behavior: 'Instrumental valuation cannot rationalize purely ceremonial behavior' (Bush, 1987, p. 1083). The ceremonial logic and operational criterion of sufficient reason and ceremonial adequacy, on the other hand, are limitless in principle: Any behavior, including instrumental behavior, may be 'rationalized', absorbed, (mis-)used, or occupied, so to speak, by ceremonial valuation, since its logic is weaker and its operational criterion less demanding. In game-theoretic terms, we might think, as a potential equivalent, of the exploitation constellations in the upper right and lower left cells of a PD normal form, where instrumental (cooperative) behavior of some agents is dominated by the ceremonial (defective) behavior of others (to their own benefit).

In cases of *ceremonial enclosure* of purely instrumental or 'dialectical' patterns of behavior, institutionalists speak of *encapsulation*: 'In these instances, instrumental behavior is "encapsulated" within a ceremonially warranted behavioral pattern, thereby incorporating instrumental behavior in a ceremonially prescribed outcome' (Bush, 1987, p. 1084).

The forms of ceremonial encapsulation are manifold, first, with pure behaviors, where purely instrumental behavior is warranted, correlated with purely ceremonial behavior, and in this way subordinated to ceremonial behavior, i.e., 'encapsulated', by ceremonial valuing:

$$B_c\text{-}V_c\text{-}B_i,$$

and the 'weaker' form (or rather a stronger assumption?) of purely instrumental behavior warranted, correlated with 'dialectical' behavior, and encapsulated by ceremonial valuation, where even 'dialectical' and purely instrumental behaviors can be encapsulated to serve a ceremonially prescribed outcome:

$$B_{ci}\text{-}V_c\text{-}B_i.$$

And, of course, also

$$B_{ci}\text{-}V_c\text{-}B_{ci} \quad \text{and} \quad B_c\text{-}V_c\text{-}B_{ci}$$

are forms of ceremonial encapsulation.

Note that B_i-V_c-B_i is no possible constellation, as ceremonial values cannot justify pure instrumental behaviors. For instance, general mutual cooperation, in our sense of problem-solving for all, cannot be considered ceremonially warrantable, although one-sided cooperative behavior can easily be ceremonially encapsulated. Similarly, as indicated, no constellation B_c-V_i-B_c is possible. Furthermore, because of the asymmetry explained, instrumental values cannot even justify *any* purely ceremonial behavior, so no constellations B_i-V_i-B_c and B_{ci}-V_i-B_c are feasible. See Figure 8.12 for an overview of forms.

	Ceremonially warranted patterns of behavior	**Instrumentally warranted patterns of behavior**
'Pure pure' forms	B_c-V_c-B_c	B_i-V_i-B_i
Pure 'dialectical' forms	B_{ci}-V_c-B_{ci} (involving some ceremonial encapsulation)	B_{ci}-V_i-B_{ci}
Mixed pure/ dialectical forms	B_c-V_c-B_{ci} (involving some ceremonial encapsulation)	B_i-V_i-B_{ci}
Pure 'encapsulation' forms	B_c-V_c-B_i B_{ci}-V_c-B_i	-/-

Source: After Bush, 1987, p. 1082.

Figure 8.12   A scheme of the variants of ceremonially and instrumentally warranted and correlated patterns of behavior

The *asymmetry* between the two logics of the ceremonial and the instrumental easily combines with the general comprehension of *institutions* in the Veblenian tradition according to which institutions are always and unavoidably past-bound and thus prone to a *ceremonial dominance* anyway. However, specific cultures and nations, in fact, differ in the 'permissiveness' of their institutions vis-à-vis new technological knowledge (or an 'increase of the social knowledge fund'), of allowing for a change towards more instrumentally warranted behavioral patterns.

So this is about graduality and degrees. A related *index of ceremonial dominance* can then be derived from a specific *network of correlated institutions*, according to the relative numbers of (instrumental vs. ceremonial) dominance relations existing in that specific institutional structure of an economy (Bush, 1983). It will be inversely related to the degree of permissiveness: The higher that index, the lower is the permissiveness of the institutional structure of an economy.

In game-theoretic terms, you may think of some 'technological' change (in the broadest sense) that may change the payoff structure in a coordination game so that the former superior coordination becomes the inferior one and vice versa, or changing a coordination game into a Prisoners' Dilemma or vice versa, or increasing the relative payoffs for common cooperation in a Prisoners' Dilemma so that common defection pays relatively less or vice versa in a 'single-shot' or population or agency approach (see Chapters 2 and 3 above). While this may appear a bit 'technical', it may nevertheless combine with the valuing aspect: The more 'permissive' the value structure of the agents in those games would be, i.e., the more the agents will be after long-run and broad (common and collective) 'problem solving' having recognized their interdependence, the more a behavioral adaptation towards the superior solution would appear feasible in all these cases. According to what we have learned so far (mainly through the single-shot solution in Chapters 2 and 3), we would assume in a game-theoretic perspective that the *degree of permissiveness* is related to both the payoff structure and the learned importance of the common future δ in the considerations of the agents – which would offer some 'rational' explanation of the relative weights of the two types of values.

8.7.4   The Process and Forms of Institutional Change

It follows from the above that *new knowledge* (technological change), together with related (newly learned or adapted) instrumental patterns of behavior, can become either encapsulated within still dominating ceremonially warranted patterns of behavior, or 'embedded' within a dominating instrumental value-behavior structure.

Basically, the asymmetry and ceremonial dominance restricts permissiveness: '(K)nowledge that cannot be reconciled with the need to justify existing patterns of status, power, and other forms of invidious distinctions would not be intentionally sanctioned' (Bush, 1987, p. 1091).

But new knowledge basically supports instrumental feasibility ('warrantability') of (newly learned or adapted) behavior. The index of ceremonial dominance (in a negative sense) or the degree of permissiveness (in a positive sense), in fact, are indicative of the degree to which new knowledge is allowed to be used in the community's problem-solving process.

The asymmetric structure of feasibilities ('warrantabilities'), in sum, now defines an *institutional space*, within which we can not only define the different sectors (subspaces, cells) according to the value-behavior constellations (instrumental and ceremonial feasibilities and infeasibilities), but also can illustrate the motions of institutional change (see Figure 8.13 below):

1. *Ongoing and enforced ceremonial encapsulation*: When (new) behavioral patterns are both *instrumentally feasible* (warrantable) and *ceremonially feasible* (warrantable), thus meeting both 'efficient cause' and 'sufficient reason', or both 'instrumental efficiency' and 'ceremonial adequacy', it is clear from the argument about asymmetry and ceremonial dominance that this is the case (and sector) of ceremonial encapsulation. Here, the institutional structure of an economy allows for benefiting from instrumentally warranted behavior that at the same time can be ceremonially justified, utilized, and encapsulated (upper left cell in Figure 8.13).

   In dynamic terms, if an increase of the knowledge fund would trigger an ongoing and even enforced ceremonial encapsulation, with no change in the degree of permissiveness, the system would remain in this sector [Case (1) in Figure 8.13].

2. Those behavioral patterns that are instrumentally feasible but ceremonially infeasible will typically be excluded under ceremonial dominance ('lost instrumental efficiency') (lower left cell in Figure 8.13). If, however, viewed dynamically, ceremonial dominance could be reduced through new knowledge and related potential of newly learned or adapted instrumental behavior, this would be indicative of *progressive institutional change*, i.e., an increasing weight of instrumental over ceremonial values, and the economy could be thought of as moving from the sector of ceremonial encapsulation into the sector of increased instrumental problem-solving, where instrumental patterns of behavior are no longer excluded but become dominant [a motion from upper left to lower left in Figure 8.13, case (2)].

3. Finally, if behavioral patterns were instrumentally infeasible and only ceremonially feasible, if they were purely ceremonial, a complete dominance of the 'myth structure' and a full 'loss of instrumental efficiency' (Bush, 1987, p. 1092) would occur, with instrumentally warranted patterns no longer existing (the upper right cell in the figure below). If, in response to new knowledge and potential new instrumental institutions, ceremonial dominance would even increase (through some counter movement) and the economy's institutional structure moved into this sector of ceremonial feasibility and instrumental infeasibility

(excluding virtually all instrumental patterns of behavior), this would be a *regressive institutional change*, i.e., an even greater dominance of ceremonial over instrumental values. This may be termed quasi-religious effects.

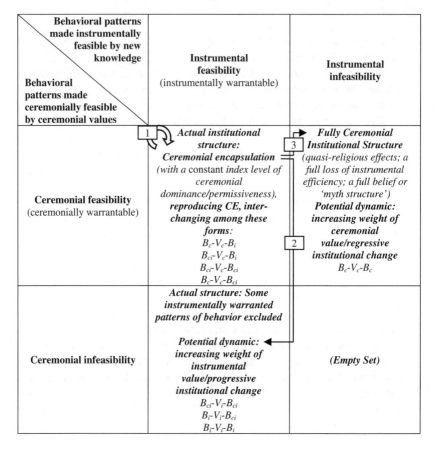

Figure 8.13   The institutional space in the interface of instrumental feasibility and ceremonial feasibility, and the basic movements of institutional change

8.7.5 The Discretionary Character of Progressive Institutional Change: A Policy Perspective

Therefore, after all, progressive institutional change will normally not emerge, particularly when systemic crises and widespread uncertainty and fears may easily lead to enforced ceremonial encapsulation. The system may move perhaps from future-binding to past-binding encapsulation and from there even to regressive institutional change. Thus, progressive change would remain an issue of proper deliberate, discretionary policy action. In the institutionalist tradition, M.R. Tool developed the theory of instrumentalism and progressive institutional change into a theory of the so-called 'social value principle', which operationalized the institutionalist conception of public policy and its formation. For institutionalists, democracy and democratic policy are substantial in the sense that decisions will have to be found in a participatory democratic negotiation process with all interests involved (the 'negotiated economy'). Thus it is not primarily about some formal majority rule but about the substantial 'process by which majorities [...] are formed' (Bush, 1987, p. 1109) – and such process would be interconnected 'with the process of inquiry upon which instrumental valuing depends' (ibid.). In this way, substantial, participative, and discursive democracy would support collective long-run rationality and action capacity, and with this the dominance of instrumental values and instrumentally warranted patterns of behavior – i.e., progressive institutional change.

FURTHER READING

For further references on distinguished recent models and developments in heterodox economics, see the textbook website www.microeconomics.us.

9.   A Universe of Economies: Interdependence and Complexity, System Trajectories, Chaos, and Self-Organization [1]

9.1   SOME BASICS OF COMPLEXITY ECONOMICS VS. NEOCLASSICAL ECONOMICS: TOPOLOGY, EVOLUTIONARY PROCESS, AND BOUNDS AND BARRIERS TO PERFECT RATIONALITY

As we have shown in the previous chapters, economies are complex, with many bilateral relations and with different possible types of relations, as soon as we allow for a most crucial characteristic of real economies, namely, *direct interdependence* and subsequent *direct interactions* among each two agents in a population.

9.1.1   The General Equilibrium Once Again

We have also mentioned the general idea of *neoclassical* 'mainstream' economics that excludes such direct interdependence through the assumption of perfectly informed agents who can *maximize* their objective functions in complete *isolation*, being dependent only on one type of external factor, namely the *price* vector (see Chapters 5 and 6). This ideal decentralized decision structure in a pure price-quantities world is called a *market*. Under this condition, agents can decide in full autonomy and isolation and are only *indirectly dependent* on each other, in the sense of being dependent only on the *sums of the quantity decisions* of all suppliers and demanders on all 'markets'. Aggregated supplies and demands on a particular market will equalize, i.e., so-called *excess demand* becomes zero, it is assumed, at a certain price. This is the equilibrium price of that partial market which leads to market clearing on that market.

The interrelations among the different market clearing prices and the quantity effects on the different partial markets that need to lead to a *simultaneous equilibrium* on all partial markets (the '*general equilibrium*'), however, remain a complex thing to solve (as shown in Chapter 6) logically and mathematically, since all agents have to recalculate their quantities (supplies and/or demands) for all partial markets if the price for only one partial market changes. This means that *all* prices and quantities in all partial markets will change as long as not all partial markets are in equilibrium simultaneously. They can only be cleared simultaneously. This is why neoclassical 'mainstream' economics is also called *General Equilibrium Economics* (or GET). Its research program was to prove that a general *pure 'market' economy* is feasible and the *optimal* thing in human history. There is nothing else needed in the economy except a 'market', if '*perfectly*' instituted and left alone, particularly by the state and other societal entities. However, as explained in Chapter 6, the interconnected quantity/price decisions of a great number of agents in a great number of partial markets may become a highly complex thing, and to ensure its feasibility at all may require a number of very specific presumptions.

That indirect interdependence mentioned is equivalent to the assumption of neoclassical 'market' economics that the *number of agents* is always so *large* that no one's decision has any realizable impact on the decision parameters of anyone else so that agents can ignore each other and pretend to be isolated maximizers. The assumption of a *very large number* of agents, in turn, is equivalent to the perspective of a *spot market* where all are present at the same time and same location, thus being always very many, an anonymous crowd.

The isolated maximizers also are *perfect* maximizers as they have everything they need for a perfect decision, particularly *perfect information*: They completely know both their 'inner' givens (their ordered objectives, costs or 'preferences') and the 'outer' givens, i.e., all prices. And if we include *intertemporal optimization*, e.g., of a given *initial stock of wealth* to be consumed over the span of a lifetime, or of *investment* of a stock of capital, agents also need to know all *future prices* in order to make optimal decisions, and to have a complex process come to a stable unique and optimal equilibrium. We will go into more detail below.

Finally, perfectly 'rational' agents need to be *all the same*, i.e., knowing one individual you basically know them all. The neoclassical agent thus is the *representative individual*. Their preferences may even be different, but this is not an issue for the ideal 'market' economy to be optimal. Particularly, the *functional forms of the objective functions* (utility functions of the consumers and profit functions of the suppliers), need to be the same, namely such that they can unambiguously be maximized. Particularly, they need to be *convex*. And optimality then basically refers to the marginal condition that all agents end up with the same marginal rate of substitution among the goods in their portfolios, given equilibrium prices.

9.1.2   Agents in Real Space: Proximity and Distance, and the Neighborhood Structure

In contrast, we have introduced above directly interdependent economies which immediately imply *initial strong strategic uncertainties* for the agents. The unavoidable subsequent interactions, nevertheless, need to be analyzed and explained, and related complex models to be specified.

For instance, real-world agents do not live in a 'spot market' but in *time* and *space*. This has fundamental implications.

First, they are *located* somewhere in a *relation* to each other, *close* or *distant* from each other, in a *geographical* and/or a *functional* (particularly economic) sense. We may consider a *lattice* (a grid, web, or net) where agents have their positions relative to each other, typically in continuously *overlapping localities* or 'regions'. Thus, some have *proximity*, some have *distance*, some are *direct neighbors*, some are *indirect neighbors* (having someone in between). It is obvious that *neighbors would interact more frequently* than indirect neighbors and/or that the behaviors of her closer neighbors in this way are weighted higher by an agent than those of more remote neighbors. The influence of indirect neighbors on an individual may nevertheless exist, although indirectly through the decisions of her direct neighbors only (who, in turn, are directly dependent on *their* neighbors' decisions, etc.).

Considering 'functional', or *economic proximities*, we may say that *direct competitors* may be 'closer' to each other (even though geographically distant) than non-competitors. In the same way, non-competitors who have a *supplier* relation with each other may also be economic neighbors (although may be geographically distant). Also, a *specialized professional group*, say those collaborating on a global inter-firm R&D project, or the top ranks of a global industry, or a group of economics professors of a specialized field, may be said to be functionally (economically) close even while dispersed over the globe.

Finally, while an agent may react to the action of a close competitor (say, an expansion of supply) in some way he may react to the same action of an (also close) supplier in a different way. Thus decisions may not be fully determined by direct neighborhood in a *functional* sense.

In social and economic systems, the topology is not necessarily a *Euclidian* space with an unambiguous *geographical distance* among agents (see Foley, 1998, 18ff.). In human socio-economies distance/closeness can be 'functional' in addition to geographical. Two agents can be *functionally close* (e.g., in the value-added chain) but at the same time geographically distant. There are also potential asymmetries involved: If *A* is a neighbour to *B* because *A*'s sales create demand for *B* upstream in the value-added chain, this is typically not true in reverse: *B*'s sales will not normally create demand for *A*. In the economy, or human society in general, therefore, an agent may react asymmetrically towards the same actions (say, a price increase) of his neighbors on two sides, *B* and *C*. Finally, economic distance may *not be additive*: The distance between *A* and *C* must not be the sum of the distances of *A* to *B* and *B* to *C*. In sum, economic distance may be non-Euclidian.

Second, agents rarely are 'very many' on a spot, but *few*, typically – an oligopolistic structure rather than a polypolistic one (as assumed in 'perfect markets'). However, agents in an oligopolistic structure are *directly interdependent*. We have applied that general characteristic of *real-world economic interaction systems* to the *typically oligopolistic structures of real-world 'markets'* in Chapter 4 above.

In Chapter 8, we have explained a number of complex models based on defined lattices or neighborhood structures, or what is called a *topology*. While the term topology denotes both topological spaces (structures with spatial properties) and the field of study of such structures as a branch of mathematics, we use the term here to specifically refer to the social structure of interaction as a spatial structure. The social structure consists of the relations between the agents. If a topology is assumed agents do not interact randomly but engage in structured interactions.

9.1.3 Knowledge, Rationality, Time: General Equilibrium and Evolutionary Process

As shown in Chapter 1, *initial strong strategic uncertainty* leads to somehow *'imperfect' rationality*. For instance, agents logically cannot know in the beginning of a repeated interaction (or in a definite one-shot interaction) the action the other one will take. As is immediately obvious from the neighborhood structure mentioned (and was in fact discussed in Chapter 8), the manifold simultaneous bilateral interactions taking place in a topology may generate a complex process throughout a whole population of agents that make up an economy. In fact, this process, if not a one-shot, will be *time-dependent* and *dynamic* in the sense that different agents may score differently in an interaction or a supergame and thus will *learn*, *imitate* or somehow else *adapt* differently, including having different *replication rates* over generations in a biological sense, dependent on their different payoff scores. In a word, the processes implied will be *evolutionary* which is why the research program of economics going beyond the special case of neoclassical economics mentioned may be labeled *Complexity Economics*.

The latter coincides in large parts with evolutionary mechanisms and processes which mostly are also complex. Thus, complexity economics largely converges with the older tradition of *Evolutionary Economics*.

In such an evolutionary process, it appears already intuitively, there are *limits to perfect 'rationality'* which exist beyond the initial strong strategic uncertainty mentioned. They stem from properties of the resulting complex dynamic, and in fact evolutionary, process. Firstly, there is what Foley has labeled *'computational complexity'* and *'bounds to rationality'* (Foley 1998, 34, 46, passim), i.e., the fact that *computation costs* may be disproportionately high as compared to the resources available (in terms of time and calculation capacity), the classical case of *'bounded rationality'* as mentioned already in Chapter 1. Secondly, the system's dynamics may be so complex as to make the calculation of 'rational' behavior even completely *logically* (i.e., mathematically) *infeasible.* An absolute *'barrier to rationality'* as termed by Foley, is where the problem at hand is *'undecidable'* or *'intractable'*, as no computer is able to come up with a solution within a finite time. We will explain and illustrate such situations later.

Note that this applies, first, to the economic researcher, being an 'impartial spectator' of a system under investigation, trying to explore the problems of 'optimal' behavior of individual agents involved as well as of the dynamics and a potential 'optimal' equilibrium of the system, and, second, to the hypothetical agents involved whose informational 'equipment' and calculation capabilities are investigated.

We will illustrate in the remainder of this chapter that with direct interaction the 'optimal rationality' as postulated by neoclassical 'market' economics is impossible to maintain – unless one sets such restrictions as to make a complex system very simple. This is not at all the end of economics but the beginning of a more relevant, substantial, realistic, and also formally analyzable economics.

In contrast to the perfect representative individual mentioned above we have already explained in Chapter 2 that the agents in a directly interdependent economy have *different options to behave* and different options to develop a *strategy*, which typically is equivalent to *different conceptions of rationality*. This already led us to argue that, with *individual interaction histories*, i.e., individual past *experiences* and related future *expectations*, as emerging in a lattice of distributed positions and recurrent interactions, under certain circumstances, *agents* easily may become *heterogeneous* – even if they started out as (a worst case) homogeneous short-run hyper-rational maximizers.

So far the current chapter repeated some aspects from earlier chapters, which are central to complexity economics. They are listed as issues (1) - (3) in Table 9.1 below; the other issues in the table, (4) and following, will form the thread, and also serve as a checklist for the student reader, for the remainder of this chapter.

Table 9.1 A universe of economies: The market-equilibrium special case and a universe of more complex interdependent-agents economies compared

Complexity Economics (e.g., Evolutionary Economics) / Directly interdependent economies	Neoclassical Economics (General-Equilibrium Economics)
(1) Direct interdependencies (between any two agents), entailing 'strategic' interactions, depending on their spatial (or economic) proximity.	(1) No direct interdependence (only indirect interdependence through equilibrium prices based on the sum of all individual excess demands (equiv. to the assumption that the no. of agents is so large that none has a realizable effect on others; thus agents can ignore each other and pretend to be isolated).
(2) 'Strong (strategic) uncertainty', with 'bounded rationality' or absolute 'barriers to rationality' in a resulting complex process.	(2) Perfect information (i.e., the equilibrium price vector is known, incl. present and future prices).
(3) Heterogeneous individual agents, possibly developing different 'rationalities' and strategies, depending on their individual past experiences and related future expectations.	(3) The 'representative individual': all agents are the same, all are perfectly 'rational', perfectly maximizing their objective (utility or profit) functions.
(4) Most information is 'local', emanating from interactions with their spatial (or economic) 'neighborhood'.	(4) Information is completely 'global' (same perfect information available to all).
(5) Local information spreads through many decentralized bilateral interactions which takes time; memory and monitoring efforts required to increase one's information ...	(5) Global information is costless and instantaneous, provided by a central and powerful agency, i.e., the 'auctioneer' (preventing exchange at non-equilibrium prices; no two-party bargaining or exchange; at equilibrium prices, decentralized, bilateral exchange is senseless: a central collective action at a spot market realizes the equilibrium).
(6) ... and to generate specific, though preliminary, expectations.	(6) 'Rational expectations'.

Table 9.1   (continued)

(7) Time-dependent action, dynamic and evolutionary system motions ('orbits').	(7) Time-independent action and system state, timeless system motion.
(8) Resulting in complex evolutionary processes with search, learning, imitation, adaptation, differential replication ...	(8) Resulting in a static general equilibrium i.e., a unique global attractor of the system.
(9) Specific system states unpredictable; inherent instability.	(9) System state is predictable; inherent static stability.
(10) Agents are (act and react) at least as complex as their environment, deploying experience, calculation, expectations and anticipation, search, creativity and experimentation; pursuing survival and evolutionary effectiveness rather than maximization.	(10) Agents are not complex, (re)act the same way, towards equilibrium; simplified trajectory.
(11) System states and orbits largely dependent on initial conditions.	(11) Equilibrium independent of initial conditions.
(12) High complexity: 'complex adaptive systems'; high 'computational complexity' and often logical infeasibility of a solution ('undecidability') ('bounds' and 'barriers' to 'rationality').	(12) Low inherent complexity; systems made simple by restrictive assumptions
(13) Even simple structures may generate complex trajectories; many different dynamics possible; a whole universe of levels of complexity opens up.	(13) Complex trajectories and different dynamics excluded by very specific assumptions.
(14) The policy 'solution': third-party (exogenous) intervention, introducing some global information; does not generate a simple stable system, though.	(14) The auctioneer is total policy (in neoclassical terms: the perfect market does not need any policy intervention).
(15) The institutional 'solution': Evolutionary-institutional emergence may stabilize processes based on complex decision structures; some self-organization as problem-solving (morphogenesis, autopoiesis) and some homeostasis become possible; particularly at 'meso'-sized platforms (populations or groups).	(15) The auctioneer also represents the social rules required for problem-solving, particularly when allowing or prohibiting 'market' exchange.

9.2 LOCAL AND GLOBAL INFORMATION, THE NEOCLASSICAL AND THE COMPLEXITY ECONOMICS APPROACHES, AND COMPLEX SYSTEM DYNAMICS

9.2.1 Local and Global Information and their Implications

In real-world direct interaction systems located in time and space, information primarily emanates from identification of other agents in the neighborhood and from *interactions with* those *neighbors*. These can be own interactions, past and present (the information on past ones depending on the agent's *memory* length), and interactions between two other agents in one's neighborhood (depending on the agent's capability to *monitor* a certain number of third-party interactions). Most *information is local* this way. And it also diffuses through countless decentral bilateral interactions. The basic difference between such local and global information is that local information is not necessarily uniform. Depending on factors of *diversification* such as search, experimentation, etc. and thus on *heterogeneous experience* from different local interactions, spreading information on cooperative behavior in some location may encounter spreading information on defective behavior emanating from some other locality. Thus, local information is unlikely to be homogeneous throughout the whole system (or population). Correspondingly, such heterogeneous experience will trigger heterogeneous *expectations* which cannot be qualified as being 'true' or 'false'. At best, they can be proper or improper for an agent in his specific environment when it comes to maximizing her long-run success. And the *algorithm* for an agent to utilize his experience with own and others' interactions in the neighborhood to *translate* it into his expectation and appropriate *behavior* needs to be specified in any model.

Note that with this already both individual action and system behavior are *time- and path-dependent*, and also inherently *unstable*, characterized by *complex evolutionary moves*, and *unpredictability*. Individual behavior obviously cannot be predetermined, given the heterogeneous information, but agents will have to be assumed as *searching* for further and more clear-cut information, as *learning*, *comparing* themselves with others, perhaps *imitating*, and *adapting* in different ways. This is equivalent to saying that *information provision is costly*, in terms of time, effort, and continuing uncertainty.

It also appears plausible already that such *agents* could easily be conceptualized as being (i.e., acting and reacting), at least as *complex* as their social environment. Such agents would clearly not maximize a one-dimensional objective function and be '*efficient*'. In complex models, agents typically have to struggle for mere *survival* in the short-run or for *long-run relative success*, improving one's relative position in the population or increasing one's evolutionary success, issues (4) - (10) in Table 9.1.

Compare the characterization above with the assumption of the neoclassical perfect 'market economy' of the '*market' providing full and costless information to everyone*. In fact, the information about prices is *genuinely collectively* generated with the help of a genuinely collective agency (the 'auctioneer') that first generates and then spreads the news about the equilibrium price vector. Since action is either formally forbidden or is not in the agent's interest, or just does not take place at non-equilibrium prices (depending on specific assumptions of the model), and thus bilateral decentralized bargaining does not occur, processing this information is quite an easy task for the agents. *Complexity* and *computation costs are low* for them, in fact zero. A solution of their optimization problem may be *feasible* with no costs. And their exchange action virtually will become a central collective action. These assumptions drastically simplify the trajectory from any initial starting point of the system: As equilibrium prices are determined and cried out, all (re-)act the 'right' way, towards equilibrium. At the equilibrium price, the same total quantity of any good will be offered and demanded, purchased and sold, meaning zero excess demand on any partial market. A static general equilibrium will result as the unique global attractor of the system.

And since, in an intertemporal model, the auctioneer also determines future prices (or, as is equivalent, the price of credit, or the 'true' real interest rate or discount factor) every agent must have true or '*rational expectations*', i.e., perfect knowledge about the future. In this way, both individual behavior and system behavior virtually are *time- (and path-) independent*. Individual behaviors and the system are inherently *stable*, their trajectories and final states *predictable*, complex trajectories excluded by assumptions (see issues (4) - (13) in the right-hand column of Table 9.1 for a check of these model properties).

9.2.2   Dynamics of a Linear System

Now, if we, in contrast to the specific neoclassical assumptions for a general equilibrium, consider and acknowledge some of the real-world properties of decentralized, multi-agent interaction systems, such as just *time dependence* (dynamics), even *simple model structures* may generate rather *complex system trajectories* (see Section 1.1 in Foley, op. cit.), i.e., different dynamics, qualitatively different from stable equilibrium. Consider a dynamic system of the form:

$$x_{t+1} = F(x_t), \tag{9.1}$$

representing the *state of a system* at time $t + 1$, where x_t is the *vector* at time t with, say, n components, changing through *time*, in a data space, or *state space X*. Each component may be in one of two possible states, say 1 for an agent who has cooperated at a certain point of time and 0 for an agent who has defected. F is an *operator* on the state space subject to important parameters of the system (for instance, certain conditions under which individual agents cooperate or defect or switch between these states).

Consider the *linear case* first. Here, F is a transformation matrix A so that

$$x_{t+1} = Ax_t. \tag{9.2}$$

The movement of this system depends on a crucial property of this matrix, i.e., its *eigenvalue* (see Box 9.1).

Box 9.1 Eigenvalues

The behavior of a *linear transformation A* is governed by its *eigenvalues* λ. If A is to transform an n-dimensional state vector x_t into an n-dimensional state vector x_{t+1} (t denoting the time),

$$x_{t+1} = Ax.$$

A takes the form of an $n \times n$ matrix. The eigenvalue λ together with a corresponding non-zero *eigenvector* v is defined as a scalar such that

$$\lambda v = Av.$$

A has n (n is the dimension) *single eigenvalues*, of which several may take the same value (double, triple, ... eigenvalues). The number of non-zero single eigenvalues is equal to the *rank* of A (its number of independent row vectors).

An eigenvalue with $|\lambda| < 1$ causes contractive motion, one with $|\lambda| > 1$ expansive motion. A complex eigenvalue (with non-zero imaginary part) causes a circular or spiral motion according to its angle from the positive real axis. A real negative eigenvalue without imaginary part (180° from the positive real axis) therefore causes an oscillation.

As an example consider a simple *Lotka-Volterra difference equation system*:

$$x_{1,t+1} = x_{1,t} + x_{2,t}$$

$$x_{2,t+1} = -x_{1,t} + x_{2,t}.$$

Therefore

$$A = \begin{pmatrix} 1 & 1 \\ -1 & 1 \end{pmatrix}.$$

This matrix is of rank 2 and must have 2 single non-zero eigenvalues. To compute these,

$$\lambda v = Av$$
$$0 = Av - \lambda v$$
$$0 = (A - \lambda I)v$$

where I is the unit matrix. Since $v \neq 0$,

$$0 = A - \lambda I$$
$$0 = det(A - \lambda I)$$
$$0 = det \begin{pmatrix} 1 - \lambda & 1 \\ -1 & 1 - \lambda \end{pmatrix}$$
$$0 = (1 - \lambda)^2 + 1$$
$$\lambda = 1 - \sqrt{-1}$$
$$\lambda_{1/2} = 1 \pm i.$$

Then we can derive the eigenvectors $v_{1/2}$ for the two eigenvalues and check whether the computation was correct with the definition of eigenvalue and eigenvector above. The eigenvectors are:

$$v_1 = \begin{pmatrix} 1 \\ i \end{pmatrix} \text{ for } \lambda_1 = 1 + i \text{ and } v_1 = \begin{pmatrix} 1 \\ -i \end{pmatrix} \text{ for } \lambda_1 = 1 - i.$$

Since both eigenvalues have a non-zero imaginary part, they yield a spiral motion, and since their absolute values are $|(1 \pm i)| = \sqrt{2} > 1$, their motion is expanding, therefore divergent.

This result is true as we can see for an example computation of the first 8 steps of such a system, starting with the initial values $x_0 = \begin{pmatrix} 1 \\ 1 \end{pmatrix}$ (see also Figure 9.1 below):

$$x_1 = \begin{pmatrix} 2 \\ 0 \end{pmatrix}; \ x_2 = \begin{pmatrix} 2 \\ -2 \end{pmatrix}; \ x_3 = \begin{pmatrix} 0 \\ -4 \end{pmatrix}; \ x_4 = \begin{pmatrix} -4 \\ -4 \end{pmatrix};$$
$$x_5 = \begin{pmatrix} -8 \\ 0 \end{pmatrix}; \ x_6 = \begin{pmatrix} -8 \\ 8 \end{pmatrix}; \ x_7 = \begin{pmatrix} 0 \\ 16 \end{pmatrix}; \ x_8 = \begin{pmatrix} 16 \\ 16 \end{pmatrix}.$$

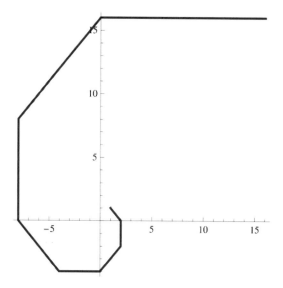

Figure 9.1   2-dimensional development of the dynamical system x(t)

Each eigenvalue (see Box 9.1) governs a component of the behavior of the system. If an eigenvalue of *A* is a *real, positive* number the system will *expand* (if the value > 1) *or contract* (if < 1) along an arrow (which, in turn, is the corresponding *eigenvector* of *A*, i.e., *x*). The action of that matrix on that (positive, non-zero) vector then changes its magnitude but not its direction. If an eigenvalue of *A* is a *real, negative* number the system will 'flip' from one side of the origin to the other, back and forth.

The third case possible is a more complicated one, in terms of numerics: For any complex value in the matrix (consisting of a *real* and an *imaginary* component) there is a pair of eigenvalues that are also *complex numbers*, where the imaginary component may, however, have either a positive or a negative sign. In the case of complex eigenvalues, it has been demonstrated in Box 9.1, that the system will *spiral inward or outward*.

Across these three cases of the system's motion, some specific *magnitudes of the eigenvalues* determine the stability of the motion: Only when the *absolute eigenvalues* are *smaller than 1* will the system be stable and move towards the origin, a *stable equilibrium* (either directly or while flipping, as explained). However, if the absolute eigenvalue is *greater than 1* the system will *move away from the origin* (again either directly or while flipping), i.e., no stable equilibrium. (The special cases are: With the eigenvalue being equal to +1, the system will remain at any initial state. If it equals -1, the system will oscillate around the origin at a stable distance. If a pair of complex eigenvalues has magnitude 1, the system will rotate around the origin on a stable circle through the starting point.)

Now, any *actual motion* of a linear dynamic system can easily be *very complex* if all three types of eigenvalues appear in the matrix. As has been proved elsewhere in the literature, such a complex actual motion will always be composed from a *combination of the three component motions* mentioned (see Foley, 1998, p. 4, for references). A general strategy to approach the analysis of the resulting system movement thus would be to consider the absolute eigenvalues of A that are greater than 1.

If all types of eigenvalues would be represented in A and all eigenvalues would be greater than 1 the system will indeed have a complex 'exploding' orbit. If only one type of eigenvalue is larger than 1 the related component motion will be quantitatively dominating sooner or later so that the system will move away from the origin according to that component motion (expansion on a ray, expanding 'flipping', or outward spiraling). If all types of eigenvalues would be exactly 1 the system would display a complex orbit that would be indefinitely repeated identically. And *only if the absolute values of all types of eigenvalues present in A would be smaller than 1 the system would converge to a stable equilibrium.*

In this way, the motions of linear dynamic systems can be decomposed, identified, analyzed, and predicted. Also, marginal and smooth changes of the parameters (i.e., the elements of A, i.e., its eigenvalues) entail marginal and smooth changes in the system's behavior, another comfortable property of linear dynamic systems: If parameters (eigenvalues) are changed (1) from positive real values < 1 through $= 1$ to > 1, or (2) from negative real values (< 0) through 0 to > 0, the system trajectories will change (1) from inward to outward motions, or (2) slow down, stop and reverse direction (for graphical illustrations, see also Foley 1998, p. 7).

In sum, you can see that even from a simple linear system structure very complex dynamics can easily emerge, and that a *stable equilibrium is to be considered a quite special case* in the range of possible dynamics of such a simple structure.

9.2.3 Dynamics of a Nonlinear System

Linear systems have the convenient property that they behave proportionally in all regions of the state space. However, this is not the case for *nonlinear dynamic systems* which behave *differently in different regions of the state space*.

The easiest way to proceed from a linear to a nonlinear system is to consider a nonlinear system as a so-called *perturbation* of the linear system (see Foley, op. cit., 7ff.), i.e., adding a 'small' term to the more easily describable (initial) linear formulation, in terms of a so-called *power series*. A power series in a variable is an infinite series of the form

$$F(x) = \sum_{n=0}^{\infty} a_n(x - c)^n = a_1(x - c)^1 + a_2(x - c)^2 + \cdots.$$

A power series typically is used to approximate a not exactly solvable problem, or a not exactly describable function, by starting from the exact description of a solvable problem, i.e., from an exactly describable function, by adding successively less important deviations from that exactly describable function. Here, a_n is a coefficient of the n-th term, c a vector of constants, and x a vector around c. Often c is equal to zero and the power series takes a simpler form of a *Maclaurin Series*:

$$F(x) = \sum_{n=0}^{\infty} a_n x^n.$$

In the case of the *representation of a function* as a power series, the added terms are calculated from the values of the known function's derivatives evaluated at a certain point. More specifically, a_n is the n-th derivative of the function which we will approximate, evaluated at the point around which we approximate, $a_n = F^{(n)}(c)$. In this case the power series assumes the form of a so-called *Taylor Series*. The Taylor Series is the following power series:

$$F(x) = \sum_{n=0}^{\infty} \frac{[F^{(n)}(c)](x - c)^n}{n!}$$
$$= \frac{F(c)}{0!} + \frac{[F'(c)](x - c)}{1!} + \frac{[F''(c)](x - c)^2}{2!} + \cdots.$$

It approximates the value of the function $F(\cdot)$ at point x which lies close to point c. In the case of the nonlinear system as described by Equation 9.2 where the operator F_a is not linear, we may suppose that the origin of the state space is a stable equilibrium:

$$F_a(0) = 0.$$

In the neighborhood of the origin, the motion of this nonlinear system can be approximated using the Taylor series:

$$F(x) = \frac{[F_a(0)]}{0!} + \frac{[F_a'(0)](x_t)}{1!} + \frac{[F_a''(0)](x_t)^2}{2!} + \cdots. \tag{9.3}$$

If the system starts at the origin it will stay there. If, however, the system starts at x_t, a point close to the origin, the system moves away from that point and its state in the next period is approximated as x_{t+1} in Equation 9.3. This functional form illustrates that the motions of the system change as the system moves in the state space.

However, contrasting to the linear systems, the eigenvalues of the system are not necessarily static. The eigenvalues are again the eigenvalues of the transformation matrix consisting of all partial derivatives of all components of the Transformation Equation 9.3 (the equation has one component for each component of the vector x_{t+1}) with respect to all components of the vector x_t resulting in a quadratic matrix. In the case of a linear system, all derivatives are scalars, and therefore all components of the transformation matrix are scalars. In the nonlinear case, the transformation matrix contains functions. Therefore the eigenvalues will in most cases also not be scalars but functions of the state vector x_t. If this function yields (for given x_t) a number with an absolute value smaller than 1, the system will behave like a stable system, if not the system will be unstable. Therefore the behavior of the system itself depends on the state vector. A stable system may become unstable and vice versa. For an example and some details of the theory of chaos and bifurcation, see Section 9.2.5 below.

The system may wander indefinitely, *never exactly repeating* its earlier orbit. The system's movement then is *unpredictable*. This is called a *chaotic* behavioral pattern.

9.2.4   Chaotic and Complex Dynamics

Generally, *chaos* can be *generated deterministically* by relatively simple systems, particularly simple *nonlinear difference or differential equations* (Equation 9.3 is an example of the latter). A more simple case than the Taylor Series above, in fact, a Taylor Series truncated to its first two terms, is the following quadratic difference equation (the much used 'logistic function' of biological growth under a resource constraint):

$$x_{t+1} = a(x_t - x_t^2). \tag{9.4}$$

For certain values of the parameter (or matrix) a, the variable (or vector) x may exhibit equilibrium-growth ('steady-state'), or periodic behavior, for other values of a, x may show an extremely complicated dynamics. Thus, chaotic fluctuations can all be produced deterministically through this function (see also, e.g., Jarsulic 1998). Chaotic systems have *asymptotic trajectories* (or *'attractors'*) *only in parts* of their state space while these are absent in others. This does not imply that they are not locally predictable or have no statistical regularities at all. We define 'chaotic' trajectories more exactly and illustrate such behavior in greater detail in Section 9.2.5 below.

From Equation 9.4 we see that, for instance, when the linear part of the function is destabilizing, according to an absolute magnitude of the eigenvalues of the matrix a being > 1, the nonlinear element may become stabilizing as the system moves further away from the origin. When these two forces incidentally may perfectly balance each other a circle orbit at some distance around the origin may emerge, a so-called *limit circle*. This, however, breaks up again as soon as we further increase a and will be replaced by ever more different cycles and, finally, by a chaotic movement.

Again, trajectories starting at different points will diverge so that *'initial conditions'* (i.e., their 'starting points' or initial parameter values) *matter*, and such divergence would lead to ever larger 'errors of prediction' if one would predict trajectories in terms of 'harmony', 'stability' and 'equilibrium'.

Chaotic systems often have been considered purely 'stochastic', i.e., without any regularities. However, they may have some regular stochastic behavior, but their stochastic regularities also may be very complex. The dynamical behavior of a chaotic system cannot be reduced or broken down into disjoint subsets of its domain. It has been said that chaotic systems 'mix' over time, which implies that periodic orbits, if they occur, cannot be stable (see, e.g., Jarsulic 1998, 60).

Note that we have introduced so far four types of complex dynamic behavior emerging from linear or nonlinear system structures (see Foley 1998, 50ff.):

- stability of (or towards) a unique, globally attracting equilibrium state;
- stability of (or towards) regular motions (*periodic oscillations or orbits*, with possibly very long distances and with complicated and even varying paths between two periodic attractors);
- chaotic behavior, trajectories are non-repeating patterns, small changes in initial conditions have large effects, statistical regularities can be observed in the evolving patterns;
- behavior at the edge of chaos, trajectories are non-repeating patterns, small changes in initial conditions spread out at first but eventually contract, statistical regularities cannot be observed.

As argued before, direct interdependence and direct interactions among agents are one condition of complex dynamics (see also Brock 1988, p. 82).

9.2.5   General Properties of Dynamic Systems

Every *dynamic system* consists of a *state vector* x_t of degree (number of *components*) D and dependent on the time t and a *transformation function F* (see Equation 9.1). From this transformation function a *transformation matrix A* is constructed containing the marginal effects of all components of the current state vector x_t on each component of the future state vector x_{t+1}. These effects are equal to the first derivatives, therefore the transformation matrix A is equal to the *Jacobi matrix of F*:

$$A = \begin{pmatrix} \dfrac{\partial x_{t+1,1}}{\partial x_{t,1}} & \dfrac{\partial x_{t+1,1}}{\partial x_{t,2}} & \cdots & \dfrac{\partial x_{t+1,1}}{\partial x_{t,D}} \\ \dfrac{\partial x_{t+1,2}}{\partial x_{t,1}} & \dfrac{\partial x_{t+1,2}}{\partial x_{t,2}} & \cdots & \dfrac{\partial x_{t+1,2}}{\partial x_{t,D}} \\ \cdots & \cdots & \cdots & \cdots \\ \dfrac{\partial x_{t+1,D}}{\partial x_{t,1}} & \dfrac{\partial x_{t+1,D}}{\partial x_{t,2}} & \cdots & \dfrac{\partial x_{t+1,D}}{\partial x_{t,D}} \end{pmatrix}.$$

For a linear dynamic system, all the derivatives are scalars, therefore A only contains scalars (see Box 9.1 again). The *eigenvalues* of the linear transformation are computed by the equation

$$\lambda v = Av,$$

where

$$v \neq 0$$

are the *eigenvectors* corresponding to the eigenvalues λ. This yields

$$0 = A - \lambda$$

and the *characteristic equation*

$$0 = det(A - \lambda)$$

from which λ may be computed. For an example see again Box 9.1. For a *nonlinear system*, the components of A, as well as its eigenvalues are likely not static but functions of x_t. Since the behavior of the system is governed by the eigenvalues, the behavior is dependent on the state vector x_t and may change, and may even switch from stability to instability and vice versa as the system develops.

The state space of the system is characterized by the *fixed points*, especially the attractors (stable fixed points) and the distribution of the *stable areas*. A fixed point in the state space is a particular value x_t with

$$x_{t+1} = x_t$$

that is, the system remains at this point, once it has reached the point. (Note that a valid set of eigenvalues for this transformation would be a set of eigenvalues that are all $\lambda = 0$).

An *attractor* is a fixed point or (for complex attractors) a set of points (1) that the system remains in forever once the set is reached (by definition, this is true for fixed points) and (2) that is surrounded by a stable area from which the trajectories contract towards the attractor.

The distribution of stable areas is determined by the eigenvalues. Every eigenvalue governs a motion of the system. The behavior is contracting if the absolute value of all eigenvalues is $|\lambda| < 1$, expansive if it is $|\lambda| > 1$. As the *trajectories* converge in the contracting case, the system tends to be stable for eigenvalues $|\lambda| < 1$. Contracting motion approaches an attractor (a stable fixed point). If an eigenvalue is $|\lambda| = 1$, the corresponding motion is neither contracting nor expanding, but a so-called *limit cycle*; the motion of the system maintains a constant distance from the attractor.

If the eigenvalues are continuous functions of x_t, the stable area is bordered by the limit cycles $|\lambda| = 1$ for all eigenvalues.

A *bifurcation* is a point in continuous parameters (or even in endogenous variables) where the properties of the system change qualitatively, for example, if one attractor becomes unstable and gives rise to a new, different attractor; in the example below a pitchfork bifurcation is shown, that replaces a stable fixed point with an attractor consisting of two period-2 fixed points.

The behavior of a system is said to be *deterministically chaotic* if no regularities, e.g., similarities of the behavior for different, at least for similar initial values are present. The direct consequence is the impossibility to make any forecast for particular initial values without exact simulation of the system for these values. There are various approaches as to how to define and consequently how to detect deterministic chaos. The most widely used are those using the *Lyapunov exponents* and *autocorrelations*. The Lyapunov exponent is a measure of the change of the distance of trajectories in time. If this distance is generally growing in a system, the system is said to be chaotic. The *autocorrelation function* for a certain time lag τ correlates values of timeseries of a dynamic variable with the same value τ time units later. The falling apart of the autocorrelation functions, i.e., the vanishing of a regular stable autocorrelation is also used as an indication of the presence of deterministic chaos.

The concept of *complexity* is broader than, but related to, deterministic chaos. The complexity of a dynamic system may be seen as the information needed for a complete description of the system. A system with maximal complexity is therefore a system that cannot be described with less information than that necessary to represent the system itself (this tends to be the case for deterministically chaotic systems); but a system can of course be much less complex.

As an example, we consider again the nonlinear, one dimensional logistic map (see Equation 9.4):

$$x_{t+1} = a(x_t - x_t^2).$$

This function depends on a parameter $0 \leq a \leq 4$ and maps a state space $0 \leq x_t \leq 1$ into itself. The properties of the system depending on the parameter a can therefore be depicted in a two dimensional plot (see Figure 9.2 below). Although it is a one-dimensional map and thus a very simple nonlinear system, it exhibits for different values of a a number of different behaviors ranging from entirely stable to a periodic system with an attractor consisting of two points with

$$x_{t+2} = x_t$$

through deterministic chaos.

We start by computing the fixed points (for simplicity neglecting the indices)

$$x = ax - ax^2.$$

The first solution is obvious $x_{FP1} = 0$. To compute a second solution different from the first one, we can divide by x:

$$1 = a - ax$$

yielding

$$x_{FP2} = \frac{a-1}{a}.$$

For $a < 1$ only the first fixed point is in the valid state space, for $a = 1$ the two fixed points are equal $x_{FP1} = x_{FP2} = 0$, for $a > 1$, the fixed points are different and both valid solutions. So which of them is stable for which values of a?

The transformation matrix of this system is one dimensional:

$$A = \frac{\partial F(x)}{\partial x} = a - 2ax.$$

The single eigenvalue of this system is therefore also easily computed from

$$a - 2ax - \lambda = 0$$

since

$$\lambda = a - 2ax.$$

The eigenvalue is a continuous, linear and strictly decreasing function of x. Thus, for each value of a, there must be an upper limit cycle $\lambda_{LC1}(x) = -1$ and a lower limit cycle $\lambda_{LC1}(x) = 1$ and with $\lambda_{LC1} > \lambda_{LC2}$. The region of the state space between the two is governed by contractive motion and will approach one of the two fixed points provided they fall into this region.

The two limit cycles are easily computed as

$$x_{LC1} = \frac{a + 1}{2a}$$

and

$$x_{LC2} = \frac{a - 1}{2a}.$$

The first fixed point is stable for $a \leq 1$, otherwise unstable, the second one is stable for a larger than or equal to 1 but smaller than or equal to an a for which the fixed point leaves the stable area crossing the upper limit cycle. As may be computed by setting the second fixed point equal to the upper limit cycle, this point is $a = 3$. For $a > 3$, both fixed points are unstable and a bifurcation occurs. A stable period-2 solution emerges (thus a pair of period-2 fixed points) that are computed by

$$x = F(F(x)) = a(ax - ax^2) - a(ax - ax^2)^2$$

which yields two period-2 fixed points

$$x_{FP3/4} = \frac{a+1}{2a} \pm \sqrt{\frac{a^2 - 2a - 3}{4a^2}}.$$

The lower one of the period-2 fixed points (x_{FP4}) enters the stable area again, only to cross the lower limit cycle towards the lower unstable area at $a_c = 1 + \sqrt{8} \approx 3.8284$. The system of x_{FP3} and x_{FP4} however becomes unstable even earlier (for a smaller a) since the eigenvalues of the period-1 system are not valid any more for the period-2 system. For a range below a_c, stable solutions for different even periods emerge (period 4, period 6, period 8, etc.); starting at a_c however, as May (1976) puts it, there are cycles with every integer period, as well as an uncountable number of asymptotically aperiodic trajectories. This situation in turn was proven to be chaotic by Li and Yorke (1975) (see Figure 9.2 for illustration).

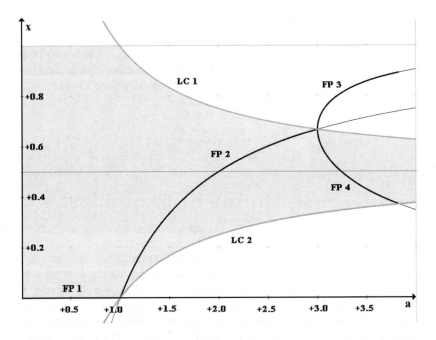

Figure 9.2   State space of the logistic map depending on the parameter a, with the fixed points FP 1–FP 4, the limit cycles LC 1 and LC 2, and the stable area shaded

9.2.6   Social Systems and Economic Space

As mentioned earlier, the neoclassical perfect-equilibrium 'market' economy restricts the real world, among others, to a *representative individual*. One of the neoclassical ideal settings is a *pure exchange economy* where every individual agent is *initially endowed* with a *stock of wealth* (in terms of exchangeable goods). Every agent then is supposed to be both buyer and seller, supplier and consumer, with no distinctive producers in the narrow sense. The market economy equilibrium requires a price vector such that all partial markets are in equilibrium, i.e., in states of *market clearance*. Every partial market then needs to exhibit a net demand (or net supply), i.e., an *excess demand of zero*.

Neoclassical economics, however, in this way generates a *paradox special case*: When the equilibrium price vector is publicly announced, agents, we would assume, find themselves in a state of being either a seller or a buyer so that their individual excess demands sum up to zero per partial market. However, if all agents strictly are the same kind (the 'representative agent') they will have to assume the same state when the equilibrium price is announced. This leads to the very special case of *every individual* agent's excess demand being zero (and not only their sum per partial market), the paradox implication being that there is *no actual exchange at all* (see Foley, op. cit., 21f.).

Therefore, Albin and Foley (1988) have modeled a decentralized exchange system *without an auctioneer* instead and in a world of *direct interaction*. Agents are still identical in their tastes and utility functions, but have *different endowments* and thus *different excess demand functions in prices*. The assumption of a spot market with a global public market price announcement is relaxed, but the agents are *arrayed in a topology* rather and do directly *exchange with their neighbors only*. In this way, the various geographical (local) submarkets are indirectly linked. As agents are allowed to exchange directly, they consequently are also allowed to *exchange at non-equilibrium prices*.

Particularly, n agents are located on a *one-dimensional topology*, i.e., a *circle* where each has $k = 1$ neighbors on each side (a 'radius-1 neighborhood'), i.e., *two neighbors* (the radius, however, may be a parameter in the model, with higher values given, e.g., two, three or more neighbors on each side). Since each agent has two possible states (the info bits 'on/off', 'buy/sell' or 'Cooperate/Defect', indicated as '0/1'), each of the interconnected local submarkets of three agents (i.e., radius 1) may have eight possible configurations (three-digit bytes: 000, 001, 010, 011, 100, 101, 110, 111) depending on an adaption algorithm (to be determined), based on one's own and one's two neighbors' actions. (The full description of the state of an agent in a certain period includes the quantities of the goods she holds and the memory of the neighbors' supplies and demands in terms of quantities and prices.) As said, agents just interact locally and have different initial endowments. In this way, even while agents are kept largely identical in terms of their objective (utility) functions, they do not have the same global information and do not behave the same way. In fact, agents have bounded rationality this way.

As said, agents have initial endowments $\{x_1, x_2\}$ of the two goods x_1 and x_2 which they can trade with their neighbors. Let their identical utility functions be $U = x_1 x_2$. At an *indifference curve* where utility is constant and thus $U' = 0$ (equivalent to the first-order condition of utility maximization), $U' = x_1 \partial x_2 + \partial x_1 x_2 = 0$ so that agents' exchange rate of the goods (their marginal rate of substitution, or their willingness to pay for a good in terms of giving a quantity of the other good, or the relative price of the goods) is $\frac{\partial x_2}{\partial x_1} = \left| \frac{x_2}{x_1} \right|$ (where ∂x_1 is the partial derivative of the utility function with respect to x_1).

Trade is motivated now by *differences in the initial endowments* of the agents i, e_{1i} and e_{2i}. The agents only know about their own endowments, though. The total endowment of the two goods in the economy is assumed to be such that the market equilibrium price will be unity, which, however, the agents do not know either. While the individual endowments are different, they are subject to the condition that the individual's wealth at the equilibrium price would be the same for all individuals, $e_1^* + e_2^*$. But the initial offer prices will differ because of the different (initial) portions of e_1 and e_2. This will motivate the agents to trade in order to improve their endowments (and utilities). Each agent, in fact, must find out about the possibilities of trading with his neighbors, about offering and buying prices and quantities.

Obviously, a very complex process of revealing the willingness to trade and the prices offered and demanded will start to evolve. Nevertheless, a simulation of such a setting could mimic the ideal neoclassical textbook model of the perfect market in equilibrium (Foley, op. cit., pp. 16, 22, 58-61, and Ch. 5). Model simulations have shown that agents in this model indeed may achieve a Pareto-efficient allocation of goods where no further mutually advantageous trading opportunities exist. A perfect 'market' can be reproduced under certain conditions on that direct-interaction basis, working, as it is supposed to, to redistribute initial endowments and to even out the proportions in which agents hold the two goods. In this way, agents may attain their household optima where their consumption structures reflect their identical preferences and the economy-wide goods supplies of x_1 and x_2 (the total endowments). This decentralized system of a 'market' thus may meet the criterion of marginal efficiency where the marginal rate of substitution of the goods, $\frac{\partial x_2}{\partial x_1} = \left|\frac{x_2}{x_1}\right|$, becomes the same across all agents and equals the economy-wide rate, so that the equilibrium price may indeed be determined in a decentralized direct-interaction process with only local information and exchanges at non-equilibrium prices. Note that this is a specific result that is *one* possibility emerging under specific conditions in that model of a market, based only on direct local interactions.

We do not delve deeper here into the details of the model, the process, and the system trajectory emerging (for more details, see Foley, op. cit., Section 1.6.4 and Chapter 5). You have learned more on the *marginal conditions of efficient equilibrium* in the conventional neoclassical 'market' economy in Chapter 5 above.

However, a notable, and unavoidable, by-product of direct interdependence, exchange at disequilibrium prices, and uneven initial distribution of wealth, is that while this 'market' may be marginally efficient it also creates a *systematic inequality of wealth* endowment. This applies in spite of the careful design of the model that would create an even wealth distribution if the system would jump to equilibrium in one step, i.e., if it were a conventional neoclassical model with an auctioneer. This effect is not much considered in mainstream economics. Mainstream economics does not care about distribution since this is not part of its efficiency conditions which are purely *marginal* conditions (while wealth distribution is not an object of marginal analysis, as reflected particularly by the *Pareto* criterion). However, as soon as we *allow for trade taking place at disequilibrium prices*, as is necessarily the case in a really *decentralized system with only local direct interactions* and information, agents *redistribute wealth* while trading and at the same time evening out their marginal rates of substitution of the goods and determining the global equilibrium price.

How does this come about? Agents with initial endowments very different from $x_2/x_1 = 1:1$ and thus with very different price offers for the goods (for instance, very high price offers for goods they have very little quantity of) will have to make most of their *exchanges at rather unfavorable prices*, since they are in particular need of one of the two goods. By paying such unfavorable prices they in fact transfer wealth to those agents whose endowments are closer to the economy-wide structure of goods and thus the prices they pay are closer to the final equilibrium prices.

Note again that this model reflects some effective 'market' that may generate a specific 'optimal' distribution, i.e., a Pareto-optimal allocation of goods at the equilibrium prices detected. But since it is *not a Walrasian market* where agents are barred from exchange at non-equilibrium prices (the one we have introduced above and explained as the usual neoclassical 'mainstream' model in more detail in Chapter 5 above), the result is less a support for the conventional neoclassical mainstream model of the 'perfect market', but rather a first indication of the *possibility of self-organization* of agents in a complex system based on local interaction and local information only (see also Foley, op. cit., 60f.). The latter is a possibility of a complex-system trajectory. We will get back to this 'institutionalized self-organization' solution at the end of this chapter.

9.3   A QUASI-NEOCLASSICAL PERFECT-EQUILIBRIUM MODEL BASED ON GLOBAL INFORMATION AND DIRECT INTERDEPENDENCE

Generating a unique stable equilibrium through agents who perfectly rationally maximize given objective functions over time requires a considerable *reduction of complexity* such that the reality content of the setting may disappear. Two crucial assumptions of this *'rational choice'* program are, first, *excluding any direct interaction* between agents (supposing none of them has any measurable impact) and, second, supposing that the *informational endowments* of agents are given as *public goods*, i.e., as *full global information*.

Well-known problems of this program with its isolated individualistic perfect maximization are, first, the fact that the objective function is 'inherently unobservable, so that it is not clear what explanatory advantage its presence in the theory confers' (Foley, op. cit., 24), and, second, 'the hypothesis of rationality puts no observational restrictions on an agent's actions. We can always rationalize behavior by positing an appropriate objective function' (id., op. cit., 23). As already discussed in Chapter 1 above, some rule-based behavior, although apparently 'irrational' as viewed through a neoclassical lens, may be better explicable and even better predictable than such hyper-rational behavior, if more realistic conditions are assumed.

The issue at hand in this chapter, however, is to consider the *costs of information processing*, given *limited computability* as existing in the real world, i.e., *boundaries to rationality*, or the logical infeasibility of a mathematical solution to an optimization problem, i.e., absolute *barriers to rationality*, both connected to certain degrees of complexity of system behavior (id., op. cit., 25). As we have explained, simple structures may lead to very complex system behaviors, where already finding some solution may imply considerable computational complexity and even computational infeasibility – and an 'optimal' solution can hardly be determined.

We will consider now how bounds and barriers to neoclassical 'rationality' may emanate even from the strict neoclassical setting.

9.3.1   An Isolated Optimal Lifetime Consumption Problem

We consider a simple neoclassical model, the decision problem of an isolated single agent – a restricted initial setting (Foley, op. cit., Section 1.3.3). Assume an isolated agent with a finite lifetime of T periods (known to him) and with an initial stock of wealth of W_0 of which he has no reason to spare something beyond his lifetime. W can be invested at an interest rate r. Alternatively, parts of W can be consumed in the magnitude C, where the following holds at any period:

$$W_{t+1} = (1 + r)(W_t - C_t). \tag{9.5}$$

For the sake of simplicity, we assume that the agent's utility function is the sum of the natural logarithms of his consumption over his lifetime, where future utility is discounted with $0 < \beta < 1$.

Thus, the agent's decision problem is to choose the *optimal consumption vector over time* $(C_0, C_1, C_2, \ldots, C_T)$ so that

$$\max \; (\log(C_0) + \beta \log(C_1) + \beta^2 \log(C_2) + \cdots + \beta^T \log(C_T)) \tag{9.6}$$
$$= \sum_{t=0}^{T} \beta^t \log(C_t)$$

where $W_{T+1} = !\, 0$ in an optimal lifetime consumption path (no bequests are made).

The *Lagrange* algorithm of which you have learned the details in Chapter 5, transforms this problem of optimally 'rational' decision-making on consumption into a dynamical system. Basically, the Lagrange function reformulates the original (objective) function, Equation 9.6, by subtracting the condition, or constraint, Equation 9.5. The latter is, first, set zero and, second, multiplied with the so-called Lagrange multiplier (called P in our case). The Lagrange algorithm is used for maximization under a given constraint (a maximum or minimum limit). Instead of the original function this Lagrange function will be maximized. The Lagrange function $\mathcal{L}$ in the case at hand is the following:

$$\max \mathcal{L}(\{W_t + 1, C_t, P_t\}_{t=0}^{T}) \tag{9.7}$$
$$= \sum_{t=0}^{T} \beta^t \{log(C_t) - P_t[W_{t+1} - (1+r)(W_t - C_t)]\}.$$

Maximizing the Lagrange function requires calculation of the first-order conditions of $\mathcal{L}$, i.e., the partial derivatives with respect to all three variables are to be set to zero:

$$(\beta^{-t})\frac{\partial \mathcal{L}}{\partial C_t} = \frac{1}{C_t} - (1+r)P_t = ! \ 0 \tag{9.8}$$

$$(\beta^{-t})\frac{\partial \mathcal{L}}{\partial W_{t+1}} = -P_t + \beta \ (1+r)P_{t+1} = ! \ 0 \tag{9.9}$$

$$(\beta^{-t})\frac{\partial \mathcal{L}}{\partial P_t} = -W_{t+1} + (1+r)(W_{t+1} - C_t) = ! \ 0. \tag{9.10}$$

Since Equations 9.8 – 9.10 have to hold for all periods t, $0 \le t \le T$, this gives us a system of $3(T + 1)$ equations which have to hold simultaneously. The first condition Equation 9.8 informs us that

$$(1+r)P_t = \frac{1}{C_t} \tag{9.11}$$

and equals the marginal utility of consumption in each period, but is not a dynamic structure. The other two conditions, however, form a dynamic system which consists of

$$\beta(1+r)P_{t+1} = P_t \tag{9.12}$$

$$(1+r)(W_t - C_t) = W_{t+1}. \tag{9.13}$$

Inserting Equation 9.5 and Equation 9.11 in Equation 9.13 we get:

$$W_{t+1} = (1+r)(W_t - \frac{1}{(1+r)P_t}). \tag{9.14}$$

The optimal, or 'rational', decision (or series of decisions, or 'strategy', 'policy', or decision path) must be one of the many trajectories of this dynamic system. Setting P_T as a parameter initially and in this way determining the whole path of P_t, and inserting this into Equation 9.14 would determine the path of W_t. An optimal path must be based on such a P_T which makes $W_{T+1} = 0$.

Typically, there are many feasible trajectories, and the agent's decision problem would be to sort out the one with the highest value of utility over his life span. When the dynamical system resulting from the intertemporal optimization problem becomes complex or even chaotic, sorting out the optimal consumption plan can become a problem where the agent (or the economist calculating this system representative of the agent) will face bounds or barriers to rationality (see Foley, op. cit., 27f.).

9.3.2 A Quasi-Neoclassical 'Market' Model with Consumption and Investment

Also, in the conventional neoclassical structure of isolated maximizing agents (the *Walrasian* model as shown in Chapter 5), the resulting system behavior may become quite complex, as already the *individual excess demand functions* in the prices may be *complex nonlinear functions*. Therefore, neoclassical economics needs to strongly *simplify* in order to meet the objective of its research program, i.e., to demonstrate the equilibrating tendencies of 'market' economies. Among these simplifications is the requirement to make *agents fully identical* in preferences, technology, and initial endowment (see Section 5.4.2 and Chapter 6). But as said above, it has the paradoxical implication that at equilibrium prices no exchange takes place at all, i.e., the specific case of a situation where all individual excess demand vectors in all partial markets need to be zero. An extreme simplification required to prove the historical superiority of the 'market'. But even here some degree of complexity can be found.

Consider the following model of intertemporal equilibrium determination (see Foley, op. cit., 29 ff.): The economy has two goods, corn, K, and steel, S. To produce 1 K next period requires a_{SK} units of steel (in terms of agricultural tools and machines). Similarly, to produce 1 S requires a_{KS} units of corn (in terms of food for steel workers). The stocks of both goods depreciate at the discount rate δ each period. The *representative agent* starts with an initial endowment of K_0 and S_0. He *consumes* only corn each period, C_t, but in order to produce more corn he needs to produce steel (i.e., to *invest*) first. So the rational decision problem is to decide how much to invest and how much to consume.

We assume the same utility function to be maximized as in the previous example, with the same discount factor β for future utility (future consumption) as before. The utility maximization problem then is to choose $\{C_t, S_{t+1}, K_{t+1}\}_{t=0}^{\infty}$ so that

$$max \ \sum_{t=0}^{\infty} \beta_t \ log(C_t),$$

given the technological constraints

$$a_{SK} \left[K_{t+1} - (1 - \delta)K_t \right] \leq ! \; S_t$$

and

$$a_{KS} \left[S_{t+1} - (1 - \delta)S_t \right] \leq ! \; (K_t - C_t).$$

Again, the usual way to solve the problem is maximizing the objective function under the restrictions given (two technological restrictions and endowment restrictions in this case), i.e., the Lagrange function:

$$max \; \mathcal{L}(\{C_t, S_{t+1}, K_{t+1}, P_{St}, P_{Kt}\}_{t=0}^{\infty}) \qquad (9.15)$$
$$= \sum_{t=0}^{\infty} \beta^t \; log(C_t)$$
$$- \sum_{t=0}^{\infty} \beta^t \; P_{St}\{a_{SK}[K_{t+1} - (1 - \delta)K_t] - S_t\}$$
$$- \sum_{t=0}^{\infty} \beta^t \; P_{Kt}\{a_{KS}[S_{t+1} - (1 - \delta)S_t] - (K_t - C_t)\}.$$

The usual first-order conditions are:

$$\beta^{-t} \frac{\partial \mathcal{L}}{\partial C_t} = \frac{1}{C_t} - P_{Kt} = ! \; 0, \qquad (9.16)$$

and similarly $\beta^{-t} \frac{\partial \mathcal{L}}{\partial K_{t+1}}$, $\beta^{-t} \frac{\partial \mathcal{L}}{\partial S_{t+1}}$, $\beta^{-t} \frac{\partial \mathcal{L}}{\partial P_{St}}$, and $\beta^{-t} \frac{\partial \mathcal{L}}{\partial P_{Kt}}$ are to be calculated and all set zero (not given here, however). Since this is an infinite horizon problem we have an infinite number of first-order conditions and methods from dynamic programming have to be used to solve this system. These methods deserve book-length treatment and will not be discussed here.

From Equation 9.16 we get $C_t = \frac{1}{P_{Kt}}$ and we can substitute $\frac{1}{P_{Kt}}$ for C_t in the equation to be formed for $\beta^{-t} \frac{\partial \mathcal{L}}{\partial P_{Kt}}$. In this way, we get a nonlinear dynamical system from the first-order conditions for an extremum of the Lagrange function

$$P_{St} = \beta \left[\left(\frac{1}{a_{SK}}\right) P_{Kt+1} + (1 - \delta)P_{St+1} \right]$$
$$P_{Kt} = \beta \left[(1 - \delta)P_{Kt+1} + \left(\frac{1}{a_{KS}}\right) P_{St+1} \right]$$
$$S_{t+1} = (1 - \delta)S_t + \left(\frac{1}{a_{KS}}\right)\left(K_t - \frac{1}{P_{Kt}}\right)$$

$$K_{t+1} = (1 - \delta)K_t + \left(\frac{1}{a_{SK}}\right)S_t.$$

As in the earlier example of optimal lifetime consumption, the *optimal joint consumption and production plan* of any individual agent must be one of the trajectories of this dynamical system. (There typically is no unique equilibrium in the neoclassical general equilibrium setting.) There are some possibilities to reduce the set of possible candidates for the optimal consumption and production path that we do not discuss here.

Generally, as in the previous 'optimal consumption' example, the agent's problem is to not to set the initial so-called '*shadow price*' of corn (i.e., the *opportunity costs* of its consumption in terms of the quantity of the steel production foregone) too low or too high. In the first case, consumption would be too high so that the stock of corn would be exhausted and eventually become zero. In the second case, consumption would be too small, steel production thus too high, which never would increase the agent's consumption because of the high depreciation costs of the high steel stock.

The rational agent is required to calculate all trajectories of this system in order to sort out suboptimal and infeasible plans. This simplified 'market' structure is, as Foley (op. cit., 32) mentioned,

> fairly simple and exhibit(s) only a small range of the possible spectrum of (the) dynamical repertoire of nonlinear systems. In these cases it is possible (…) that the discovery of the market equilibrium is computationally feasible for highly motivated and clever agents, who might use methods of trial-and-error extrapolation to determine the consistent current prices of assets.

Note again that the clever auctioneer who calls out the current prices, consistent with current and future market clearings, can be substituted by the clever economist who runs the model or by the clever agent himself who calculates his optimal infinite behavioral sequence. If any of them is able to solve the problem, all of them are. But note also, that the conventional neoclassical 'market equilibrium' wisdom, with its implicit auctioneer, particularly gives no way in which 'the' market equilibrium (let alone complex equilibrium paths) would be arrived at. The Lagrange algorithm thus represents the representative individual's potential optimal decision. It has been illustrated above that even this setting (isolated individuals) leads to a dynamical system that may generate complex trajectories and prohibit any unique and stable equilibrium.

But even more so, such intertemporal rational choice models can exhibit very complex trajectories as soon as we loosen even the slightest restriction, as has been shown by Boldrin and Montrucchio (1986) and Benhabib and Day (1981). Any complex dynamical system may arise from an intertemporal identical-agent optimal-consumption model as soon as, for instance, several capital goods are allowed for (see Foley, ibid.). Trajectories arising then may be chaotic, for instance.

It is well known that chaotic behavior can arise in a wide range of economically relevant intertemporal models. 'These mathematical facts raise serious questions for the methodological plausibility of the Walrasian equilibrium concept that underlies these models (...) what warrant do we have for regarding Walrasian equilibrium as a relevant model of real market interactions?' (Foley, op. cit., 33).

9.4   A POLICY SOLUTION AND THE EMERGENT-INSTITUTIONS SOLUTION

Within the wide range defined by the extremes of pure local information emerging exclusively from neighborhood interaction and pure global knowledge provided by some central agency (the 'auctioneer'), system stability and trajectory predictability might emerge from 'some' global information in a decentralized direct-interaction system. Some global information may be either generated and provided through an *exogenous agency* (a *policy* agent, a neutral advisor or a public policy agent), i.e., the 'policy solution', or through the emergence of a social rule (or institution) from a process of interactively and informally solving the complex stability and coordination (or often cooperation) problem through interactively learning to behave rule-based and to follow a long-run and thoughtful rationality rather than 'autistic' short-run maximization.

9.4.1   Emergent Institutions with Policy

Albin and Foley (op. cit., 18, passim and Ch. 4) have modeled the 'exogenous-agent'/third party idea within a direct-interdependence topology. They model a public agent (a central bank, for instance, in the case of monetary policy), the measures of which are common knowledge available to each private agent. Such global information is considered 'weak' in the sense that it does not replace the local information but comes on top of it. They introduce into the topology of private agents a *public agent* at a special site (on a different plane) which is a *neighbor to all private agents*. In this way all private agents receive some same, common and public, information. The informational unit is of the same dimension and size as the information that the individuals receive as a result of their decentralized interactions in their neighborhoods.

Consider that agents can assume the states +1 and -1 only (or C=cooperate and D=defect) and will do so according to an *algorithm* based on their current own, their memorized own, and their monitored third-party interactions in a neighborhood, past and present. Then the public policy agent can add another informational unit (confirmation or challenge of the state an agent has assumed on that informational basis, i.e., a 'pro-cyclical' or 'anti-cyclical' policy) by adding another '+1' or '-1' to each agent's information stock, which somehow has to be processed by the agent, who will then have to reconsider her latest decision.

Depending on the algorithm governing that transformation of experienced and perceived local interactions into individual decisions, simulations of this model yield the result that the impact of policy is not at all clear and uniform. Complexity levels can be reduced but also increased by the public information supplement. Therefore, 'solutions' in terms of equilibrating and stabilizing tendencies may become easier or more difficult.

Obviously, an issue here is the relative weight the public decision has for the decisions of the individuals, be it either the same weight as any private interaction or any greater weight (say, the value of 100 private interactions), i.e., the degree of the weakness or strength of the global compared to the local information. Foley concludes that still 'we have very little feel for the impact of weak global interactions in these contexts (of direct-interaction systems – WE)' (Foley, op. cit., 18).

Note that in the conventional neoclassical 'market'-equilibrium world the *auctioneer* in fact represents also a *total policy*, i.e., full information provision. Agents do not need to collect information from interactions with others. Since the auctioneer metaphor has not been considered by neoclassical economists to be also a metaphor of total policy, the prevailing way to view the 'market economy' by the economic 'mainstream' (and the everyday consciousness) has been that the (perfect) 'market' does not need any policy intervention or frame setting and regulation (see Table 9.1 above, Issue 14).

9.4.2 The Game-Theoretic Solution with Emergent Institutions again

In the real world, interactions are always somehow *local*, with *information* consequently generated also locally only, i.e., with a *limited number of agents* rather than 'very many' agents on a spot simultaneously, and, thus, with always some *scope for bargaining* on price, quantity, quality, and other dimensions of a transaction or relation between agents.

Living organisms and the social systems of human beings rarely exhibit full-fledged chaotic behavior. They typically have some *stabilizing*, particularly *structure-generating* ('*morphogenetic*' or '*autopoietic*') and self-reproducing ('*homeostatic*') properties. This is a 'behavior qualitatively different both from simple stability and chaos' (Foley, op. cit., 14). As human beings do perceive, interpret, explore, consciously reflect, imitate, learn, expect, plan, anticipate, and adapt in manifold ways social systems are called *complex adaptive systems*. Their trajectories can exhibit extremely high *computational complexity* and thus *computational costs*, and often even a computational *infeasibility* and *logical insolvability* (see, e.g., id., op. cit., 13ff.). Again, high computational complexity delineates 'bounds' to rationality while logical infeasibility is equivalent to absolute 'barriers' to rationality.

The research program to demonstrate how exactly the behavior of a large system converges on some asymptotic trajectory (i.e., an 'attractor' in a complex system trajectory), in the sense of *self-organization* as described above, while the number of agents can be arbitrarily large, is connected with *game theory*, particularly *evolutionary* game theory. You have learned some things about this already in Chapters 3 and 8. Also, we have applied this research program to *real-world markets* with *few agents* and with some scope for *bargaining* in the *Cournot–Nash oligopoly* in Chapter 4. As already explained, *complexity is inherent* in game-theoretic modeling, and *simplistic rationality impossible* to maintain therein.

A *full strategy* for a supergame would explicitly tell what the agent would do in every single interaction, depending on what has been done so far in the game. Developing an '*optimal' strategy choice in advance* would imply considerable computational *complexity* and, in fact, computational infeasibility. Strategies will typically be some *truncated version* of an ideal full strategy, i.e., a *more simple rule* to calculate and behave. This already indicates that there is no ideal rationality since agents have a smaller brain and memory capacity already than that required for a complete strategy for every individual interaction to come – which, in turn, relates to the bounded computational capacity of the human brain which is biological in this respect.

As mentioned, real *human beings* basically are at least as complex as their surrounding social interaction systems, they may be capable of very *complex reasoning*, but at the same time may also display a quite *simple behavior*.

In typical and recurrent complex situations, agents often need to, and in fact tend to, *reduce complexity*. They often *have to* reduce complexity in order to make undecidable problems (i.e., computationally infeasible solutions of systems) tractable. The simplest example of this was the 2x2 *Prisoners' Dilemma* supergame and the paradigm of its institutionalized cooperative solution, as explained and applied in Chapter 1 and Chapter 3.

While game theory provides basic devices for mathematical modeling, system trajectories of a certain level of complexity are no longer tractable in deterministic mathematical ways (see, e.g., Foley, op. cit., 50ff.). They then require complex computation, i.e., model *simulation*, as introduced in Chapter 7.

We have seen already in Chapter 3 that, and how, *complexity reduction* through the agents themselves is a *prerequisite of problem-solving* in typical complex multipersonal decision settings such as a Prisoners' Dilemma, a coordination game, and other games. Problem-solving here does not mean that agents realize a predetermined unique stable system equilibrium as suggested by the 'optimal market economy'. On the contrary, they enter a *complex process of experiencing and learning* where they develop *social institutions* as less complex ways of behavior and as alternatives to recurrent counterproductive short-run rationality. This is to solve a problem, perceived as individual, in a rather egoistic way, just because they have to realize that they are not isolated individuals, that the problems at hand typically are collective ones, and that they have to consider the others if they want to improve their very own payoffs and status in the long run.

Evolutionary-institutional economics in this way may provide 'an explicit theory of the ways in which agents achieve simplified representations of complex social interactions' (Foley, op. cit., 67) as needed in these contexts. And in the complex social and economic contexts described typically 'optimization of an objective function (is) less important than avoidance of disaster' (ibid.), as can easily be seen by considering a Prisoners' Dilemma or Coordination supergame. Thus, the perspective and 'vanishing point' of complexity analysis is agents rationally developing some (somehow evolving) 'equilibrium' (or attractor area), i.e., some stable *self-organization*, through proper behavioral regularities (see also Foley, op. cit., 67 ff.).

In contrast, as mentioned in Table 9.1 above [see issue (15)], the implicit auctioneer of the neoclassical interpretation of the classical idea of the invisible hand not only would implicitly represent, and thus explicitly redundantize, a policy agent (as mentioned above), but also the set of social rules as a required problem-solving device in complexity economics. In complex modeling, institutions emerge in a process of *morphogenesis* (or autopoiesis), i.e., self-organization, and the structure emerging often exhibits properties of *homeostasis*. That is, socio-economic systems often display some stability, even after some circumstances have changed, or return to their paths even after some external shock.

The contemporary crises, particularly the financial 'markets' crisis, have revealed most complex system properties and trajectories, i.e., an evolution with often changing behavioral regimes (bifurcations, see above), rather than smooth deterministic or simply distributed stochastic motions (as in option-price or hedge theories). One of the problems of, and reasons for, the financial markets and their meltdowns may be that both financial economists and agents in the financial 'markets' perceive and model them with lower complexity levels, such as systems with periodic orbits or of the chaotic type, amenable to analyses based on statistical regularities (see, e.g., Foley, op. cit., 71).

To sum up: A universe of complex economies and processes exists – but this is not a situation where economic agents are 'lost in complexity' or economic science would have to become agnostic. On the contrary, a new world of analysis and praxis is to be learned.

9.5   A FINAL WORD

What we may keep in mind from the foregoing analyses for the rest of our lives is that socio-economic 'reality' is mostly not what it appears to be at the surface of the immediate phenomena, but has a particular microeconomic 'deep structure' behind that. We must always look behind that veil of immediate impressions; this is why we have received an academic education. So always think twice, and try to apply what you have learned here. Particularly, the 'market' or 'market economy' are not what we are usually told they were, and what powerful opinion leaders claim them to be. 'Markets' can be nothing and everything. Being just decentralized, limited forms, they usually are underdetermined and undetermined in their structures, processes, and results. Also, often, they are overly complex and generate overcomplexity and over-turbulence, they often are idiosyncratic or locked-in situations or cycles. Therefore, they may become useful, functioning tools (among other or alternative useful tools) of coordination only if properly embedded in sets of what are their counter-principles, such as complexity-reducing sets of rules and institutions. The latter may take the form of networks of cooperation, sometimes to be combined with some hierarchy (not necessarily that much hierarchy, though, hierarchies being very complex sets of rules and institutions themselves). Last not least, it should have become clear throughout this textbook that the analysis of complex structures and of dynamic, evolutionary and often 'chaotic' processes, and their institutional, complexity-reducing solutions, can under no circumstances justify a hope for a general 'good' (let alone 'optimal') self-sustainability of any decentralized system with due certainty and within due course of time. Thus, in the end, we are reminded that we also are, and for some reason have evolved into, 'political animals'. As such we may hope to be able once to generate proper politics and policies, much better informed than those we have nowadays, in order also to set some formal rules and institutions to both, better restrict and empower 'markets' and any other spontaneous decentralized systems.

NOTES

1. This chapter is widely based on Duncan Foley's introduction chapter to 'Barriers and Bounds to Rationality' (Foley 1998) a collection of works by Peter Albin edited by Foley. The authors would like to thank Duncan Foley for comments on this chapter.

FURTHER READING

For a list of selected textbooks, monographs and articles on complexity economics, see the textbook website www.microeconomics.us.

References

Albin, Peter S. and Duncan K. Foley (1988), 'Decentralized, Dispersed Change Without an Auctioneer: A Simulation Study', in Peter S. Albin and Duncan K. Foley (eds), *Barriers and Bounds to Rationality. Essays on Economic Complexity and Dynamics in Interactive Systems*, Princeton, NJ, USA: Princeton University Press, pp. 157–180.

Albin, Peter S. and Duncan K. Foley (1992), 'Decentralized, Dispersed Exchange Without an Auctioneer', *Journal of Economic Behavior and Organization*, **18** (1), 27–51.

Arrow, K.J. and F.H. Hahn (1971), *General Competitive Analysis*, San Francisco, CA, USA: Holden-Day.

Arthur, W. Brian (1989), 'Competing Technologies, Increasing Returns, and Lock-In by Historical Events', *Economic Journal*, **99** (394), 116–131.

Arthur, W. Brian, Yuri M. Ermoliev and Yuri M. Kaniovskii ([1982] 1983), 'A Generalized URN Problem and Its Applications', *Cybernetics*, **19**, 61–71.

Axelrod, Robert ([1984] 2006), *The Evolution of Cooperation*, New York City, NY, USA: Basic Books.

Ayres, Clarence E. ([1944] 1978), *The Theory of Economic Progress,* Kalamazoo, MI, USA: New Issues Press, Western Michigan University.

Benhabib, Jesse and Richard Day (1981), 'Rational Choice and Erratic Behavior', *Review of Economic Studies*, **48**, 459–471.

Bertrand, Joseph L.F. (1883), 'Théorie Mathématique de la Richesses Sociale', *Journal des Savants*, **67**, 499–508.

Blinder, Alan S., Elie R.D. Canetti, David E. Lebow, and Jeremy B. Rudd (1998), *Asking About Prices: A New Approach to Price-Stickiness*, New York City, NY, USA: Russell Sage Foundation.

Boldrin, Michele and Luigi Montrucchio (1986), 'On the Indeterminacy of Capital Accumulation Paths', *Journal of Economic Theory*, **40** (1), 26–39.

Brock, William D. (1988), 'Nonlinearity and Complex Dynamics in Economics and Finance', in Philip W. Anderson, Kenneth J. Arrow, and David Pines (eds), *The Economy as an Evolving Complex System. The Proceedings of the Evolutionary Paths of the Global Economy Workshop*, Santa Fe Institute Studies in the Sciences of Complexity, Vol. 5, Redwood City, CA, USA: Addison Wesley, pp. 77–97.

Buchanan, Marc (1 October 2008), 'This Economy Does Not Compute', *New York Times*, OP-ED.

Buiter, Willem (3 March 2009), 'The Unfortunate Uselessness of Most "State of the Art" Academic Monetary Economics', *The Financial Times*.

Bush, Paul D. (1983), 'An Exploration of the Structural Characteristics of a Veblen-Ayres-Foster Defined Institutional Domain', *Journal of Economic Issues*, **17** (1), 35–66.

Bush, Paul D. (1987), 'The Theory of Institutional Change', *Journal of Economic Issues*, **21** (3), 1075–1116.

Calkin, Melvin G. (1996), *Lagrangian and Hamiltonian Mechanics*, Singapore: World Scientific Publishing.

Cass, David (1965), 'Optimum Growth in an Aggregative Model of Capital Accumulation', *The Review of Economic Studies*, **32** (3), 233–240.

Chamberlin, Edward H. (1933), *The Theory of Monopolistic Competition*, Cambridge, MA, USA: Harvard University Press.

Chen, Ping (2002), 'Microfoundations of Macroeconomic Fluctuations and the Laws of Probability Theory: The Principle of Large Numbers vs. Rational Expectations Arbitrage', *Journal of Economic Behavior and Organization*, **49** (3), 327–344.

Cohen, Patricia (4 March 2009), 'Ivory Tower Unswayed by Crashing Economy', *New York Times*.

Dahlem-Report (2009), *The Financial Crisis and the Systemic Failure of Academic Economics*, available at: http://www.debtdeflation.com/ blogs/wp-content/uploads/papers/Dahlem_Report_EconCrisis021809.pdf.

David, Paul A. (1985), 'Clio and the economics of QWERTY', *American Economic Review*, **75** (2), 332–337.

David, Paul A. and Julie Ann Bunn (1988), 'The Economics of Gateway Technologies and Network Evolution: Lessons From Electricity Supply History', *Information Economics and Policy*, **3** (2), 165–202.

David, Paul A. and W. Edward Steinmueller (1994), 'Economics of Compatibility Standards and Competition in Telecommunication Networks', *Information Economics and Policy*, **6** (3–4), 217–241.

Debreu, G. (1959), *Theory of Value: An Axiomatic Analysis of Economic Equilibrium*, New York City, NY, USA: Wiley.

Easley, David and Jon Kleinberg (2010), *Networks, Crowds, and Markets: Reasoning About a Highly Connected World*, Cambridge, UK: Cambridge University Press.

Elsner, Wolfram (2012), 'The Theory of Institutional Change Revisited: The Institutional Dichotomy, Its Dynamic, and Its Policy Implications in a More Formal Analysis', *Journal of Economic Issues*, **46**, 1–44.

Fehr, Ernst, Urs Fischbacher, and Simon Gächter (2002), 'Strong Reciprocity, Human Cooperation and the Enforcement of Social Norms', *Human Nature*, **13** (1), 1–25.

Foley, Duncan K. (1998), 'Introduction', in Peter S. Albin and Duncan K. Foley (eds), *Barriers and Bounds to Rationality. Essays on Economic Complexity and Dynamics in Interactive Systems*, Princeton, NJ, USA: Princeton University Press, pp. 3–72.

Frenken, Koen and Alessandro Nuvolari (2004), 'Entropy Statistics as a Framework to Analyse Technological Evolution', in John Foster and Werner Hoelzl (eds), *Applied Evolutionary Economics and Complex Systems*, Cheltenham, UK and Northampton, MA, USA: Edward Elgar, pp. 95–132.

Fullbrook, Edward (ed.) (2009), *Pluralist Economics*, London, UK: Zed Books.

Hargreaves-Heap, Shaun and Yanis Varoufakis ([1995] 2004), *Game Theory: A Critical Introduction*, London, UK and New York City, NY, USA: Routledge.

Jarsulic, Marc (1998), 'Chaos in Economics', in John B. Davis, D. Wade Hands, and Uskali Maeki (eds), *The Handbook of Economic Methodology*, Cheltenham, UK and Northampton, MA, USA: Edward Elgar, pp. 59–64.

Kaletsky, Anatole (5 February 2009), 'Economists are the Forgotten Guilty Men', *The Times (TIMESONLINE)*.

Katz, Michael L. and Carl Shapiro (1985), 'Network Externalities, Competition and Compatibility', *American Economic Review*, **75** (3), 424–440.

Kauffman, Stuart A. (1993), *The Origins of Order*, Oxford, UK: Oxford University Press.

Kauffman, Stuart A. (1995), *At Home in the Universe*, New York City, NY, USA: Viking Press.

Kauffman, Stuart A., José Lobo, and William G. Macready (2000), 'Optimal Search on a Technology Landscape', *Journal of Economic Behavior and Organization*, **43** (2), 141–166.

Keen, Steve (2009), 'A Pluralist Approach to Microeconomics', in Jack Reardon (ed.), *The Handbook of Pluralist Economics Education*, London, UK and New York City, NY, USA: Routledge, pp. 120–150.

Keen, Steve (2011), *Revised and Expanded Edition: Debunking Economics – The Naked Emperor Dethroned?*, London, UK: Zed Books.

Kirman, Alan P. (1997), 'The Economy as an Interactive System', in Brian W. Arthur, Steven N. Durlauf, and David A. Lane (eds), *The Economy as a Complex Interactive System*, Boulder, CO, USA: Westview Press, pp. 491–531.

Kirman, Alan P. ([2009] 2010), 'The Economic Crisis is a Crisis for Economic Theory', paper presented at the CESifo Economic Studies Conference *What's wrong with modern macroeconomics?*, Munich: ifo.

Kochen, Manfred (1989), 'Toward Structural Sociodynamics', in Manfred Kochen (ed.), *The Small World*, Norwood, NJ, USA: Ablex, pp. 52–64.

Koopmans, Tjalling C. (1965), 'On the Concept of Optimal Economic Growth', *Cowles Foundation Paper*, **238**, reprinted from *Academiae Scientiarum Scripta Varia*, **28** (1), 225–300.

Korte, Charles and Stanley Milgram (1970), 'Acquaintance Linking between White and Negro Populations: Application of the Small World Problem', *Journal of Personality and Social Psychology*, **15** (1), 101–118.

Kurz, Heinz D. and Neri Salvadori (1997), *Theory of Production*, Cambridge, UK: Cambridge University Press.

Lee, Frederic S. (2004), *Post Keynesian Price Theory*, Cambridge, UK: Cambridge University Press.

Li, Tien-Yien and James A. Yorke (1975), 'Period Three Implies Chaos', *The American Mathematical Monthly*, **82** (10), 985–992.

Liebowitz, Stan J. and Stephen E. Margolis (1990), 'The Fable of the Keys', *Journal of Law & Economics*, **33** (1), 1–25.

Lindgren, Kristian (1997), 'Evolutionary Dynamics in Game-Theoretic Models', in W. Brian Arthur, Steven N. Durlauf, and David A. Lane (eds), *The Economy as an Evolving Complex System II*, Reading, MA, USA: Addison Wesley, pp. 337–367.

Marglin, Stephen A. (2008), *The Dismal Science: How Thinking Like an Economist Undermines Community*, Cambridge, MA, USA: Harvard University Press.

Mas-Colell, A., M.D. Whinston, and J.R. Green (1995), *Microeconomic Theory*, New York City, NY, USA: Oxford University Press.

May, Robert M. (1976), 'Simple Mathematical Models With Very Complicated Dynamics', *Nature*, **261**, 459–467.

Maynard Smith, John and George R. Price (1973), 'The Logic of Animal Conflict', *Nature*, **246**, 15–18.

Means, Gardiner C. (1939), *The Structure of the American Economy. Part I: Basic Characteristics*, Washington, DC, USA: Government Printing Office.

Milgram, Stanley (1967), 'The Small World Problem', *Psychology Today*, **2** (1), 291–308.

Mirowski, Philip (1989), *More Heat Than Light – Economics as Social Physics, Physics as Nature's Economics*, Cambridge, UK: Cambridge University Press.

Mischel, Kenneth (1998), 'Sticky Prices as a Coordination Success', *Atlantic Economic Journal*, **26** (2), 162–71.

Mitchell, James Clyde (1969), 'The Concept and Use of Social Networks', in James Clyde Mitchell (ed.), *Social Networks in Urban Situation*, Manchester, UK: Manchester University Press, pp. 1–50.

Nadeau, Robert (2008), 'The Economist Has No Clothes', *Scientific American,* **298** (4), p. 42.

Nash, John (1950), 'Equilibrium Points in N-Person Games', *Proceedings of the National Academy of Sciences*, **36** (1), 48–49.

Negishi, Takashi (1960), 'Welfare Economics and Existence of an Equilibrium for a Competitive Economy', *Metroeconomica*, **12** (2–3), 92–97.

Nell, Edward (1998), *The General Theory of Transformational Growth – Keynes after Sraffa*, Cambridge, UK: Cambridge University Press.

Nelson, Richard and Sidney Winter (1982), *An Evolutionary Theory of Economic Change*, Cambridge, MA, USA: Harvard University Press.

Neumann, John von (1946), 'A Model of General Economic Equilibrium', *The Review of Economic Studies*, **13** (1), 1–9.

Neumann, John von and Oscar Morgenstern (1944), *Theory of Games and Economic Behavior*, Princeton, NJ, USA: Princeton University Press.

Nowak, Martin A. (2006), *Evolutionary Dynamics: Exploring the Equations of Life*, Cambridge, MA, USA and London, UK: Belknap Press of Harvard University Press.

Pool, Ithiel de Sola and Manfred Kochen (1978), 'Contacts and Influence', *Social Networks*, **1** (1), 1–48.

Ramsey, Frank P. (1928), 'A Mathematical Theory of Saving', *The Economic Journal*, **38** (152), 543–559.

Reardon, John E. (ed.) (2009), *Handbook of Pluralist Economics Education*, London, UK and New York City, NY, USA: Routledge.

Ricardo, David (1817), *On the Principles of Political Economy*, London, UK: John Murray.

Robinson, Joan (1933), *The Economics of Imperfect Competition*, London, UK: Macmillan.

Romer, D. (2005), *Advanced Macroeconomics*, New York City, NY, USA: McGraw Hill.

Rubinstein, Ariel (1979), 'Equilibrium in Supergames With the Overtaking Criterion', *Journal of Economic Theory*, **21** (1), 1–9.

Schelling, Thomas C. (1971), 'Dynamic Models of Segregation', *Journal of Mathematical Sociology*, **1** (2), 143–186.

Schelling, Thomas C. (1978), *Micromotives and Macrobehavior*, New York City, NY, USA and London, UK: W.W. Norton & Company.

Schotter, Andrew (1981), *The Economic Theory of Social Institutions*, New York City, NY, USA: Cambridge University Press.

Schumpeter, Joseph A. ([1911] 1997), *Theorie der wirtschaftlichen Entwicklung – Eine Untersuchung über Unternehmergewinn, Kapital, Kredit, Zins und den Konjunkturzyklus*, Berlin: Duncker und Humblot.

Shapiro, Nina and Malcolm Sawyer (2003), 'Post Keynesian Price Theory', *Journal of Post Keynesian Economics*, **25** (3), 355–365.

Simon, Herbert A. (1956), 'Rational Choice and the Structure of the Environment', *Psychological Review*, **63** (2), 129–138.

Skvoretz, John (1985), 'Random and Biased Networks: Simulations and Approximations', *Social Networks*, **7** (3), 225–261.

Smith, Eric and Duncan K. Foley (2008), 'Classical Thermodynamics and Economic General Equilibrium Theory', *Journal of Economic Dynamics & Control*, **32** (1), 7–65.

Sraffa, Piero (1926), 'The Laws of Returns under Competitive Conditions', *The Economic Journal*, **36** (144), 535–550.

Sraffa, Piero (1960), *The Production of Commodities by Means of Commodities*, Cambridge, UK: Cambridge University Press.

Starr, Ross M. (1997), *General Equilibrium Theory: An Introduction*, Cambridge, UK: Cambridge University Press.

Stigler, George (1957), 'Perfect Competition, Historically Contemplated', *Journal of Political Economy*, **65** (1), 1–17.

Sweezy, Paul (1939), 'Demand Under Conditions of Oligopoly', *The Journal of Political Economy*, **4**, 568–573.

Tversky, Amos and Daniel Kahneman (1973), 'Availability: A Heuristic for Judging Frequency and Probability', *Cognitive Psychology*, **5** (2), 207–232.

Vatiero, Massimiliano (2009), 'An Institutionalist Explanation of Market Dominances', *World Competition: Law and Economics Review*, **32** (2), 221–227.

Veblen, Torstein B. (1898), 'Why is Economics Not an Evolutionary Science?', *The Quarterly Journal of Economics*, **12** (4), 373–397.

Walsh, Carl E. (2003), *Monetary Theory and Policy*, Cambridge, MA, USA: MIT Press.

Watts, Duncan J. (1999a), 'Networks, Dynamics, and the Small-World Phenomenon', *American Journal of Sociology*, **105** (2), 493–527.

Watts, Duncan J. (1999b), *Small Worlds: The Dynamics of Networks between Order and Randomness*, Princeton, NJ, USA: Princeton University Press.

Watts, Duncan J. and Stephen H. Strogatz (1998), 'Collective Dynamics of "Small-World" Networks', *Nature*, **393** (4), 440–442.

Wellhöner, Volker (2002), *Ökonomik – Physik – Mathematik: Die Allgemeine Gleichgewichtstheorie im interdisziplinären Kontext*, Frankfurt: Verlag Peter Lang.

Wilensky, Uri (1997), *NetLogo Segregation Model*, Center for Connected Learning and Computer-Based Modeling, Evanston, IL, USA: Northwestern University, available at: http://ccl.northwestern.edu/netlogo/ models/segregation.

Wilensky, Uri (1999), *NetLogo*, Center for Connected Learning and Computer-Based Modeling, Evanston, IL, USA: Northwestern University, available at: http://ccl.northwestern.edu/netlogo/.

Woodford, Michael (2003), *Interest and Prices: Foundations of a Theory of Monetary Policy*, Princeton, NJ, USA: Princeton University Press.

Name Index

Subject Index